D1275597

Errata

The publisher apologizes for the printing on pages 17 and 19 of typesetter's notes ("choice," etc.) that are irrelevant to the text and were intended for production purposes only.

Page 78

Iproniazid

Nialamide

Page 96

Tofisopam

Introduction
to psychopharmacology

A SCOPE® PUBLICATION

Malcolm Lader, DSc, PhD, MD, FRC Psych, Dipl Psych Med
Professor of Clinical Psychopharmacology, Institute of Psychiatry,
University of London.
Member of External Scientific Staff, Medical Research Council, U.K.
Honorary Consultant, Bethlem Royal and Maudsley Hospitals.
Honorary Research Fellow, Department of Pharmacology,
University College London.

The views expressed in this monograph are not necessarily those of the
publishers, and the author gives no endorsement of The Upjohn Company
products by reason of his work appearing under the Company's imprint.

Library of Congress Card Number 80-51225 ISBN 0-89501-032-1

Copyright 1980, The Upjohn Company, Kalamazoo, Michigan 49001
Printed in The United States of America

8801-26

Contents

Preface

Drugs have become an important part – many would say the mainstay – in the management of many psychiatric conditions. The general practitioner, the psychiatrist, and the internist prescribe psychotropic drugs in large quantities to large numbers of patients. Yet many of these prescribers, judging by the questions I am asked after lecturing on the topic, are not confident that they have sufficient knowledge to use these drugs efficiently. The psychotropic drugs were discovered mainly by accident, and their pharmacology is complex – involving as it does brain mechanisms that are poorly understood.

This book is an attempt to present succinctly the pharmacological basis for the clinical use of psychotropic drugs. It is based on lectures and seminars I have given in the Institute of Psychiatry and elsewhere and, in particular, on a more detailed account comprising chapters in the *Handbook of Biological Psychiatry* (edited by Van Praag, Lader, Rafaelsen, and Sachar, and published by Marcel Dekker, New York). The reader I have particularly in mind is the psychiatrist-in-training, and I have tried to provide for his needs in specialist-qualifying examinations. However, I hope that a wider readership including psychiatrists, general practitioners, psychologists, and pharmacologists will have access to the book and will find it useful.

I must stress that it is not meant as a textbook of therapeutics. I intend to write such a book in the near future. However, this introductory book should be of direct help to the prescribing physician in providing him with the scientific rationale for drug treatment in psychiatry. Doses are given on occasion, but these recommendations must not be accepted unreservedly. The prescriber must check other sources of information such as the drug data sheet.

In writing about drugs for an international audience, I am aware that some of the drugs discussed are not available in some countries. Moreover, therapeutic usage varies from country to country. Consequently, any advice about clinical practice must be modified by the reader in the light of local usage. Nevertheless, the scientific principles underlying therapeutic manoeuvres are universal, and these should not be compromised. Rather than detailed references throughout the text, a list of further reading has been provided at the end of each chapter.

I acknowledge my indebtedness to colleagues who generously gave their time to read various chapters. I am grateful for their many suggestions, which have greatly improved the book, but I take full responsibility for any remaining errors.

Malcolm Lader
December 1980

Introduction

To better understand the current state of psychopharmacology and its potential development, it is useful to set some historical perspective. The subject in its clinical form is still less than 30 years old, dating from the introduction of the antipsychotic medication chlorpromazine in the early 1950s. This was a milestone because chlorpromazine, as with the antidepressants and lithium, proved to have hitherto unique pharmacological properties. It could not be fitted into the then-current simple classificatory schema of psychotropic drugs, namely, depressants, stimulants, and deliriants. Even now, many physicians find the psychotropic agents puzzling because of their empirical nature.

The accidental discovery and subsequent introduction of novel therapies is, of course, not confined to psychopharmacology. However, the complexities of the brain could have obstructed the study of these new drugs. That it proved a challenge illustrates the immense development of the brain sciences in the past quarter century. Brain mechanisms were uncovered that seemed particularly relevant to psychotropic drug action, the elucidation of dopamine pathways being an example. Indeed, as will be amplified later, the drugs themselves proved to be invaluable tools in neurochemistry, neurophysiology, and psychology.

The antecedents of psychopharmacology are various — anthropological, biophysical, physiological, biochemical, psychological, and, of course, clinical. These various threads still run through the subject but serve to bind it together rather than to divide it into compartments. For example, biochemical monitoring of drug effects on animal behaviour has been much more helpful than either biochemical or behavioural observation alone. This book stems from the belief that an understanding of the clinical actions of the psychotropic drugs must be based on a knowledge of their fundamental mechanisms. Psychopharmacology is rapidly moving from the empirical to the rational, so that further advances become increasingly probable rather than having to be left to the vagaries of chance observations.

However, this book is directed towards the clinician, and it is in the clinical context that the drugs have proved so beneficial. In the "pre-drug era," before the mid-1950s, the primary treatment centre was the large regional mental hospital with its thousands of patients, many of whom were permanent residents. Each year, their numbers increased and conditions became more demoralizing for patients and staff. Schizophrenic patients with bizarre behaviour, talking to their own voices or striking catatonic postures, were mingled with chronic depressives or the dementing. Violence or at least the fear of it was common, and often there was hostility and suspicion between patients and staff. Restraint was common, with padded cells and straitjackets in constant use.

Conditions varied from hospital to hospital and from country to country. By the 1940s, in some enlightened instances, compassionate management policies had minimized the use of restraints and had led to an optimistic atmosphere in the wards and to increased rates of discharge. In other places, the pejorative term "snake pit" was an understatement.

The advent of the antipsychotic agents such as chlorpromazine, used essentially as powerful tranquilizers, interacted with the attempts at reform. In hospitals in which a liberal and therapeutic policy was already producing gratifying results, the drugs' impact was minor. In hospitals exercising a solely custodial role, change was often dramatic. Disturbing behaviour became less common, not only in those patients given tranquilizers but in their companions as well. The number of broken windows, the amount of other damage, and the use of restraints dwindled; nursing and medical staff could devise methods of rehabilitation, confident of some hope of success. Attitudes of the community towards mental illness changed. There was more acceptance of the mentally and socially disabled, although even now there is a long way to go. And yet the revolution was incomplete. Patients were discharged from hospital but they often relapsed. The number of inpatients decreased but the numbers of admissions and especially of readmissions increased rapidly. Initial enthusiasm and even euphoria has been tempered by the sober appraisal that schizophrenia is not conquered, not even contained. Its ravages have been merely lessened, yet life in the community is possible for many who without drugs would have been condemned to an institutional existence.

The antidepressants had their first impact in psychiatric outpatients. Since the early 1940s, depressed inpatients had been treated with electroconvulsive therapy (ECT), and their prognosis, usually good, was not altered by imipramine, iproniazid, or their congeners. Indeed, as psychiatrists became increasingly reluctant to use ECT and persisted with drug therapy, it is conceivable that some patients remained depressed longer. For the less severely depressed, however, it became obvious that the antidepressants, both "tricyclics" and monoamine oxidase inhibitors, were a vast improvement over the disappointing amphetamines. More recently, family practitioners have become increasingly expert in the use of the antidepressants, and the psychiatrist is seeing an increasingly selected group of patients who have failed to respond for one reason or another. In the treatment of anxiety, tension, and related states, the barbiturates have been superseded by the benzodiazepines, which are more effective, have fewer side effects, and are much safer. Again, this is primarily the domain of the family practitioner, who now refers only a small proportion of his anxious patients for a specialist's opinion.

The widespread use of the benzodiazepines has led to much disquietude among clinical pharmacologists. The overuse, misuse, and abuse of psychotropic substances is nothing new. Noah unwisely imbibed his wine to excess, and other intoxicants have been known since prehistory. More recently, opium, bromides, and the barbiturates have all been widely used for nonmedical purposes. When more than 10% of the adult population have recourse to the benzodiazepines, it is not surprising that cautionary voices are raised. However, recent advances in our understanding of sedative and narcotic drug mechanisms may allow us to separate the therapeutic and dependence-producing properties of new drugs.

Other possible therapeutic indications for psychotropic drugs have hardly been explored. Drugs are available to lessen behavioural disturbances in children, to curtail the sex drive, and to combat obsessions, but their usefulness is still poorly established. Some priority is being given to drugs that curb aggressive behaviour and impulses. Again, the wider social, moral, and political implications of being able to control people's behaviour pharmacologically have not been seriously debated. The spectre of an Orwellian future is some way off despite recent advances in brain biochemistry. Nevertheless, the use of drugs to control disturbed behaviour does raise ethical issues concerning the definition of social deviation; those issues lie outside our present scope.

Pharmacologists and biochemists were at first slow to recognize the implications of the new psychotropic drugs. At times, those drug effects first to be discovered were regarded automatically as underlying the clinical mode of action. Indeed, the finding of an unusual biochemical action has occasionally led to the resurgence of interest in a drug that had been discarded on clinical grounds. The monoamine oxidase inhibitors are a case in point. Discarded as "activators" in schizophrenics, their ability to block the widespread enzyme monoamine oxidase (MAO) led to a reappraisal of their properties, and claims of their effectiveness in atypical de-

pression followed. Nevertheless, explaining their clinical actions in terms of monoamine oxidase inhibition leaves many questions unanswered. In the case of the tricyclic antidepressants, discovery of their ability to block the re-uptake of serotonin, dopamine, and noradrenaline from synaptic clefts led to the assumption that this blocking explained their mode of action. When newer drugs were developed that seemed to have clinically observable antidepressant properties but minimal effects on amine re-uptake, great astonishment was expressed. It is very probable that amine re-uptake blockade is only the first step in a long chain of biochemical consequences that relate to the antidepressant effect, and it is not inconceivable that other drug actions could lead to these secondary effects. One wonders how many potentially useful drugs have been discarded because they did not conform to the rigidly established profile of action.

The psychotropic drugs have proved as valuable in the laboratory as in the clinic. They have provided powerful means of analysing brain physiology and animal behaviour. In turn, as the properties of a drug have been unravelled, they have provided the basis for elucidating the actions of other drugs. For example, reserpine was found to deplete nerve endings of their neurotransmitter amines. Drugs that rectify this deficit often have antidepressant properties, so the reserpine-treated animal has been used as a screen for such drugs and as a preparation with useful biochemical characteristics.

Psychopharmacology has been helped greatly by advances in other areas of pharmacology, both technical and theoretical. If the 1960s were the decade of the synapse, then the 1970s were the decade of the receptor. One might speculate that the 1980s will be the decade of postreceptor intraneuronal mechanisms.

It is instructive that for ten years after their introduction in 1959, the antidepressants were more interesting to psychopharmacologists than the neuroleptics had been. Synapse pharmacology was being rapidly worked out, particularly with regard to the storage and release mechanisms for cerebral monoamines. Receptors were a heuristic concept with great explanatory power but few direct means of study. The advent of radioactive labelling provided receptor pharmacology with the necessary tool. Now, our understanding of the actions of the neuroleptics as dopamine antagonists on the receptor outstrips our understanding of the antidepressants as interfering with amine disposition in the synaptic cleft.

The major success in this area has been the discovery of opiate receptors and of their effect in pain and other pathways. So the narcotics and their antagonists now join the ranks of drugs whose mechanism of action is at least partly understood instead of being the legacy of a folk remedy, the product of a serendipitous observation, or the lucky outcome of sheer wrong-headed reasoning. At times, receptor pharmacology has outstripped our knowledge of transmitter functions. For example, the benzodiazepines bind strongly to certain protein molecules widespread in the central nervous system, and the drugs' affinities closely match their clinical potencies. No endogenous, natural substance that uses those receptors has yet been convincingly identified, however, and the relationship to benzodiazepine actions on transmitters is unclear. The demonstration of receptor involvement in a physiological function or pharmacological action bodes well for the eventual development of rational remedies. Receptors seem more easily and selectively influenced by chemical molecules than, say, synapses or cells. The examples of beta-adrenoceptor and histamine-2 receptors show how symptomatic remedies can be beneficially developed.

Psychopharmacology has perhaps been less successful in its relationships to psychology, both animal and human. Behaviour is so complex a topic and any drug so multifarious in its actions that the conjunction of the two could hardly be expected to be enlightening. Often, neurological side effects have been carefully studied in the mistaken belief that they were somehow related to the therapeutic actions. The cataleptic states induced by neuroleptics in animals were regarded as particularly significant, although catatonia is a rare feature of schizophrenia and anyway bears only a superficial resemblance to the drug-induced condition. Often, the mixed actions of psychotropic drugs were insufficiently recognized. Chlorpromazine is both antipsychotic and sedative, and flupenthixol is both antipsychotic and stimulant. The lack of useful animal models of psychiatric illnesses has handicapped the search for relevant drug effects. Admittedly, the study of drug effects in animals has given rise to the large topic of animal psychopharmacology, a speciality in its own right, but it is doubtful whether behavioural studies, in contrast to biochemical studies, have greatly advanced our understanding of the therapeutic actions of psychotropic drugs. Similarly, studies in normal humans can be expected to yield only limited information, although that information can be invaluable in interpreting parallel data regarding patients.

Finally, psychopharmacology has revived the flagging subject of so-called biological psychiatry. This approach to psychiatry assumes that some structural or functional abnormality is associated with certain psychiatric conditions – in particular, the major psychoses. Its successes in elucidating the pathophysiology of vitamin deficiencies such as pellagra and of infective conditions such as general paralysis of the insane led to expectations that all major psychiatric conditions resulted from causes that would be discoverable using available techniques. Countless brain slices were examined by neuropathologists, numerous family trees were constructed by geneticists, and as each new body constituent was identified, its concentration in the biological fluids of schizophrenic patients was meticulously estimated by biochemists. But advances were few and often limited, the discovery of a relation between periodic catatonia and nitrogen balance being an example. Enthusiasm waned with brief flickerings of interest as new techniques of investigation such as the electroencephalogram were introduced. Genuine advances were made in neuropsychiatry, but the hard core of the major functional psychoses remained.

The advent of, first, electroconvulsive therapy and leucotomy, and later, the modern psychotropic drugs rekindled belief in the importance of the biological concomitants and perhaps antecedents of psychiatric disease. The logic is simple: If a drug provides symptomatic relief for a condition, then because it acts on biological mechanisms, those mechanisms must be operative in the condition. But of course the logic is not flawless: Diuretics help heart failure but the kidneys are not at fault; anticholinergics help parkinsonism but dopamine pathways and not cholinergic mechanisms are primarily affected. Even more far-reaching claims depend on the assumption that the psychotropic drugs alter basic disease processes rather than symptoms. If those claims were true, then unfolding the ways by which the drugs act would tell us not about the expression of the disease in terms of its symptoms but rather about the fundamental abnormal process giving rise to those symptoms.

Nevertheless, scientific studies of psychiatric disorders have received an enormous fillip from the discovery of the antipsychotics, antidepressants, and other agents. Not only do the drugs provide invaluable tools but their existence also provides some guarantee that biochemical and other biological mechanisms are important and perhaps crucial. These mechanisms are outlined in the next two chapters, which are followed by a chapter devoted to pharmacokinetics, still a rather neglected topic in psychopharmacology. The remaining chapters then deal systematically with the various classes of psychotropic drugs.

FURTHER READING

Avery GS (ed): *Drug Treatment.* Sydney, Adis Press, 1976.

Ayd FJ, Blackwell B (eds): *Discoveries in Biological Psychiatry.* Philadelphia, Lippincott, 1970.

Barchas JD, Berger PA, Ciaranello RD, Elliott GR (eds): *Psychopharmacology. From Theory to Practice.* New York, Oxford University Press, 1977.

Hollister LE: *Clinical Pharmacology of Psychotherapeutic Drugs.* New York, Churchill Livingstone, 1978.

Jeste DV, Gillin C, Wyatt RJ: Serendipity in biological psychiatry – A myth? *Arch Gen Psychiatry 36*:1173-1178, 1979.

Lipton M, DiMascio A, Killam KF (eds): *Psychopharmacology. A Generation of Progress.* New York, Raven Press, 1978.

Silverstone T, Turner P: *Drug Treatment in Psychiatry.* London, Routledge and Kegan Paul, 1978.

Van Praag HM: *Psychotropic Drugs. A Guide for the Practitioner.* London, MacMillan, 1978.

Neurotransmitters

INTRODUCTION

Conduction *along* nerves is by electrical processes that entail fluxes of cations, in particular sodium and potassium. Conduction *between* nerves is not electrical but depends on the release of specific chemicals called neurotransmitters. These chemical "messengers" diffuse across the synaptic cleft to the postsynaptic neuron, where they activate specific sites on the cell membrane called receptors. This in turn causes the postsynaptic neuron to alter its standing electrical charge. Decrease in polarization (excitatory postsynaptic potential, EPSP) tends to excite the neuron, with possible discharge and electrical conduction along the axon to the next synapse. Hyperpolarization (inhibitory postsynaptic potential, IPSP), on the contrary, lessens the likelihood of the neuron firing, ie, it is inhibited. Whether neurotransmitter release produces excitation or inhibition is a property not of the individual neurotransmitter but of the particular postsynaptic neuron. Most synapses have large numbers (1,000 to 10,000) of presynaptic nerve endings ("boutons terminaux") impinging on them, and whether a neuron fires or not is thus the resultant of a large number of influences. Most synapses are axodendritic but some are axoaxonic. It has been generally accepted that each neuron releases only one neurotransmitter although some evidence to the contrary has been presented.

The importance of the synapse is that it is a complex structure in biochemical terms, as compared with the axon. It furnishes a site where drugs can exert actions most easily inasmuch as so many processes take place there, some of which are critically balanced. Thus, the neurotransmitter must be synthesized, stored, and released, must act on the receptor, and then must be broken down; various drugs can interfere with or facilitate any of these processes.

HISTORICAL NOTE

In the 19th century, various organ extracts were found to mimic the effects of nervous activity. For example, in 1895, Oliver and Schafer reported that the effects of stimulating sympathetic nerves could be reproduced, at least in part, by the injection of adrenal extracts. Soon after, adrenaline* was isolated and identified as the apparently active principle. Dale, Barger, and others implicated acetylcholine in parasympathetic transmission, and Dale proposed the division of the autonomic nervous system into the cholinergic parasympathetic and the adrenergic sympathetic systems.

The crucial demonstration that chemical transmission

*In the United States, "epinephrine" is the generic term, and "Adrenalin" is a brand name. In the United Kingdom, "Epinephrine" is a brand name.

was involved came from the experiments of Loewi in the 1920s. Stimulation of the vagus nerve in an isolated perfused frog's heart released a substance, "Vagusstoff," which slowed a second denervated heart. This messenger substance was identified as acetylcholine. Sympathetic nerves were found to release not adrenaline, as originally thought, but noradrenaline, although the latter was not finally identified until 1946 by von Euler.

Almost all this early work centered on the peripheral nervous system, and the identification of central neurotransmitters has in many cases been a success of biochemical techniques of the past 20 years or so. Some of the impetus for these neurochemical advances came from the realization of the complex actions of the modern generation of psychotropic drugs.

NEUROTRANSMITTER MECHANISMS

Synthesis

As with most body cells, the nucleus of the nerve cell contains deoxyribonucleic acid (DNA), which enables it to control the synthesis of proteins, including enzyme molecules. The enzymes needed for the synthesis of the neurotransmitter are manufactured in the cell body and then migrate down the axon to the nerve terminal. The cell body and nerve terminals also have mechanisms for taking up the appropriate precursor needed to synthesize the particular neurotransmitter – choline, for example, in the case of those cholinergic nerves that release acetylcholine. However, these uptake mechanisms are not completely specific, and high concentrations of related substances can result in their uptake into the neuron. The transport and uptake systems depend on energy-providing mechanisms (Figure 2-1).

The uptake of precursors at the nerve terminals activates the synthesizing enzymes that produce the neurotransmitter. In general, the neurotransmitter is synthesized more rapidly than repetitive nerve impulses can release it, so that the neurotransmitter store does not become depleted.

Storage

The synthesized neurotransmitter is taken up into specialized synaptic vesicles, or granules, which in electron micrographs can be seen in large numbers inside the nerve terminals. Each nerve ending has thousands of vesicles that contain high concentrations of neurotransmitter, each granule containing several thousand molecules.

Release

When the neuronal membrane is depolarized by the nerve action potential, major fluxes of sodium, potassium, and calcium occur. The last in particular is required in the activation of the storage vesicles, which then migrate to the cell boundary, where they fuse to the membrane. The vesicle contents are extruded into the synaptic cleft by a process of exocytosis. As well as the neurotransmitter, other substances contained in the synaptic vesicles may be released. For example, noradrenaline, adenosine triphosphate (ATP), and dopamine-β-hydroxylase (a synthesizing enzyme) are released together from peripheral adrenergic nerves.

Action on receptors

The synaptic cleft is quite narrow (10 to 50 nm – 1 nm is 10^{-9} m), so that soon after release the neurotransmitter diffuses across to the postsynaptic membranes, where it binds to specific protein receptors. This aspect of neuropharmacology is rapidly growing, but much of our knowledge of receptor physiology is indirect and inferential. The specificity of the receptor is usually high. For example, dopamine may activate it, but not noradrenaline, and vice versa, although the molecular structures of dopamine and noradrenaline differ by only a hydroxyl group. In particular, the receptors are highly stereospecific, so that the laevo-isomer of a drug or transmitter may be many times more active than the dextro-isomer.

Binding of the appropriate transmitter externally to the receptor alters the molecular configuration of the protein in such a way as to cause changes in the postsynaptic neuron, either internally or within the cell membrane. For example, membrane permeabilities ("ionophore channels") to sodium, potassium, chloride, and other ions may change, the upshot being a change in excitability. "Gearing" is very high: one molecule of acetylcholine on its receptor can result in the flux of 50,000 cations.

Inactivation

Obviously, neurotransmission would be impossible if the transmitter were to activate the receptor permanently. The association of a transmitter to its receptor molecule is an equilibrium, with the transmitter molecules constantly dissociating and reassociating with the receptors. Mechanisms do exist, however, to remove the neurotransmitter from the vicinity of the receptors.

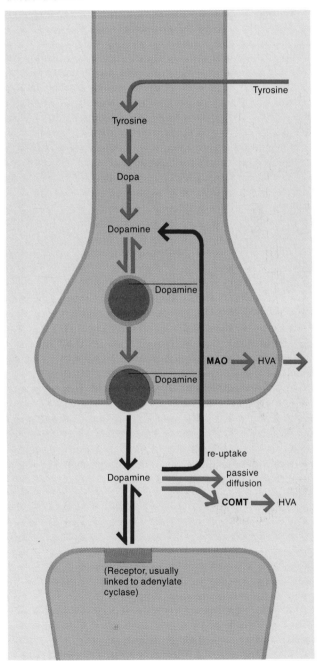

Figure 2-1. Release and inactivation of dopamine, a neurotransmitter.

14

One such mechanism is enzymatic breakdown, which transforms the neurotransmitter to inactive metabolites. Such enzymes are located either in the synaptic cleft or in the postsynaptic membrane itself. Another mechanism is the physical removal of transmitter from the synaptic cleft by diffusion away from and subsequent absorption into the circulation or by an active re-uptake through the presynaptic membrane back into the neuron, where it can reenter the storage granules. Finally, intracytoplasmic enzymes in the presynaptic neuron can break down any neurotransmitter that remains free in the cytoplasmic fluid.

Inactivation processes vary among neurotransmitters. Thus, acetylcholine is broken down by cholinesterase, whereas the catecholamines are mostly taken back into the releasing neuron.

Regulatory mechanisms

At the biochemical level, mechanisms exist to regulate the synthesis of transmitters. One such device is "end-product inhibition," in which the synthesized substance acts back on one or more of the enzymes in the chain of synthesis, inhibiting further synthesis.

Neuronal circuits, including their synapses, are in dynamic biochemical equilibrium. If that balance is disturbed, mechanisms come into play to redress, at least partly, that imbalance.

One such "feedback loop" is intrasynaptic. Many neurotransmitter systems are believed to incorporate receptors on the *pre*synaptic as well as on the *post*synaptic membranes. Activation of these "autoreceptors" is believed to initiate processes that ultimately inhibit further neourotransmitter synthesis and release. Consequently, excessive traffic across the synapse diminishes the amount of neurotransmitter available, which diminution tends to lessen trans-synaptic activity.

A second synaptic regulatory mechanism concerns the postsynaptic receptors. Underactivity across the synapse results in a proliferation in numbers of receptors and perhaps an increase in sensitivity of the receptors. This is seen at its extreme in the peripheral phenomenon of "denervation supersensitivity." The converse also occurs to some extent: excessive trans-synaptic activity culminates in fewer available receptors (Figure 2-3).

"Long-loop feedbacks" consisting of a chain of neurons also exist. Thus, the nigrostriatal pathway is believed to excite a striatonigral pathway, which in turn inhibits the first neuron. Thus, a balance is maintained.

Figure 2-2. Dopamine autoreceptors.

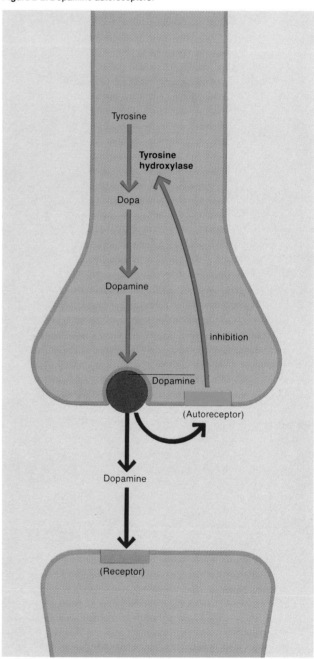

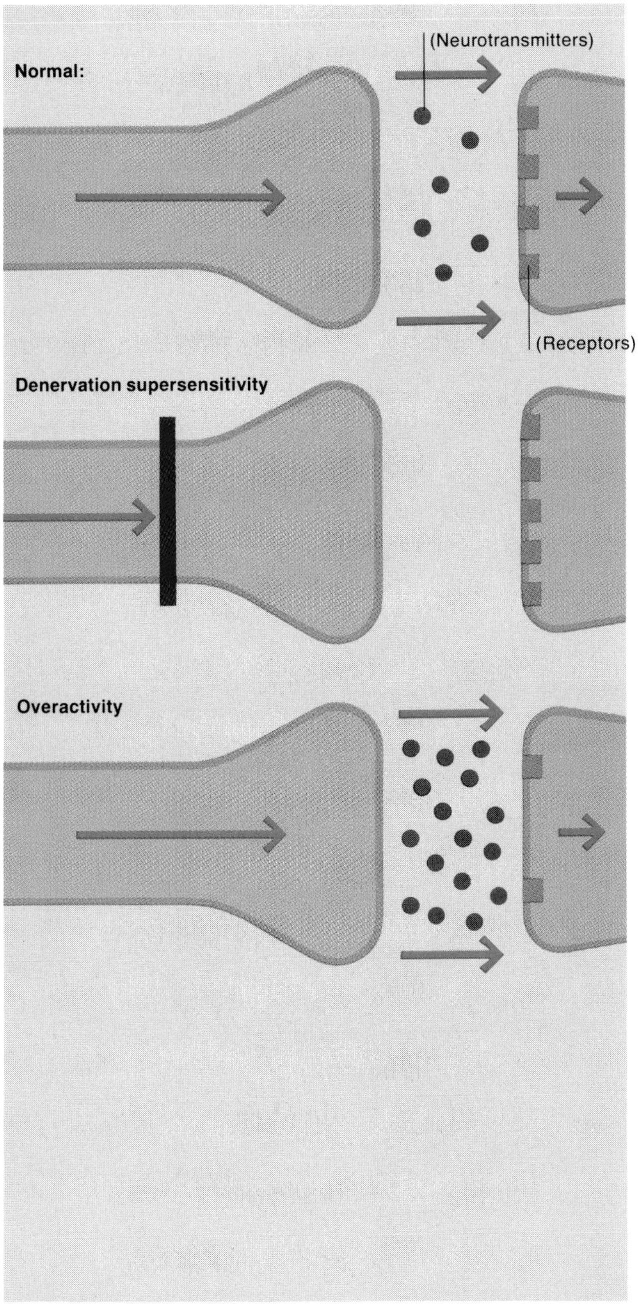

Figure 2-3. Receptor sensitivity.

Normal:

(Neurotransmitters)

(Receptors)

Denervation supersensitivity

Overactivity

Figure 2-4. Sites of drug action at the synapse.

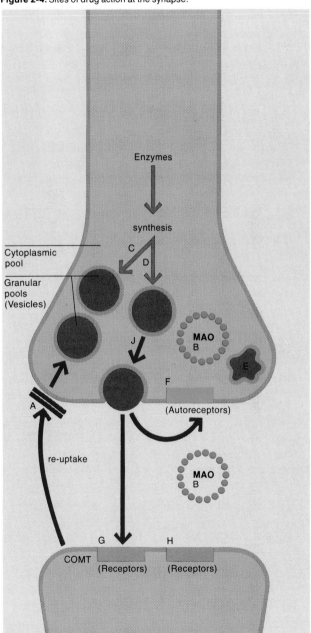

Enzymes

synthesis

Cytoplasmic pool

Granular pools (Vesicles)

MAO B

E

C

D

J

A

F

(Autoreceptors)

re-uptake

MAO B

G

H

COMT

(Receptors)

(Receptors)

A Tricyclics block re-uptake
B MAOIs destroy MAO
C Methyldopa forms a false transmitter
D L-dopa enhances catecholamine synthesis
E Reserpine depletes granular pools (vesicles)
F LSD acts on autoreceptors
G Chlorpromazine and propranolol are receptor antagonists
H Bromocriptine and isoprenaline are receptor agonists
J Lithium interferes with discharge of vesicles

16

Sites of drug action

Before discussing each neurotransmitter in turn, it is useful to list the sites where drugs can exert an action. Drugs can act at several places, and such effects may vary from species to species (Figure 2-4).

First, drugs can interfere with synthesizing mechanisms by stimulating or blocking catabolic enzymes. Drugs can also act as precursors, resulting either in increased amounts of the natural neurotransmitter or in the synthesis of a transmitter-like substance. Usually this "false" transmitter is much less effective than the natural molecule, but it could be more potent. The uptake and storage of neurotransmitters can be impeded, resulting in depletion at the nerve endings.

Some drugs act by releasing the neurotransmitter from storage granules. Others block the intracytoplasmic enzymes responsible for breaking down any transmitter that has leaked into the cytoplasmic fluid. Similarly, some drugs can act on the catabolic enzymes in the synaptic cleft, usually inhibiting them and thus prolonging the neurotransmitter's action. The re-uptake of the transmitter into the presynaptic neurons can also be blocked by some drugs.

Many important drugs act directly on transmitter receptors, either activating them directly (agonists) or blocking them from the action of the natural neurotransmitter (antagonists). Some drugs possess both properties, being either agonist or antagonist according to dose and conditions. These actions can be either competitive or noncompetitive with the natural transmitter, but the two properties are more matters of degree than absolute distinctions. Some drugs act preferentially on presynaptic or postsynaptic receptors. The receptors can be "sensitized" by some drugs so that neurotransmission is facilitated, and, finally, some drugs may act directly on synaptic membranes, especially in altering ionophore permeability.

It may be emphasized that no drug has just a single effect, and what is usually described is its principal properties. Psychotropic drugs in particular have a multitude of actions.

SPECIFIC NEUROTRANSMITTERS

Transmitter processes have been mostly worked out in the peripheral nervous system, in particular at neuroeffector sites such as the neuromuscular junction. Establishing that similar mechanisms exist at synapses in the central nervous system has proved far more difficult. The general lines of evidence taken to support the identification of a specific substance as a neurotransmitter are:

1. A physiologically active substance can be identified in appropriate regions, together with the enzymes needed for its synthesis and breakdown.
2. The compound can be identified in the perfusate of a region when stimulated but not when it is inactive.
3. The putative neurotransmitter applied locally is fully capable of mimicking the effects of nerve stimulation.
4. The effects of the substance and of nerve stimulation can be modified, enhanced, or attenuated in the same manner by appropriate drugs.

Some of these criteria depend heavily on the development of sensitive techniques for the measurement of neurotransmitters, their metabolites, and associated enzymes. The stability of the substance in biological material is another factor; acetylcholine, for example, is labile. Furthermore, some substances that apparently act as neurotransmitters are also widespread throughout the brain, the amino acid glycine providing such an instance. Finally, neurotransmitters localized to fairly well-defined tracts are easier to study than are more diffusely organized substances. For all these reasons, the degree of interest in and knowledge of the various central neurotransmitters does not necessarily reflect their physiological importance. The catecholamines, especially in view of their implication in psychiatric conditions, have been investigated in the central nervous system more than has acetylcholine, despite much of our knowledge of neurotransmission deriving from studies of acetylcholine in the periphery.

After reviewing the synthesis, storage, release, breakdown, regulation, and receptors for each major neurotransmitter, we will consider the main drug interactions with each substance.

Acetylcholine

Very sensitive biological assays for acetylcholine have been developed. For example, as little as 5×10^{-15} mole can be detected in the clam heart preparation. Chemical methods are sometimes even more cumbersome, but useful ones have been introduced recently. Measurements of turnover and release of acetylcholine have tended to displace simple and rather uninformative estimates of tissue content.

Synthesis (Figure 2-5): Acetylcholine is synthesized from choline and acetyl radicals by the enzyme choline acetyl transferase. Choline is synthesized in the liver and is taken up into the axon by active transport from the extracellular fluid. The acetyl radical is provided by acetyl coenzyme A, derived from general metabolic functions. It seems likely that choline acetyl transferase is not saturated under normal conditions, so that the concentration of choline determines the rate of synthesis of acetylcholine. The implication is that increasing the amount of choline will increase acetylcholine production, although increased production seems difficult to attain in practice.

Storage and release: Acetylcholine is sequestered in the synaptic vesicles. Small numbers of vesicles discharge spontaneously during resting conditions and are detected at the neuromuscular junction as minute spontaneous depolarizations – "miniature end-plate potentials." However, when an axon potential arrives at the nerve ending (after a latent period of about 0.75 milliseconds), several hundred vesicles discharge simultaneously into the synaptic cleft. Calcium ions are essential for the process, which is antagonized by magnesium ions.

Cholinergic terminals are able to support a very high rate of acetylcholine synthesis and release. In the superior cervical ganglion of the cat, supramaximal electrical stimulation results in an hourly acetylcholine output of six times the resting content. Depletion of acetylcholine, therefore, does not seem to occur.

Breakdown: Body fluids and tissues contain cholinesterases that can split acetylcholine into choline and acetic acid. Acetylcholinesterase, also called true or specific cholinesterase, occurs in neurons and neuroeffector junctions. Butyrylcholinesterase (pseudocholinesterase) is widely distributed throughout the body, including body fluids. True acetylcholinesterase hydrolyses acetylcholine more rapidly than it does any other choline ester; butyrylcholinesterase hydrolyses butyrylcholine with maximum velocity. Suxamethonium, a muscle relaxant, is rapidly hydrolysed by butyrylcholinesterase in the

Figure 2-5. Synthesis and breakdown of acetylcholine.

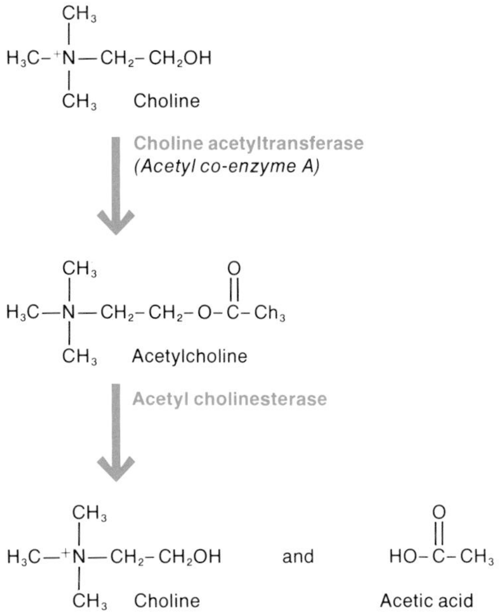

Choice:

$$H_3C-{}^+N-CH_2-CH_2OH$$

plasma, except in the one of 3,000 persons in whom the enzyme is atypical (genetically determined) and has little affinity for suxamethonium. Consequently, neuromuscular blockade can last three hours or more.

Regulation: Choline concentrations may govern the rate of synthesis of acetylcholine, but the rate of uptake of choline into the nerve terminal may also be important.

After acetylcholine is hydrolysed, up to half of the choline produced is taken back into the nerve terminal. Acetylcholine itself seems to impede this re-uptake, so a regulatory feedback loop is possible. Otherwise, little is known of synaptic regulatory mechanisms, neuronal feedback loops being better understood.

Receptors: The acetylcholine receptors have been extensively studied, especially those at the neuromuscular junction. Classically the receptors have been divided into the muscarinic type (activated by the alkaloid muscarine) and the nicotinic (activated and later blocked by nicotine). Muscarinic activation results in a rapid action, whereas nicotinic activation is rather slower and more sustained. Acetylcholine produces both effects, but many drugs are fairly specific to one or the other population of receptor. Further subdivision of both muscarinic and nicotinic receptors has been proposed.

Pharmacological considerations: Hemicholinium, a synthetic drug, interferes with the choline uptake system and thus lowers acetylcholine content. Botulinus toxin prevents the release of acetylcholine and kills by respiratory paralysis. Specific inhibitors of choline acetyl transferase have been developed, but little is known of their clinical actions.

A wide variety of drugs can block acetylcholinesterase, thereby increasing and prolonging acetylcholine actions. Physostigmine (eserine) is the prime example, and later members of this class include neostigmine, pyridostigmine, and edrophonium. Irreversible inactivators of acetylcholinesterase were developed as insecticides and nerve-gas poisons; they comprise the organophosphates such as parathion. Physostigmine is the only therapeutic agent that penetrates the brain, and its actions can be deduced from Table 2-1. It can be used in a dose of 0.5 to 2 mg intravenously to counteract many of the peripheral and central effects of poisoning by atropine and similar anticholinergic drugs and by psychotropic drugs with secondary anticholinergic actions such as amitriptyline.

Substances acting directly on cholinergic receptors include methacholine, carbachol, and the alkaloids pilocarpine and muscarine. The most widely used cholinomimetic is nicotine from tobacco, but nicotine has complex actions: it later blocks cholinoceptors and also releases catecholamines from the adrenal medulla.

The most important group, therapeutically, consists of the antimuscarinic agents, which directly block acetylcholine receptors. These agents include atropine, hyoscine, and scopolamine among the alkaloids; methantheline and propantheline among the synthetics; and benztropine and trihexyphenidyl among the antiparkinsonian agents. Antipsychotic drugs such as chlorpromazine and thioridazine, and tricyclic antidepressants such as amitriptyline and prothiaden, also have powerful cholinoceptor-blocking properties.

Catecholamines

This category includes *dopamine*, an important neurotransmitter in the basal ganglia, limbic system, and other parts of the brain; *noradrenaline*, the transmitter at most sympathetic postganglionic fibres and in certain tracts in the brain—especially the hypothalamus and the cerebral and cerebellar cortices; and *adrenaline* (epinephrine), the major hormone of the adrenal medulla and, possibly, a central neurotransmitter as well. Because they are active in a common chain of synthesis, they will be dealt with together.

Synthesis: The precursor is the amino acid tyrosine (monohydroxyphenylalanine), which is taken up into the nerve ending (Figure 2-6). The precursor is hydroxylated to dihydroxyphenylalaline (L-dopa) by the enzyme tyrosine hydroxylase, which is located in the cytoplasm and on cell membranes. Tyrosine contains iron and utilizes tetrahydrobiopterin as its cofactor. The next step is the conversion of L-dopa to dopamine by the soluble enzyme L-aromatic amino acid decarboxylase (sometimes called dopa decarboxylase), which needs pyridoxal phosphate as its cofactor.

Dopamine is then taken up into vesicles, which in noradrenergic neurons contain dopamine-β-hydroxylase, an enzyme that adds a hydroxyl group to the side chain. The enzyme contains copper, and its cofactor is ascorbic acid. Finally, in the adrenal medulla and in certain parts of the brain, noradrenaline is methylated to adrenaline by the cytoplasmic enzyme phenylethanolamine N-methyltransferase, using S-adenosylmethionine as the methyl donor.

These synthetic enzymes are believed to be fairly non-specific. Thus, L-aromatic amino acid decarboxylase also converts 5-hydroxytryptophan to 5-hydroxytryptamine, and histidine to histamine. Similarly, tyramine can be hydroxylated to octopamine (which is noradrenaline minus one hydroxyl on the ring), a transmitter substance in certain invertebrates.

The rate of synthesis of catecholamines depends on the amount of available tyrosine hydroxylase, ie, it is the rate-limiting enzyme. Thus, only major manipulations of the other synthesizing enzymes would be expected to have any effect on the amount of catecholamine synthesized.

Storage and release: The catecholamines are stored in granules that contain high concentrations (up to a fifth) of the substance, probably as a complex with adenosine triphosphate, four molecules of catecholamine to one of ATP. Chromogranin (a specific protein) and dopamine-β-hydroxylase are also present in the granules.

Catecholamines are also found free in the cytoplasmic fluid and in the granules, thus forming two mobile pools as well as the intragranular reserve pool. Catecholamines move by active uptake from the cytoplasmic mobile pool into the granules.

The nerve impulse causes ion fluxes, which mobilize the reserve pool, dissociate the catecholamine-ATP-protein complex, and release the neurotransmitter by exocytosis into the synaptic cleft. ATP, chromogranin, and dopamine-β-hydroxylase are also released from peripheral sympathetic endings and presumably from central ones as well.

In the adrenal medulla, noradrenaline is released into the cytoplasm from the granules in which it has been synthesized from dopamine. In the cytoplasm it is methylated and the adrenaline is taken up into separate storage granules.

Inactivation: The most important mechanism whereby dopamine and noradrenaline are removed from the synaptic cleft and their influence on receptors terminated is by re-uptake, first across the presynaptic membrane into the cytoplasm and thence into the storage vesicles. Simple diffusion also accounts for some of the transmitter inactivation.

Enzymatic breakdown requires several enzymes, both intracellular and extracellular (Figures 2-7 and 2-8). The two enzymes of major importance are monoamine oxidase (MAO) and catechol-o-methyltransferase (COMT). Both enzymes

Figure 2-6. Synthesis of catecholamines.

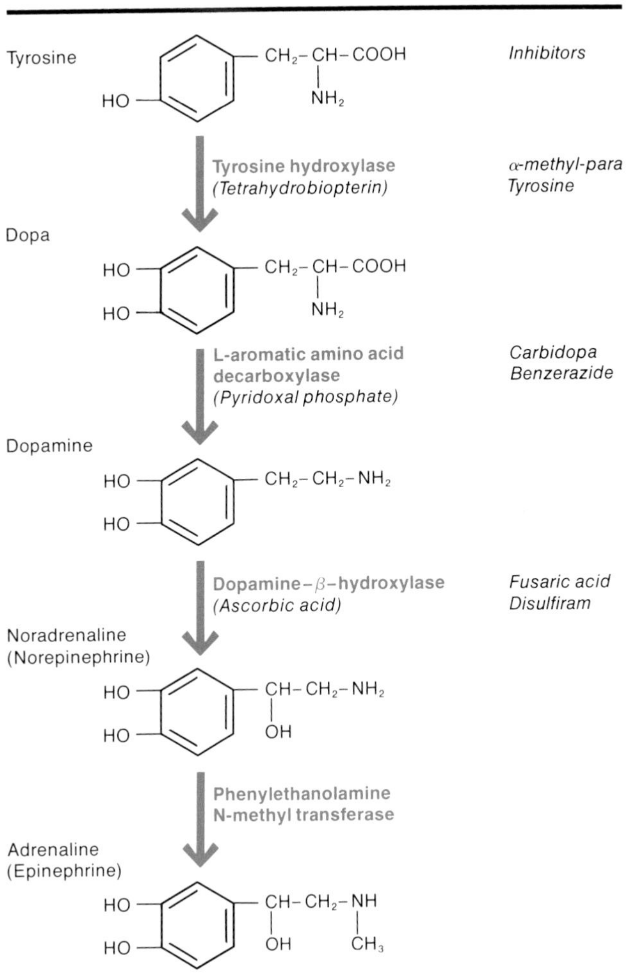

Choice:

Tyrosine hydroxylase
(Tetrahydrobiopterim)

20

Figure 2-7. Breakdown of dopamine.

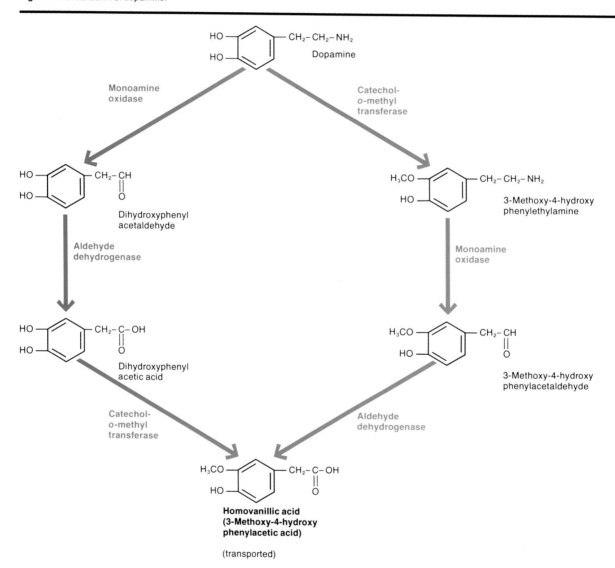

21

Figure 2-8. Breakdown of noradrenaline.

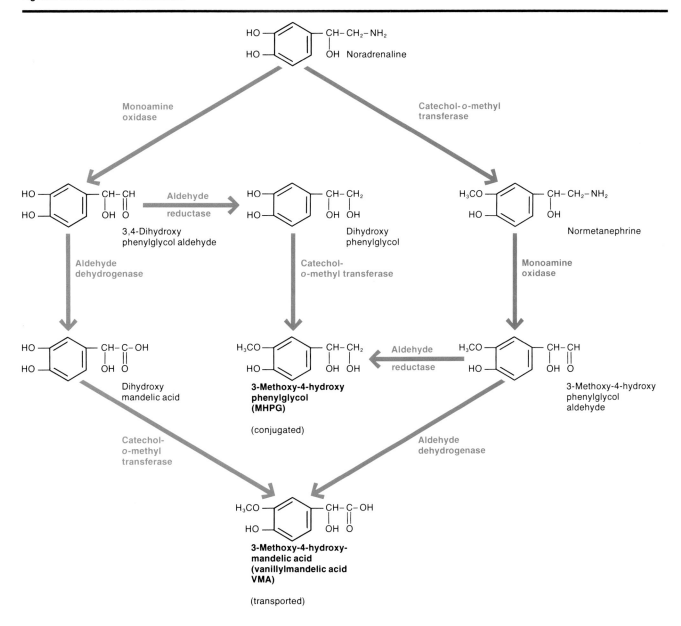

are widespread throughout the body, especially the liver and kidney. MAO is a mitochondrial enzyme that converts the catecholamine to its corresponding aldehyde by oxidative deamination. Thus, dopamine forms dihydroxyphenylace-taldehyde, and noradrenaline and adrenaline form 3,4-dihydroxyphenylglycolaldehyde. COMT in the synapse occurs largely in relation to the postsynaptic membrane and synaptic cleft itself. It uses S-adenosylmethionine as a methyl donor to convert dopamine into 3-methoxy-4-hydroxyphenyl-ethylamine and noradrenaline into normetanephrine; ie, COMT changes one of the hydroxyl groups into a methoxy (CH_3O) group.

Further breakdown takes place involving MAO, COMT, and aldehyde reductase and dehydrogenase. The outcome of all these complex processes is that dopamine is converted mainly to its acidic derivative 3-methoxy-4-hydroxyphenyl-acetic acid (also called homovanillic acid, HVA), and to a minor extent to dihydroxyphenylacetic acid (DOPAC).

The metabolites of noradrenaline are more complex. The main acidic metabolite is 3-methoxy-4-hydroxy mandelic acid (also somewhat erroneously called vanillyl-mandelic acid, VMA). In the rat and possibly in the human brain, the main metabolite is the alcohol derivative formed from the intermediate aldehydes by aldehyde reductase. This substance is 3-methoxy-4-hydroxy phenylethylglycol (MHPG), which is finally conjugated as the sulphate or glucuronide and is excreted. Adrenaline follows mostly the same metabolic pathways as noradrenaline, inasmuch as the terminal methyl group does not affect the process.

Both the alcoholic and acidic breakdown products can be detected in the cerebrospinal fluid (CSF) as well as in the urine. The acidic products move out of the CSF by means of an active transport mechanism that can be blocked by the drug probenecid. Thus, measurement of CSF metabolite concentrations before and after administration of probenecid can give a gross index of amine turnover in the brain.

Regulation: Several mechanisms regulate the synthesis of catecholamines. Two pertain to the rate-limiting enzyme tyrosine hydroxylase. First, end-product inhibition can occur, noradrenaline inhibiting its own synthesis by competing with tyrosine for the cofactor tetrahydrobiopterin. Thus, with a decrease in noradrenaline concentration in the mobile pool (a decrease that would follow noradrenaline's uptake into granules and release on repetitive firing), tyrosine conver-

sion to L-dopa would be enhanced. The second mechanism entails a sustained activation of tyrosine hydroxylase and dopamine-β-hydroxylase after sustained activity of noradrenergic neurons.

The glucocorticoids play an important role in regulating adrenaline synthesis. The adrenal glands have a portal vascular system organized so that secreted steroids from the cortex pass through the medulla on their way into the systemic circulation. In the medulla, the glucocorticoids induce the synthesis of the enzyme phenylethanolamine-N-methyltransferase and hence increase the synthesis of adrenaline.

Receptors: Much work using radioactive-isotope-labelled agonists and antagonists has been carried out to characterize catecholamine receptors. Dopamine receptors have been identified and have been shown to be most sensitive to dopamine and less sensitive to noradrenaline, adrenaline, and isoprenaline (isoproterenol). It has been suggested that these receptors exist in two states, one in which they are preferentially bound to agonist drugs and the other in which they are bound to antagonist drugs, but different populations of receptors may exist. It is also possible that some receptors (D_1) are in close association with the enzyme adenylate cyclase, which when activated will increase the amount of cyclic adenosine monophosphate in the cytoplasmic fluid. Others (D_2) seem not to be associated with adenylate cyclase.

The noradrenergic receptors are divisible into α and β categories. The α-adrenoreceptors are activated more potently by adrenaline and noradrenaline, whereas the β-adreno-receptors are maximally activated by isoprenaline. The latter receptors can be further divided into β_1, chiefly at cardiac sites, and β_2, which occur elsewhere including the bronchi. Both α and β receptors can be excitatory or inhibitory, depending on the location (Table 2-1). The brain appears to possess both α and β receptors, but their characteristics are not always entirely typical. Some β receptors may be on blood vessels rather than neurons.

Drug effects: Drugs that interact with the synthetic enzyme tyrosine hydroxylase profoundly alter catecholamine function. Tyrosine analogues such as α-methyl-para-tyrosine impair the synthesis of dopamine and noradrenaline by blocking this enzyme.

Noradrenaline synthesis is also diminished after the administration of fusaric acid or disulfiram, drugs that can

Table 2-1. Effector organ responses to autonomic
nerve impulses.

Effector organ	Type	Adrenergic impulses	Cholinergic impulses
Heart			
S-A node	β	heart rate increases	heart rate decreases
Atria	β	contractility increases	contractility decreases
Ventricles	β	contractility increases	
Arterioles			
Skin and mucosa	α	constriction	some dilatation
Skeletal muscle	α, β	usually dilatation	some dilatation
Lung			
Bronchial muscle	β	relaxation	contraction
Eye			
Radial muscle, iris	α	mydriasis	
Sphincter muscle, iris			miosis
Ciliary muscle			contraction for near vision
Stomach and intestine			
Motility	β	decrease	increase
Sphincter	α	contraction	relaxation
Secretion			stimulation
Bladder			
Detrusor	β	relaxation	contraction
Sphincter	α	contraction	relaxation
Sweat glands	α	localized secretion	generalized secretion
Male sex organs		ejaculation	erection
Liver	β	glycogen breakdown	synthesis
Salivary glands	α	some water secretion	marked water secretion
Lacrimal glands			secretion
Nasopharyngeal glands			secretion

interfere with dopamine-β-hydroxylase. Disulfiram also inhibits aldehyde dehydrogenase, causing the accumulation of aldehydes such as acetaldehyde after ethanol ingestion.

Precursor administration will increase catecholamine synthesis, provided that tyrosine hydroxylase is by-passed. Thus, administration of L-dopa increases the synthesis of dopamine in dopaminergic neurons and of noradrenaline in noradrenergic neurons. Concomitant administration of a peripherally acting dopa decarboxylase inhibitor such as carbidopa or benserazide results in even higher brain concentrations of dopamine. Large doses of L-dopa also affect other neurotransmitters by swamping uptake mechanisms and enzymes. Conversely, the administration of L-α-methyl dopa results in the synthesis of α-methyl-noradrenaline, which acts as a false transmitter to cause a diminution in central noradrenergic function, with hypotension and sedation.

The storage of catecholamines is disrupted by reserpine and tetrabenazine, which destroy the mechanism whereby catecholamines are transported from the cytoplasmic pool to the granules. Furthermore, catecholamines are released, but not by exocytosis (inasmuch as dopamine-β-hydroxylase concentrations do not increase). Several other antihypertensive agents act by depleting the nerve endings of noradrenaline. To do so, the drugs (guanethidine, debrisoquine, and bethanidine, for example) are taken up into the neuron by the transmembrane-catecholamine-uptake system. Bretylium also depletes noradrenergic terminals, but only after repeated dosing.

Many sympathomimetic agents act indirectly by displacing noradrenaline from its granule stores without impairing synthesis. Ephedrine and amphetamine are important examples. Tyramine also releases noradrenaline, but probably by displacement from the mobile pool. These drugs exhibit tachyphylaxis, that is, their effects diminish on repeated administration as the catecholamine pools become depleted.

The major inactivation pathway, re-uptake, is blocked by the tricyclic antidepressants and related drugs. These compounds affect the catecholamines and serotonin to varying extents: the re-uptake of dopamine is usually least impaired. Cocaine and amphetamine can also inhibit re-uptake whereas lithium may facilitate it.

Monoamine oxidase inhibition results in a failure to catabolize catecholamines in the cytoplasmic pool. The catecholamines are therefore available for uptake into the stores and subsequent release. MAO is believed to exist in two forms,

A and B. Noradrenaline is inactivated mostly by type A, and dopamine by both types. No known drugs effectively block COMT.

Many drugs act directly on catecholamine receptors. Dopamine agonists include apomorphine, piribedil, and bromocriptine, whereas the antipsychotic drugs ("major tranquilizers") are very effective dopamine antagonists, acting by blockade of the receptors. Agonists on the α-adrenoceptor include noradrenaline and the directly acting sympathomimetic agents phenylephrine and phenylpropanolamine; β-adrenoceptor agonists include isoprenaline, terbutaline, isoxsuprine, and salbutamol. The α-adrenoceptors are blocked by phenoxybenzamine, phentolamine, some ergot alkaloids, and some antipsychotic agents such as chlorpromazine and haloperidol. β-adrenoceptor blockade is the major action of the large and important group of drugs of which propranolol was the first to be widely used. Some β-adrenoceptor blocking agents preferentially affect β_1 or β_2 receptors.

5-Hydroxytryptamine (serotonin)
For many years it was known that a vasoconstrictor substance is present in the plasma; the substance, named serotonin, was identified about 30 years ago as 5-hydroxytryptamine (5-HT) and found to be widely distributed in the body. Eventually, 5-HT was discovered in the brain and gradually established as a neurotransmitter. It is still not as well studied as the catecholamines are.

Synthesis: the precursor of 5-hydroxytryptamine is the essential amino acid tryptophan, an indolic compound (Figure 2-9). Tryptophan is the only amino acid bound largely to plasma albumin, and it is taken up into the brain by an active transport process. Hydroxylation to 5-hydroxytryptophan then takes place, using the enzyme tryptophan hydroxylase and tetrahydrobiopterin as the cofactor. This is the rate-limiting step, and concentrations of tryptophan are normally below maximal so that the availability of tryptophan and the extent of its binding to plasma proteins govern the amount of neurotransmitter synthesized. The 5-hydroxytryptophan is decarboxylated by L-aromatic amino acid decarboxylase to 5-HT.

Storage and release: Like the catecholamines, 5-HT is taken up and stored in granules at the presynaptic ending. The storage is in association with adenine nucleotides, mainly ATP.

25

Figure 2-9. Synthesis and breakdown of 5-hydroxytryptamine.

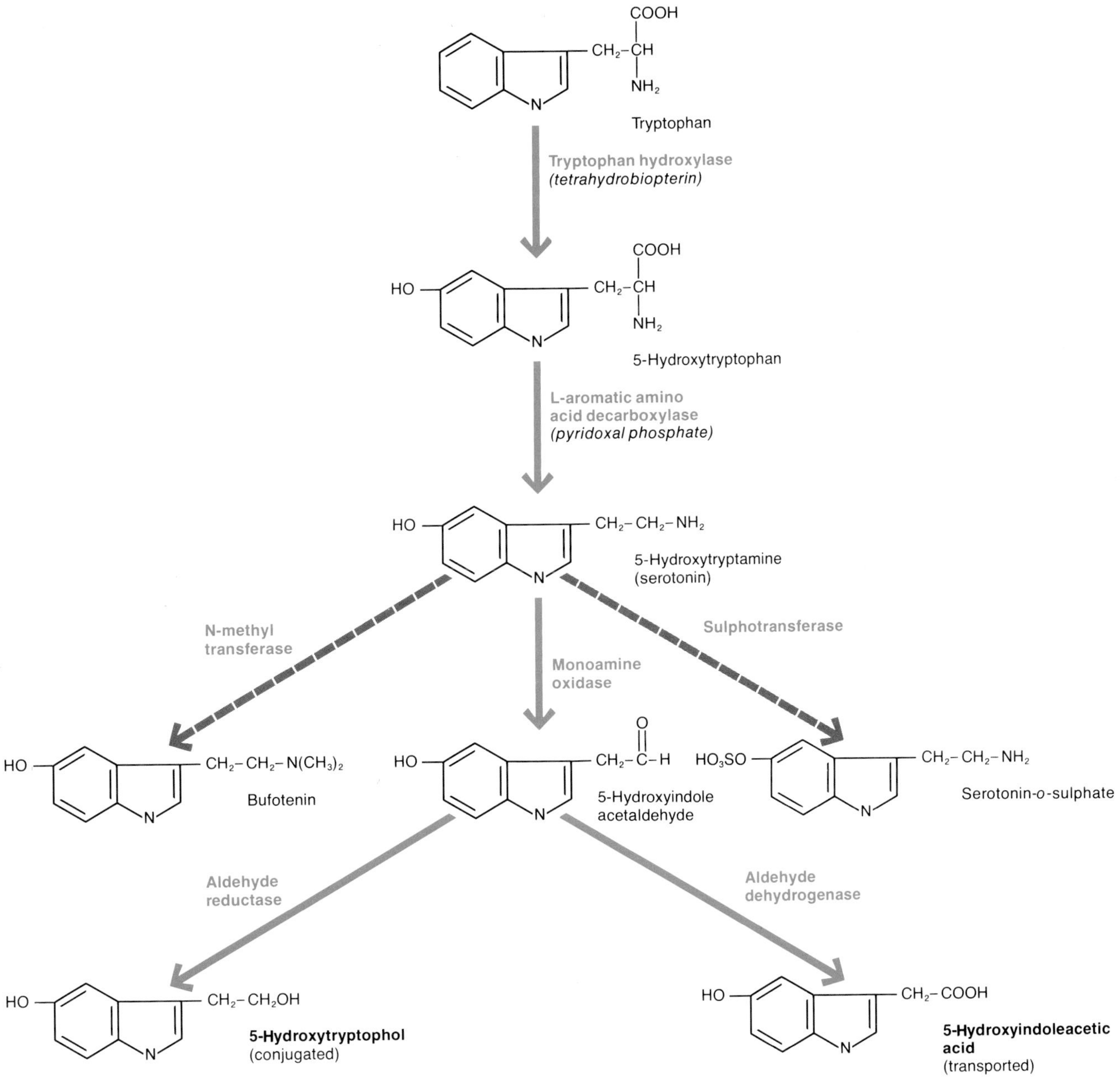

Some 5-HT probably exists in a mobile extragranular pool. Other tissues such as blood platelets can take up and store 5-HT.

The discharge of 5-HT into the synaptic cleft is by ionic activation and exocytosis.

Inactivation: Re-uptake into nerve terminals is the primary route of inactivation of 5-HT. The process is energy dependent and can work against a considerable concentration gradient. Similar uptake mechanisms exist in the blood platelet, which has been proposed as an accessible model in man of central serotonergic processes.

Intracytoplasmic 5-HT can form a substrate for MAO, type A especially. The substrate converts 5-HT into 5-hydroxy-indoleacetaldehyde, which can then be oxidized by aldehyde dehydrogenase to the acidic metabolite 5-hydroxyindole-acetic acid (5-HIAA). Like those of HVA and VMA, the egress of 5-HIAA from the cerebrospinal fluid can be blocked by probenecid, thus giving a rough measure of 5-HT turnover.

Under certain conditions, 5-HIAA can be reduced to the alcoholic derivative 5-hydroxytryptophol. Other minor metabolic pathways include conjugation to a sulphate derivative and perhaps action by N-methyl transferase to methylated compounds, which are believed to be hallucinogenic (eg, 5-hydroxy-N-dimethyltryptamine, or bufotenin, and dimethyltryptamine, DMT).

Regulation: Very little is known of the control of synthesis. Only about 2% of dietary tryptophan is converted to 5-HT, and the wide fluctuations in plasma tryptophan seem to have little influence on central 5-HT function. End-product feedback inhibition also seems unimportant.

Receptors: Little is known of 5-HT receptor characteristics. There is some evidence that different types or at least different configurations of receptor exist.

Drug mechanisms: The synthesizing enzyme tryptophan hydroxylase can be blocked by para-chlorophenylalanine, thus decreasing concentrations of 5-HT. Conversely, L-tryptophan can be administered and will increase 5-HT concentrations in the brain. However, large doses are needed to attain this, possibly interfering with the brain uptake of other amino acids. The administration of 5-hydroxytryptophan can also increase 5-HT synthesis. As it does with the cate-

cholamines, reserpine depletes the nerve endings of 5-HT and prevents its storage.

The re-uptake of 5-HT into the presynaptic endings and vesicles can be effectively blocked by some of the tricyclic antidepressants such as chlorimipramine and amitriptyline. Monoamine oxidase inhibitors increase 5-HT concentrations by preventing the breakdown of the intracytoplasmic pool.

Hallucinogens such as LSD and mescaline have complex actions on 5-HT systems. These drugs inhibit serotonergic cell firing, probably by blocking autoreceptors on these cells and thereby producing inhibition. Hallucinogens have much less effect on tryptaminergic postsynaptic receptors. Non-hallucinogenic analogues such as methysergide show no such selectivity, blocking both types of receptor. Cyproheptadine is a potent 5-HT (and histaminic) receptor antagonist.

Gamma-aminobutyric acid (GABA)

GABA was identified first as an important constituent of the crustacean nervous system and later of the mammalian central nervous system. GABA was eventually proved to be a powerful inhibitor and has fulfilled most of the criteria for a neurotransmitter. Progress in research has been slow because of the lack of drugs acting specifically on GABA mechanisms. It has been estimated that 40% of synapses in the brain are GABA ergic, making GABA the most ubiquitous neurotransmitter.

Synthesis: GABA is synthesized by decarboxylation of the amino acid glutamic acid by the enzyme glutamic acid decarboxylase (GAD) (Figure 2-10). The cofactor is pyridoxal phosphate. GAD seems to be localized exclusively in neurons that contain GABA.

Storage and release: Glutamate metabolism in the brain is complex, and GABA appears to be apportioned into several "pools." Newly synthesized GABA is released preferentially over stored GABA. GABA release in response to electrical stimulation is dependent on calcium ions.

Inactivation: Like the monoamine transmitters, GABA is taken back into the presynaptic nerve endings by a high-affinity uptake mechanism. Interestingly, some glial cells also possess a powerful uptake mechanism, but the role of this process in GABA regulation remains unclear.

Enzymic breakdown entails transamination to succinic semi-

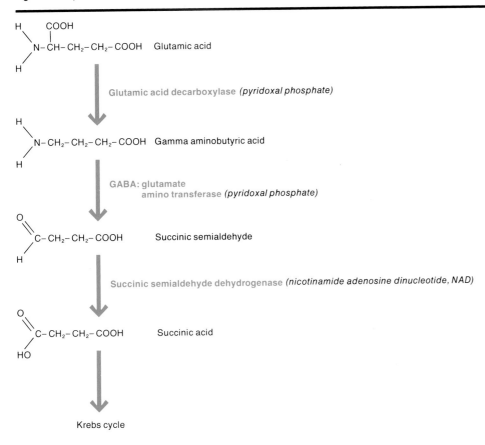

Figure 2-10. Synthesis and breakdown of GABA.

aldehyde by GABA: glutamate aminotransferase. This mitochondrial enzyme is widespread in the central nervous system, including neurons and glial cells, and uses pyridoxal phosphate as coenzyme. The next step is oxidation to succinic acid by succinic semialdehyde dehydrogenase, the succinic acid then entering the Krebs cycle.

Receptors: The brain contains many short interneurons, many of which appear to exert an inhibitory function, and GABA is the neurotransmitter in many instances. Through the use of radioactive-isotope-labelled GABA, postsynaptic GABA receptors have been detected in brain extracts. Evidence suggests that in the spinal cord, GABA may act as well on presynaptic receptors to inhibit the release of some other neurotransmitters.

Drug mechanisms: Some convulsants are believed to inhibit GABA synthesis, and many other drugs interfere with the GABA uptake mechanism. Fluspirilene, an antipsychotic agent, is one of the most potent. The anticonvulsant drug sodium valproate may slow GABA breakdown by inhibiting succinic semialdehyde dehydrogenase.

The research alkaloid muscimol is a specific receptor agonist, whereas bicuculline and picrotoxin are receptor antagonists. The benzodiazepines and perhaps the barbiturates potentiate the actions of GABA, but the mechanism of that effect is bafflingly obscure; it is not by direct receptor agonism.

Other Neurotransmitters

The amino acid *glycine* is a strong candidate as an inhibitory neurotransmitter, especially in the spinal cord. One of strychnine's actions is powerful antagonism of glycine receptors.

Glutamic acid and *aspartic acid*, both dicarboxylic amino acids, have widespread excitatory functions in the crustacean and mammalian nervous systems and fulfill some of the criteria for a neurotransmitter role.

Histamine has been rather neglected as a possible central neurotransmitter despite its undoubted importance in the periphery. However, some neurons respond to histamine, and it stimulates adenylate cyclase in the hippocampus. This stimulation is competitively inhibited by H_2 receptor antagonists such as cimetidine.

Among the vast number of actions of the various *prostaglandins*, effects on neuronal cells have been documented.

There has been much interest in the possible neuroregulatory functions of *polypeptides*. Some, such as luteinizing-hormone-releasing hormone (LHRH), thyrotropin-releasing hormone (TRH), and growth-hormone-release-inhibiting hormone (somatostatin), are released by the hypothalamus and transported by the hypophyseal portal system to the anterior pituitary where they regulate endocrine secretions. However, these releasing factors are found in other areas of the brain and may "modulate" neurotransmission, ie, modify neuronal responses to other neurotransmitters. ACTH also seems to have functions in the central nervous system and is distributed in the hypothalamus and limbic system. Substance P, an 11 amino acid peptide, has a definite distribution in the brain and spinal cord and may be implicated in pain transmission. Other peptides found in the central nervous system include neurotensin, vasoactive intestinal polypeptide (VIP), cholecystokinin, bradykinin, and angiotensin II. The central nervous system functions of these peptides, many of which were originally discovered in the gut, remain unclear.

Finally, one of the most important developments in recent years has been clarification of the mechanisms of narcotic drugs. Specific binding sites for opiates have been found in the central nervous system, particularly in sites known to be associated with pain transmission. Specific narcotic antagonists such as naloxone also bind to these receptor sites with high affinity. The endogenous ligand or neurotransmitter eluded identification for about a year and was then reported by Hughes and Kosterlitz to be two pentapeptides that they termed "enkephalins." It was noted that the amino acid sequence of one of the enkephalins occurred in fragments of β-lipotropin, a pituitary polypeptide believed to be the precursor of β-melanocyte-stimulating hormone. These fragments also possess opioid activity and are now termed "endorphins," but β-endorphin itself is possibly the only naturally occurring endorphin. Intensive research is now directed towards identifying the natural functions of these opioid peptides, the leucine[5]- and the methionine[5]-enkephalins and β-endorphin (see also page 109).

FURTHER READING

Axelrod J: Neurotransmitters, in Thompson RF (ed): *Progress in Psychobiology.* San Francisco, Freeman, 1976, pp 122-129.

Bachelard HS: *Brain Biochemistry,* London, Chapman and Hall, 1974.

Cooper JR, Bloom FE, Roth RH: *The Biochemical Basis of Neuropharmacology,* ed 3. New York, Oxford University Press, 1978.

von Euler US: Historical background for studies on neurotransmitter release, in Fields W (ed): *Neurotransmitter Function: Basic and Clinical Aspects.* New York, Stratton, 1977, pp 1-10.

Iversen LL, Iversen SD, Snyder SH: *Handbook of Psychopharmacology,* volumes III and VI. New York, Plenum Press, 1975.

Jones DG: *Synapses and Synaptosomes. Morphological Aspects.* London, Chapman and Hall, 1975.

Lipton MA, Di Mascio A, Killam KF (eds): *Psychopharmacology. A generation of Progress.* New York, Raven Press, 1978.

Snyder SH, Innis RB: Peptide neurotransmitters. *Ann Rev Biochem 48*: 755-782, 1979.

Usdin E, Kopin IJ, Barchas J: *Catecholamines: Basic and Clinical Frontiers.* New York, Pergamon Press, 1979.

Brain Organization and Behaviour

The translation of the drug effects on biochemical mechanisms (outlined in the previous chapter) into alterations in holistic behaviour is a difficult one, primarily because the relationship of neurotransmitters to various aspects of brain functioning is dauntingly complex. In this chapter, drug effects on physiological systems such as the reticular activating system will first be summarized. Next, what is known of the relationship of specific neurotransmitters to identifiable brain tracts will be outlined, and, finally, some of the more important drug effects on behaviour will be presented.

SINGLE-UNIT ACTIVITY

Single-unit activity comprises the spike potential from a single neuron that can be recorded through the use of minute electrodes. Drugs can be administered either locally by means of a micropipette or systemically. With local administration, carefully gauged amounts of drug can be released close to the neuron by means of electrical pulses.

The effects of drugs on the single unit informs us about the localization of drug-sensitive neurons and their type of activity. For example, serotonergic neurons in the midbrain raphé nuclei are reversibly inhibited by the local administration of lysergic acid diethylamide (LSD). Similarly, noradrenaline reduces the spontaneous discharge of Purkinje neurons in the cerebellum. Cyclic AMP produces a similar reduction and may be the mediator for the effects of noradrenaline at that site.

RETICULAR ACTIVATING SYSTEM

With larger electrodes, multiple-unit activity within a larger structure can be measured. The reticular activating system is a diffuse core of ventral neuronal chains that extends from the spinal cord to the thalamus. Electrical stimulation of these polysynaptic pathways produces behavioural and electrical signs of increased alertness and arousal. The arousal continuum ranges from deep sleep, light sleep, wakening, an inactive state, conditions of heightened alertness, emotion, and, finally, to emotional extremes. Insomnia and anxiety are overarousal states.

Amphetamines activate the reticular system, whereas barbiturates depress it. Chlorpromazine increases the filtering effect of the reticular system, which normally dampens inessential sensory signals by modulating (facilitating or inhibiting) afferent inputs.

THE LIMBIC SYSTEM

The limbic system is a complex, ill-defined group of nuclei and tracts that includes the septal area, the hippocampus, the hypothalamus, and parts of the rhinencephalon and cerebral cortex. The limbic system is concerned with integrating emotional and motivational behaviour, particularly motor coordination in emotional responses. Stimulation of the hippocampus or amygdala in animals is followed by spontaneous after-discharges with concomitant behavioural effects that resemble a psychomotor attack in man. Chlorpromazine reduces the threshold for the amygdaloid after-discharge whereas phenobarbitone raises it. The benzodiazepines have various effects on the limbic system, although there are definite differences among these drugs. For example, chlordiazepoxide but not diazepam alters spontaneous activity in the hippocampus.

CEREBRAL CORTEX

The electrical activity of the cerebral cortex is the resultant of potential changes in many neurons, dendrites, and axons. In animals, cortical recordings enable some localizing of function; in man, scalp recordings are blurred by much spatial summation but, instead, an integrated estimate of cortical activity is possible.

The EEG in man is analysed in several ways. Visual analysis into the clinical wavebands (delta, 0.5-3.5 Hz; theta, 3.5-7.5 Hz; alpha, 7.5-13 Hz; and beta, 13-40 Hz) is fairly crude and will detect only major drug effects such as drowsiness and suppression of epileptic discharges. The interpretation of the recordings is empirical but, nevertheless, based on a wealth of clinical experience.

Computer analysis of EEG takes several forms, some of which entail esoteric mathematics. Most simpler methods consist of analysing the EEG into wavebands of various widths and measuring the energy in those wavebands.

Psychotropic drugs produce fairly characteristic patterns of change in the EEG (Table 3-1). These patterns have been described empirically, and the relationship between EEG changes and underlying drug effects on neuronal function is unknown. Some of the effects may be misleading. For example, tricyclic antidepressives produce effects similar to those of atropine, and the EEG may be partly reflecting anticholinergic rather than antidepressive effects. Some drugs with atypical profiles in animals have been tested in man, and their probable psychotropic properties have been predicted from their EEG effects: mianserin, an antidepressant, is an example of such a drug.

The EEG is among the most sensitive detectors of psychotropic drug actions. Thus, it can be used in studies of bioavailability and duration of action, for example, and because it reflects changes in nervous tissues it is often more appropriate than are plasma concentration estimations.

As well as quantifying spontaneous EEG activity, computers can be used to distinguish responses to individual stimuli. The evoked response at the scalp comprises early waves (less than 50 msec after the auditory, visual, or tactile stimuli), which represent the primary afferent volley, and later waves, which reflect secondary association processes. The latter components are altered by psychological processes such as attention, arousal, expectation, and stimulus novelty; drugs that affect these functions alter the evoked responses.

AUTONOMIC NERVOUS SYSTEM

Psychotropic drugs have many actions on the peripheral nervous system, so it is important to know the organization of the main branches of the autonomic nervous system. Reference should be made to a relevant and authoritative textbook for details, but the following is a résumé:

The afferent fibres from the viscera are mostly nonmyelinated fibres; they form the first links in the autonomic reflex arcs subserving vasomotor, respiratory, and other functions. The autonomic nervous system is functionally integrated in the spinal cord and the medulla oblongata, but the principal site of integration is the hypothalamus. The posterolateral hypothalamic nuclei are mainly sympathetic in their connexions; those more medial and ventral are the head ganglia of the parasympathetic system. Among other areas concerned with autonomic activity are the basal ganglia, some cortical areas, and some parts of the limbic system.

On the motor side, the autonomic nervous system consists of the sympathetic (or thoracolumbar) outflow and the parasympathetic (or craniosacral) outflow. The cells that give rise to the preganglionic fibres of the sympathetic division lie in the intermediolateral columns of the spinal cord from the eighth cervical to the second or third lumbar segments. These axons pass into the anterior roots and synapse in the vertebral and prevertebral, or terminal, sympathetic ganglia. They are cholinergic. The postganglionic fibres reach all the visceral structures of the thorax, abdomen, head, and neck, often by means of terminal plexuses such as the cardiac. With the ex-

Table 3-1. EEG patterns induced by psychotropic drugs.

Drug example	Effect on amplitude waveband				
	1-3.5	3.5-7.5	7.5-13	13-22	22-32
Chlorpromazine	+	+ +	0	0	−
Trifluoperazine	+	+	+	0	−
Reserpine	+	+	−	0	0
Amylobarbitone	0	0	0	+ +	+
Diazepam	0	−	0	+ +	+
Amphetamine	0	−	−	+	+ +
Atropine	+ +	+	−	+	+ +
Imipramine	+	+ +	−	+	+
Iproniazid	0	0	−	0	0
Alcohol	0	0	+	0	0

+ + marked increase; + increase; 0 no effect; − decrease

ception of the sweat-gland innervation, which is cholinergic, these postganglionic sympathetic fibres are noradrenergic. The adrenal medulla is embryologically and anatomically similar to sympathetic ganglia, but its cells, homologous to the postsynaptic sympathetic ganglion cells, release mainly adrenaline rather than noradrenaline.

The parasympathetic nervous system comprises three outflows of preganglionic connexions. All these neurons are cholinergic. The midbrain outflow innervates the ciliary ganglion of the orbit; the medullary outflow runs in the facial, glossopharyngeal, and vagus nerves; and the sacral outflow originates in the second, third, and fourth segments of the spinal cord. The organs innervated by these outflows are listed in Table 2-1.

The sympathetic system is widely and diffusely distributed to effectors throughout the body, whereas the parasympathetic is much more discretely innervating to effector organs. The autonomic ganglia have nicotinic-type receptors for acetylcholine; the effector organs have muscarinic receptors.

SPECIFIC PATHWAYS
Cholinergic pathways
The cholinergic pathways have not generally been worked out in detail, mainly because of the lack of appropriate techniques. Instead, indirect evidence is used, such as the presence of synthetic and breakdown enzymes and uptake and binding mechanisms for choline and acetylcholine.

Several cholinergic pathways have been proposed; they may be interconnected by a major ascending tegmental-mesencephalic-cortical system. One fairly well-defined pathway runs from the septum to the hippocampus, another from the habenular nucleus to the interpeduncular nucleus. Cholinergic neurons occur widely in the brain and spinal cord and hence influence many neuronal and behavioural functions.

The diffuse activating system of the brain has important cholinergic components, being activated by cholinergic drugs and blocked by atropine and its analogues. Muscarinic pathways appear to have a diffuse function; nicotine pathways are more specific in the brain stem. Nevertheless, the cholinergic pathways are complex, and cholinergic stimulation is by no means identical with EEG arousal.

Cholinergic mechanisms are operative in seizures, but as part of several interconnecting systems. Cholinergic agonists and anticholinesterases are epileptogenic. Sleep mechanisms include cholinergic pathways; for example, atropine blocks REM sleep. Cholinergic agonists improve memory and learning, at least experimentally in animals. Conversely, atropine impairs learning, the hippocampus perhaps being involved.

The cholinergic mechanisms in the striatum have been particularly well studied. Cholinergic striatal interneurons inhibit a GABA-mediated feedback loop to the substantia nigra. Cholinergic agonists increase this inhibition, which results in increased dopaminergic activity in the striatum. If these drugs are injected into the striatum unilaterally, the animals circle. Increased cholinergic activity in the basal ganglia can also lead to catalepsy or to stereotyped gnawing, biting, and compulsive jumping. Another cholinergically affected motor behaviour is tremor.

Aggressive behaviour, eating, drinking, and sexual behaviour can all be influenced by activity of cholinergic pathways, but the details of the pertinent mechanisms are poorly understood. The role of acetylcholine in sensory pathways has been worked out in more detail. Both visual and auditory pathways entail cholinergic transmission. In man, anticholinesterases alter visual thresholds and adaptation to the dark. Pain perception is altered by drugs that act on cholinergic synapses; for example, cholinergic agonists potentiate opiates.

The diffuse nature of many cholinergic pathways militates against a facile allocation of specific behavioural and physiological functions to particular pathways. The acetylcholine system is active in general functions such as sleep, arousal, biorhythms, and sensation, and it contributes to many other aspects of brain function.

Dopaminergic pathways
Detailed information is available concerning catecholamine pathways in the brain because specialized histological techniques in which cytofluorescence and immunofluorescence are used have been successful.

Dopamine receptors and, possibly, dopaminergic neurons are found in the vomiting center (area postrema). Thus, dopaminergic blockade exerts an antiemetic effect. In the brain stem, dopaminergic neurons emanate from what are termed the A8- and A9-region cell bodies in the pars compacta of the substantia nigra (Figures 3-1 and 3-2). These dopamine cell bodies merge imperceptibly with the A10-region cells located in the medial region above the interpeduncular nucleus.

The axons of A8 and A9 cells form the nigrostriatal pathway, which runs in the crus cerebri and internal capsule to innervate the caudate nucleus, putamen, globus pallidus,

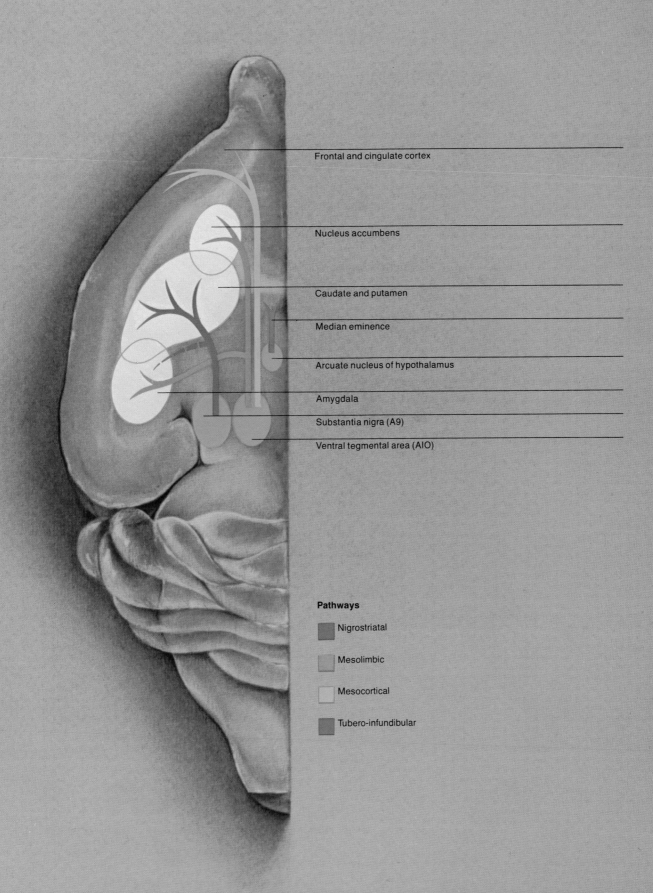

Frontal and cingulate cortex

Nucleus accumbens

Caudate and putamen

Median eminence

Arcuate nucleus of hypothalamus

Amygdala

Substantia nigra (A9)

Ventral tegmental area (AIO)

Pathways

Nigrostriatal

Mesolimbic

Mesocortical

Tubero-infundibular

34

Figure 3-2. Some dopamine tracts in rat brain (sagittal representation).

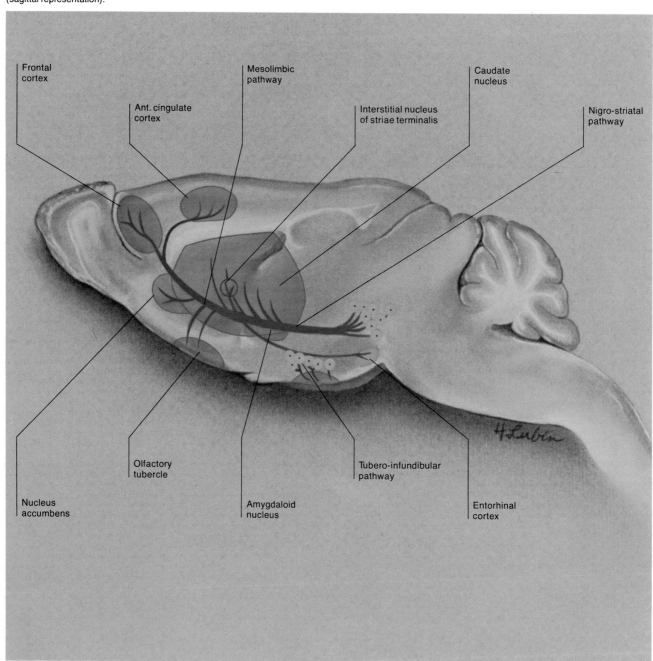

Frontal cortex

Ant. cingulate cortex

Mesolimbic pathway

Interstitial nucleus of striae terminalis

Caudate nucleus

Nigro-striatal pathway

Olfactory tubercle

Tubero-infundibular pathway

Nucleus accumbens

Amygdaloid nucleus

Entorhinal cortex

and, possibly, the amygdala. This is the pathway that degenerates in idiopathic parkinsonism and those forms of the disease that follow exposure to toxic substances such as carbon monoxide. Neuroleptic drugs produce the parkinsonian syndrome by competitively blockading the dopamine receptors on the cholinergic interneurons in the striatum. The motor abnormalities such as stereotyped movements induced by amphetamines are mediated through excessive dopaminergic activity in the basal ganglia.

The A10 cell bodies form the mesolimbic projection system, which runs more medially to terminate in the nucleus accumbens just anterior to the caudate, the olfactory tubercle, the septum, and related areas. This tract is believed to act in the regulation of emotional behaviour, especially its motor components. Axons from A10 neurons and from the medial part of the A9 group also project to the frontal, cingulate, and entorhinal cortices. Thus, dopaminergic synapses exert influences at the highest levels of cerebral function.

Finally, there are several short dopaminergic pathways close to the midline. These run from the central grey area to various nuclei in the thalamus and hypothalamus. The best-defined short tract is the tuberoinfundibular, with its cell bodies in the arcuate nucleus and its axons running into the median eminence and pars intermedia of the pituitary. The tuberoinfundibular tract inhibits the release of prolactin from the anterior pituitary. Thus, dopamine agonists decrease prolactin concentrations whereas dopamine antagonists such as neuroleptics elevate them.

Noradrenergic pathways

All noradrenergic cell bodies are confined to the hind brain, in the pons and medulla (Figures 3-3 and 3-4). A1, A2, and A5 cells are located in the ventral medulla and project both to the spinal cord and rostrally. The clearest cell-body grouping is the locus coeruleus, the "blue site," situated in the floor of the fourth ventricle. It constitutes A6 cells, with A7 cells located ventrolaterally to it and A4 cells just caudally. The locus coeruleus contains the most abundant noradrenergic cell population and is responsible for noradrenergic innervation of all the cortices, geniculate bodies, colliculi, thalamus, and all parts of the hypothalamus.

The rostral projection pathways are the dorsal and the ventral. The dorsal pathway arises in the locus coeruleus and projects ventrolaterally to the central grey area. Its main component runs in the medial forebrain bundle to innervate all the cortices, the thalamus, geniculate bodies, colliculi, habenula, some hypothalamic nuclei, and the olfactory bulb. The ventral pathway is formed from A1, A5, and A7 cell bodies and runs through the medullary reticular formation, the pons, and mesencephalon, gradually overlapping the dorsal bundle. It extends through the cuneate nucleus and the A8 cell region to innervate the septal area, preoptic area, hypothalamus, periventricular area, mammillary bodies, and substantia nigra. A4 cells caudal to the locus coeruleus probably project to the cerebellum.

The translation of such diffuse pathway innervation into physiological functions has proved difficult. Indeed it is not yet clear whether the projection pathways are excitatory or inhibitory. Lesions of the locus coeruleus result in surprisingly little disturbance of overt behaviour. However, studies of the cerebellum, hippocampus, diencephalon, and cerebral cortex suggest that the noradrenergic innervation is inhibitory, being slow in onset with latencies greater than 50 msec, prolonged with actions over 350 msec, and mediated by beta receptors coupled to adenylate cyclase. Note, however, that all the systems detailed are components of the dorsal tract and that the ventral system may be different. Finally, noradrenergic influences in the brain may be more akin to neuromodulation than to classical neurotransmission, ie, the effects of other neurotransmitters may be modified.

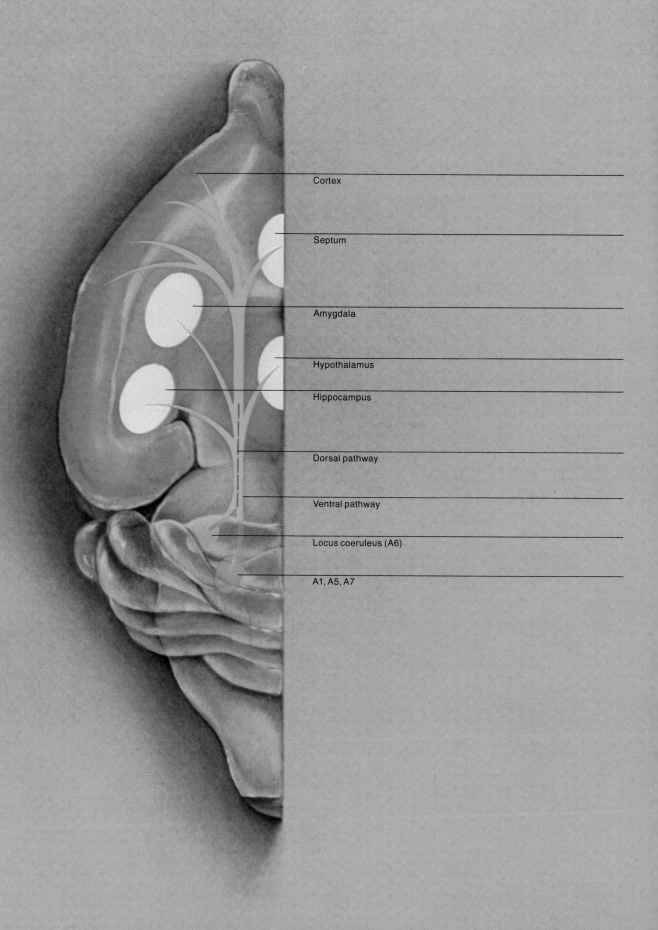

Figure 3-3. Some noradrenaline tracts in rat brain (longitudinal representation).

Cortex

Septum

Amygdala

Hypothalamus

Hippocampus

Dorsal pathway

Ventral pathway

Locus coeruleus (A6)

A1, A5, A7

37

Figure 3-4. Some noradrenaline tracts in rat brain
(sagittal representation).

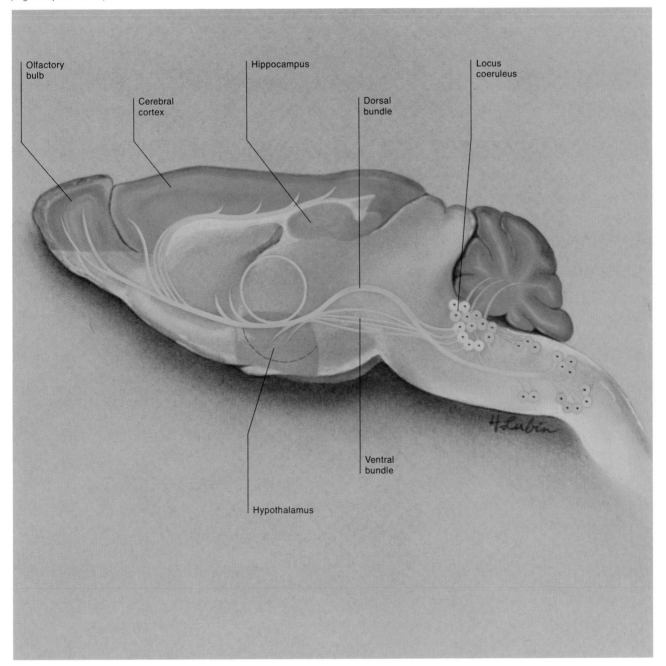

Olfactory
bulb

Cerebral
cortex

Hippocampus

Dorsal
bundle

Locus
coeruleus

Ventral
bundle

Hypothalamus

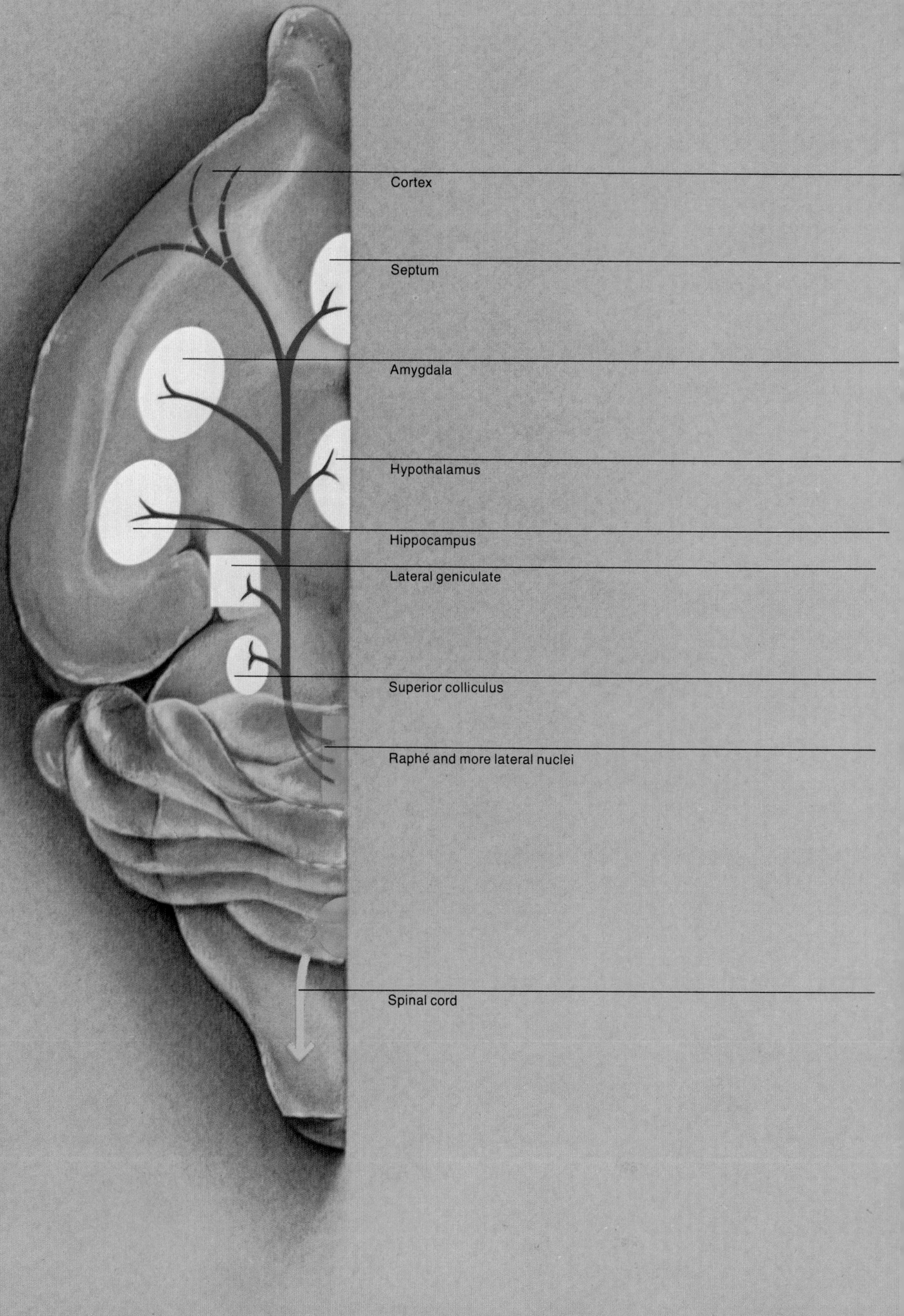

Figure 3-5. Some serotonergic pathways in rat brain (longitudinal representation).

Cortex

Septum

Amygdala

Hypothalamus

Hippocampus

Lateral geniculate

Superior colliculus

Raphé and more lateral nuclei

Spinal cord

Serotonergic pathways

The serotonergic pathways emanate from cell bodies designated groups B1 to B9, situated mainly in the midline raphé nuclei (Figure 3-5). B3, B6, and B9 are situated a little more laterally to the raphé nuclei. The rostral projections are not clearly known, but diffuse innervation to the forebrain, possibly through a projection in the medial forebrain bundle, has been shown. Serotonergic fibres project from the raphé to the limbic system (hippocampus and amygdala), lateral geniculate, and superior colliculus. Another serotonergic pathway runs caudally from midline regions in the brain stem to innervate the spinal cord.

A most striking property of serotonergic neurons is their tonic firing activity, which may subserve some pacemaker function. Some of these neurons cease firing only during rapid-eye-movement (REM) sleep. Thus, the serotonergic pathways have been implicated in sleep regulation and also (with less evidence) in arousal, sexual, and aggressive activities. Tricyclic antidepressive drugs increase central serotonin turnover by blocking re-uptake, and they also suppress REM sleep.

GABA pathways

The importance of GABA as an inhibitory neurotransmitter in the brain and spinal cord has been recognized so recently that the neuronal pathways of GABA have been studied only tentatively. GABA nerve endings are active in both presynaptic and postsynaptic inhibition in the spinal cord. These pathways seem in part to descend from the medulla, and short interneurons also participate.

The Purkinje cells of the cerebellum are GABA neurons and are themselves under inhibitory influences from other short GABA interneurons in the cerebellar cortex. The entire output of the cerebellar cortex is through the GABA inhibitory axons of the Purkinje cells to the deep cerebellar and vestibular nuclei.

Another GABA pathway originates in the caudate nucleus and terminates in the substantia nigra, exerting an inhibitory influence on the nigrostriatal dopaminergic neurons.

GABA neurons are widespread throughout the brain, including the cortices. Inhibitory influences are believed to be exerted more specifically on the noradrenergic locus coeruleus cells and the serotonergic cells of the raphé nuclei. Dopaminergic (mesolimbic) and cholinergic projection pathways are also thought to be influenced by GABA inhibition.

Other pathways

Immunocytochemical studies have suggested that a single β-endorphin system exists with cell bodies in the arcuate nucleus and long axons innervating the midbrain and limbic structures. Enkephalin-containing cell bodies and axons are, by contrast, widely distributed in the spinal cord and brain, especially areas concerned with sensory transmission, endocrine control, and motor activity. The gastrointestinal tract is richly innervated by enkephalinergic neurons and, in turn, peptides first found in the gut are now known to be present in the CNS. For example, vasoactive intestinal peptide (VIP) and cholecystokinin have been detected in the cortex.

ANIMAL BEHAVIOUR

Studies of the effects of drugs on animal behaviour have three main goals: (1) to inform about the mechanism of action of the drug, (2) to elucidate behavioural processes through the use of behaviour-altering drugs, and (3) to discover new drugs of potential value for treating human mental illness. Many factors make these goals difficult. They include variation between species, variation between strains within species, individual variation, differences in prior experience amongst animals, and problems in maintaining uniform experimental conditions. Nonetheless, a wide range of techniques has been devised. The biochemical and physiological findings have been summarized earlier and in Chapter 2. Here, a few behavioural techniques will be outlined.

Animal studies range from the general observation of drug effects on behaviour occurring under conditions as natural as possible to the analysis of drug effects on highly artificial but quantifiable laboratory tests. Gross behavioural measures include posture, running, rearing, and stretching, and abnormal effects such as convulsions and exophthalmos. More specific behavioural observations include measures of social interaction, excitement, and hostility. Taming effects have been particularly studied. Maze-running, perception, and discrimination have also been a focus of interest. Conditioning techniques – both classical (Pavlovian) and operant – have been used extensively. For example, chlorpromazine abolishes the conditioned avoidance response without impairing simple escape behaviour.

Special animal models have been developed to mimic human mental illness. Infant monkeys deprived of their mothers, and dogs exposed to inescapable electric shocks, develop states of inactivity and apparent despondency claimed to resemble human depressive illness. Experimental neuroses have been more extensively studied: Pavlov's dogs given increasingly complex discrimination tasks eventually showed disrupted behaviour patterns. In the conditioned emotional response, a neutral stimulus paired to a shock can eventually on its own suppress normal behaviour.

The most commonly used models are pharmacological: a known drug is administered and the test drug is expected to prevent, attenuate, or reverse the effects of the first. For example, a widely used screening test for putative antidepressants is the prior or subsequent administration of reserpine or tetrabenazine. Antidepressants can prevent or reverse the typical reserpine syndrome. Similarly, a test for neuroleptics concerns their ability to block apomorphine-induced stereotypies in rodents.

Despite a wide variety of such screening tests, new compounds are sometimes discovered not routinely but by accident as part of some other development program. The most interesting drugs are often those with the most atypical profiles of action on the battery of animal tests.

HUMAN BEHAVIOUR
Normal subjects
Again, many tests have been devised or adapted to assess drug effects in normal subjects. However, it must be stressed that information about effects in normal subjects is limited to knowledge about relatively simple (in psychological terms) stimulants and depressants and to the detection of secondary psychotropic effects, eg, sedation with amitriptyline. Antipsychotic and antidepressant actions in normal subjects cannot be studied in any depth.

Techniques available include assessment of sensory thresholds; perceptual tests such as critical flicker fusion; psychomotor tests such as simple tapping, reaction time, and steadiness; tests of conceptual and higher mental functions, eg, mental arithmetic and problem solving; observation of responses under stress conditions; subjective reports of moods and feelings, often gratifyingly sensitive to drug effects; assessment of effects on group functioning; and, as in animal tests, observation of drug interactions. Batteries of tests are usually used to build up a profile of drug action and of dose-effect and time-effect curves.

Patients
All the above techniques are available for use in patients.

However, some adaptation to clinical conditions is usually necessary, and allowance has to be made for the generally poor psychological performance of many groups of psychiatric patients. Social and occupational measures are of obvious importance in view of the frequency and severity of handicaps in these areas shown by many psychiatric patients, and yet few such measures have been studied.

However, the keystone of patient assessment remains the rating scales. These take many forms, but the major divisions concern the diagnostic and the assessment scales. In the former, the schedule is designed to elicit mental symptoms and signs, with the aim of standardizing the diagnosis. A well-known example, the Present-State Examination has been widely used internationally. The second type of scale is concerned not with diagnosis but with rating the severity of particular symptom clusters; the Hamilton Depression and Anxiety Scales are cases in point and are applicable to patients diagnosed as suffering from depressive and anxiety illnesses respectively (Figure 3-6).

Rating scales are also classifiable in terms of whether they are administered by an examining psychologist or psychiatrist or completed by the patient himself. Also important is the "time-focus" of the scale, ie, whether the patient's state is assessed with respect to the previous day, week, or month.

Clinical Trials
It is now accepted that the ultimate criterion for the effectiveness of a new drug is the demonstration of its therapeutic efficacy within the framework of a controlled clinical trial. This is not to deny the usefulness of uncontrolled observations, systematic prospective patient monitoring, and single-case reports, but the conclusions from such studies are limited. *The main features of the controlled trial are:*
1. The test drug must be compared with a control, either a dummy treatment (placebo) or a standard medication (such as amitriptyline in the case of an antidepressant, or diazepam as an anxiolytic).
2. The comparison experiment must be self-sufficient. It is not permissible to compare one treatment with another given in another context or at another time.
3. The patient groups treated must be carefully characterized so that other clinicians can draw firm conclusions concerning the type of patient who responds or does not respond to the test drug.
4. Allocation of treatments to the patients must be random to

prevent biases from creeping in (such as, for example, the more severely ill patients being allocated to the standard treatment because the clinician is reluctant to expose them to a new untried drug).

5. Neither the patient nor the examining clinician can be aware of which treatment is being given, ie, the trial is "double-blind."
6. Appropriate and sensitive rating scales must be used.
7. Adequate statistical techniques are used to estimate the level of probability that genuine and not chance effects are being detected: individuals vary with respect to the items being rated and to drug responsiveness.
8. Any features in the patients predictive of differential responsiveness to one or other treatment should be delineated if possible.

Nonspecific Factors

In the evaluation and testing of new drugs, two groups of factors are important. In one group are those factors associated with the specific pharmacodynamic action of the drug (eg, dosage, mode of administration, and length of action). In the second group are the nonspecific factors that comprise:

1. The placebo effect, which is the therapeutic effect associated with the giving of any tablet, elixir, or injection.
2. The opinions of the clinician about the place and value of a particular treatment in a specific type of patient, which opinions will heavily bias the results. (Similarly, nurses, ancillary staff, relatives, friends, and other patients can alter the patient's treatment response by influencing his expectations, motivation, and attitudes.)
3. The patient's adherence to the treatment regimen, which is of paramount importance in determining drug response. Obviously, if the patient is unimpressed with the therapeutic effects of the drug or is discommoded by the side effects, he may cease taking the medication.
4. The environment in which the drug is taken and other social factors, which can modify drug actions. An antipsychotic agent may be less effective if social circumstances are adverse.
5. Other forms of treatment (psychotherapy, occupational therapy, and social management, for example), which can interact with drugs to increase or decrease therapeutic effects.
6. The personality of the patient, which may greatly alter his response to drugs.

Figure 3-6. Brief rating scale for anxiety derived from the Hamilton Anxiety Scale. The psychiatrist marks the lines as in the example.

Brief rating scale for anxiety

Name: Date:
Sex: Age:

Symptom		Rating		Score
1. Anxious mood		absent	very severe	
Worries	✓			
Anticipation of the worst				
Apprehension (fearful anticipation)				
Irritability	✓			
2. Tension		absent	very severe	
Feelings of tension				
Fatiguability				
Inability to relax	✓			
Startle response				
Moved to tears easily				
Trembling	✓			
Feelings of restlessness	✓			
3. Autonomic symptoms		absent	very severe	
Dry mouth	✓			
Flushing				
Pallor				
Tendency to sweat	✓			
Giddiness	✓			
Tension headache				
Raising of hair				
4. Cardiovascular symptoms		absent	very severe	
Tachycardia				
Palpitations	✓			
Pain in the chest				
Throbbing of vessels	✓			
Fainting feelings				
Missing beat				
5. Behaviour at interview		absent	very severe	
Tense, not relaxed	✓			
Fidgeting and restlessness	✓			
Hands				
Picking fingers				
6. Behaviour physiological		absent	very severe	
Tremor of hands				
Furrowed brow	✓			
Strained face				
Facial pallor				
Swallowing	✓			
Belching				
Sweating	✓			
Eye-lid twitching	✓			

FURTHER READING

Aghajanian GK: LSD and CNS transmission. *Ann Rev Pharmacol, 12*:157-168, 1972.

Barchas J, Usdin E: *Serotonin and Behavior.* New York, Academic Press, 1973.

Beaumont A, Hughes J: Biology of Opioid Peptides. *Ann Rev Pharmacol Toxicol, 19*:245-267, 1979.

Bradford-Hill A: *Short Textbook of Medical Statistics.* London, Hodder, 1977.

De Feudis FV: *Central Cholinergic Systems and Behavior.* New York, Academic Press, 1974.

Hamilton M: *Lectures on Methodology of Clinical Research.* Edinburgh, Churchill Livingstone, 1974.

Iversen SD, Iversen LL: *Behavioral Pharmacology.* London, Oxford University Press, 1975.

Lipton MA, DiMascio A, Killam KF (eds): *Psychopharmacology. A Generation of Progress.* New York, Raven Press, 1978.

McNair DM: Anti-anxiety drugs and human performance. *Arch Gen Psychiatry 29*:611-617, 1973.

Roberts E, Chase TN, Tower DB (eds): *GABA in Nervous System Function.* New York, Raven Press, 1975.

Saletu B: Classification of psychotropic drugs based on human evoked potentials, in Itil TM (ed): *Psychotropic Drugs and the Human EEG.* Basel, Karger, 1974.

Ungerstedt U: Stereotaxic mapping of the monoamine pathways in the rat brain. *Acta Physiol Scand,* suppl 367, 1971, pp 1-48.

Pharmacokinetics

INTRODUCTION

Pharmacokinetics – in essence, the study of the body's effects on drugs – has become increasingly important in recent years. It is impossible for the psychiatrist to know all the pharmacokinetic details about every psychotropic agent, its absorption characteristics, distribution, liver metabolism, kidney excretion, and drug interactions. Where relevant, the important pharmacokinetic features are dealt with in the chapters on the individual drugs. The purpose of this chapter is to introduce some basic principles and to point out the relevance of these basic principles to the rational use of therapeutic agents. This chapter follows the traditional headings of absorption, distribution, metabolism, and excretion.

ABSORPTION

Most drugs are distributed in the body in the water phase of the plasma. Hence, apart from local application, eg, to skin or conjunctiva, drugs must first enter the bloodstream by crossing lipoprotein cell membranes. The rate at which a drug reaches its site of action, such as the brain, is thus dependent on (a) the blood flow through the organ and (b) the speed with which the drug can pass across lipoprotein membranes.

A drug enters the circulation either by being placed there directly or by absorption from depots or "sumps" such as the gastrointestinal tract, the muscles, or subcutaneous tissue. The latter two sites represent the parenteral mode, and the gut represents the enteral mode (see Figure 4-1).

An obvious advantage of the intravenous method of drug administration is that the drug enters the circulation with the least delay. Moreover, intravenous administration is easy to control, especially if an infusion rather than a bolus injection is used. The use of intravenously infused drug to induce abreaction is an example of controlled injection. Intravenous infusions are a useful way of building up body concentrations as has been advocated in the case of clomipramine.

The disadvantages of intravenous injection are that dangerously high concentrations can occur during the bolus injection and that once injected the drug cannot be removed, whereas an emetic or stomach lavage can remove an oral overdose.

Intramuscular injections are commonly used by psychiatrists not only to quiet the disturbed patient with tranquilizers but also as long-acting depot injections. Blood flow through resting muscles is about 0.02 to 0.07 ml/min/gm tissue and may increase tenfold during emotional excitement. Thus, the agitated or frenzied, disturbed patient should rapidly absorb antipsychotic injections. However, some drugs are poorly absorbed on intramuscular injection, diazepam being an example. Highly lipid-soluble formulations of drugs such as fluphenazine decanoate in oil are absorbed very slowly from their depot in the muscle, probably because they dissolve in the fatty tissues of the muscle.

Drugs are traditionally given by mouth, absorption being possible along the whole length of the gastrointestinal tract from buccal mucosa to rectum. The absorption in the stomach and jejunum is the most important, but the site of most rapid absorption depends on the chemical properties of the drug. Gastric absorption is favoured by an empty stomach, the drug coming into unimpeded contact with the mucosal walls. A full stomach can also postpone absorption of drugs from the intestine by causing delayed gastric emptying. Thus, if rapid action is required, drugs (except for gastric irritants such as aspirin) should be given on an empty stomach. For a smoother, delayed absorption, the drug should be taken after meals.

Some drugs such as iron, methyldopa, and several amino acids are actively absorbed by specific carrier mechanisms. Most, however, diffuse into the body. To do so the molecule must be either very small or nonionized and lipid soluble. Gastric juice is acid (pH about 1), and intestinal contents are neutral or slightly alkaline. Many drugs are weak acids or bases; most psychotropic drugs are weak bases that exist in two forms – the nondissociated (or nonionized) form, and the dissociated (or ionized) form, eg:

Drug base + HCl $\rightleftharpoons$ Drug base • H⁺ + Cl⁻
(nonionized)   (ionized)

The degree of dissociation depends on the pH of the medium. The drug is half ionized at the pH of the solution indicated by its pK_a (negative logarithm of the dissociation constant). In practice, weak bases are absorbed better in the higher pH conditions of the jejunum, where their ionization is largely suppressed.

Absorption also depends critically on the lipid solubility (better termed "lipophilicity") of the undissociated drug. Thus, barbitone and quinalbarbitone (secobarbital) have almost the same pK_a, yet the latter is more rapidly absorbed because of its higher lipophilicity.

Some drugs intended for oral use are formulated in sustained-release preparations so that the tablet slowly dissolves or the drug leaches out of an inert matrix. If release is too slow and the rate of movement through the gut too rapid, the drug will be incompletely absorbed.

44

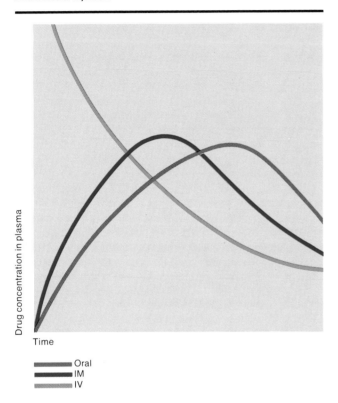

Figure 4-1. Model curves for drug concentration against time for intravenous, intramuscular, and oral administration. Note that these curves vary from drug to drug, eg, diazepam is slowly absorbed after intramuscular injection.

Drug concentration in plasma

Time

▬▬▬ Oral
▬▬▬ IM
▬▬▬ IV

As a rule, psychotropic drugs are well absorbed because they are highly lipophilic and mainly nonionized at physiological pHs. However, some antacids may reduce the bioavailability of drugs, probably by absorption of the drug in the gut. Many psychotropic drugs have autonomic effects that usually slow gut motility, thus favoring total absorption.

DISTRIBUTION

The body water may be regarded as being divided into several functional compartments such as the plasma water (about 3 litres), extracellular fluid (9 litres), and intracellular fluid (30 litres), totalling 42 litres in a 70 kg man. The apparent volume of distribution of a drug (V_d) is the fluid volume throughout which it seems to be distributed. To estimate the V_d, one gives a standard dose (X) of a drug, allows time for equilibration, and estimates the plasma concentration (C). Assuming complete absorption, $V_d = X/C$. If $V_d = 3$ litres, then drug is confined to plasma water; if it is 42 litres, then it is uniformly distributed throughout the body water. If V_d is greater than 42 litres, then C, the plasma concentration, is low and the drug is being taken up preferentially into body tissues such as the brain.

Distribution is affected by plasma binding. Iron and copper are bound to specific proteins in the blood, transferrin and ceruloplasmin B, respectively, and vitamins A and D and steroid hormones are bound to lipoproteins. Drugs are bound mostly to plasma albumin and glycoproteins, the degree of binding depending on the chemical nature of the drug. Binding is reversible, and drugs can compete for the binding sites on the albumin molecule.

Psychotropic drugs are fairly highly bound. Diazepam is about 98% bound, chlorpromazine 95% to 98%, and amitriptyline and imipramine 96%. Barbiturates are less highly bound (eg, phenobarbitone 20%). Because the concentration at the site of action depends on the free (unbound) drug, quite small variations in the degree of binding of highly bound drugs can make a great difference in drug action. Binding also varies among individuals, again an important factor with the highly bound psychotropic drugs.

When albumin is denatured, drugs no longer bind to it. As precipitation is a standard first step in chemical drug estimations, total drug concentrations are obtained. Free drug concentrations can be measured by dialysis or ultrafiltration techniques, but these are not routinely applied. Bioassay techniques that do not entail protein precipitation will estimate free drug, providing equilibrium is not upset.

Another implication of plasma binding is the treatment of overdose. Dialysis is least useful in highly bound drugs because the free concentrations and hence the diffusion gradients are low.

Passage of drugs into brain

A drug may enter the brain directly from the circulation or indirectly from the cerebrospinal fluid. Areas of brain vary in vascularity, the cortex having a richer blood supply than has white matter. The brain is the best supplied of all organs; it comprises only 2% of the body weight but receives 15% of the cardiac output. Thus, drugs should equilibrate rapidly between brain and blood. Some drugs, however, do not enter the brain easily, giving rise to the concept of the "blood-brain barrier." However, more recently it has become recognized that there is no such absolute barrier and that the rate of diffusion from blood to brain depends on a number of factors:

1. *Protein binding.* Highly bound drugs will diffuse into the brain slowly because unbound-drug concentrations, which determine the rate of diffusion, are low. After equilibration, the concentration in the CSF is usually close to the free plasma water concentration because the fluid is virtually protein-free. Brain tissues, by contrast, can strongly bind many psychotropic drugs, forming a central pool.

2. *Ionization.* As with absorption from the gut, the drug diffuses into the brain in its nonionized form. Thus, at the plasma pH of 7.4, or the slightly lower pH values of extracellular fluid, knowledge of the pK_a of the drug allows one to calculate the nonionized proportion.

3. *Lipophilicity.* The brain is a highly lipid tissue, and the lipid solubility of a drug gives a good indication of how rapidly the drug will enter the brain. This factor is the most important of the three. Most psychotropic drugs are highly lipophilic and enter the brain expeditiously (see Figure 4-2 and Table 4-1).

Because they are highly ionized, quaternary ammonium compounds such as neostigmine are not taken into the brain. Dopamine and serotonin have low lipophilicity and also fail to diffuse into the brain. Finally, simple cations or anions such as lithium and bromide diffuse readily because the molecules are small.

METABOLISM

Some drugs, mainly those that are relatively lipid insoluble or ionized, are excreted unchanged by the kidney; barbitone

and lithium are examples. However, most highly lipophilic drugs diffuse readily across body membranes and are reabsorbed by diffusion from the glomerular filtrate in the kidney. Such substances have a very low renal-clearance rate and persist in the body. To be eliminated, drugs of this type must be metabolized to derivatives that are more polar, ie, more soluble in water and less in lipids. This process is not "detoxication," since the metabolite may be more active than its parent.

Drug metabolism takes place mainly in the liver and is by four main processes:

1. *Oxidation* is the most common form of drug metabolism. Liver microsomal enzymes catalyze a variety of reactions, including hydroxylation, N-dealkylation, O-dealkylation, and sulphoxide formation. Examples of such reactions are shown with chlorpromazine, in Chapter 5, and also with the metabolic pathways of the biogenic amines, in Chapter 2.

Some drug oxidations are not catalyzed by the typical liver microsomal enzymes. Examples are the alcohol and aldehyde dehydrogenases, which oxidize ethanol to acetaldehyde and then to acetic acid. The monoamine oxidases, another example, are widely distributed mitochondrial enzymes that oxidatively deaminate a whole range of substances.

2. *Reduction* as by the aldehyde reductases (mentioned in Chapter 2) is not common.

3. *Hydrolysis* is also uncommon, metabolism by cholinesterases being an example.

4. *Conjugation* consists in the coupling of molecules such as glucuronic acid, acetyl radicals, and sulphate to form less lipid-soluble and hence easily excretable metabolites. The molecular weight of the complex is increased so that active transport excretion can also take place.

"First-pass metabolism"

The rate of liver metabolism can be high. For example, more than 90% of orally administered fluphenazine is oxidized in the liver after absorption before even reaching the systemic circulation. Individuals vary in their capacity for such "first-pass metabolism" and some seem to metabolize phenothiazines almost entirely. These patients in particular may benefit most from a switch to depot administration of neuroleptics, which obviates first-pass metabolism.

Inhibition of drug metabolism

Disulfiram inhibits aldehyde dehydrogenase, thus causing the accumulation of acetaldehyde after the ingestion of ethanol.

Table 4-1. Penetration time of barbiturates to the brain depends on degree of protein binding and pK$_a$ but especially on lipid solubility.

	Thiopentone	Pentobarbitone	Barbitone
Percent bound	75	40	2
pK$_a$	7.6	8.1	7.5
Percent nonionized at pH 7.4	61	83	56
X	X	X	X
Lipid solubility	3.3	0.05	0.002
=	=	=	=
Effective partition coefficient	200	0.42	0.001
Penetration half-time (minutes)	1.4	4.0	27.0

Figure 4-2. Lipophilicity and site of action.

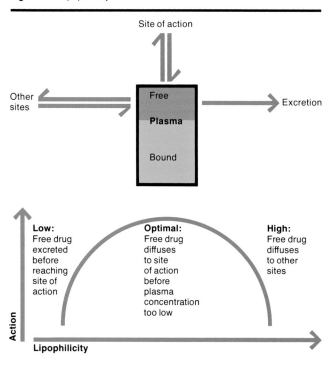

Acetaldehyde accumulation is believed to produce the unpleasant flushing, throbbing, nausea, and vomiting of the "disulfiram reaction."

The MAO inhibitors are another example. The inhibition is irreversible, and the effects of the drug wear off only when a new enzyme has been synthesized. The MAO inhibitors thus potentiate the action of amines that are broken down primarily by MAO (see also Chapter 2). The prime example is tyramine, a constituent of fermented foods such as cheese. On ingestion, tyramine is not metabolized by the inhibited MAO, but instead reaches the circulation and releases noradrenaline from the noradrenergic nerve endings. Thus, a potentially fatal hypertensive crisis may ensue from the combination of an MAO inhibitor and a tyramine-containing food.

Stimulation of drug metabolism

Several drugs administered for a few days induce an increase in synthesis of microsomal drug-metabolizing enzymes. The drugs most studied include phenobarbitone, steroid hormones, some insecticides, and the carcinogen hydrocarbon 3,4-benzpyrene.

Induction usually occurs within a few days of drug administration and wears off a week or so after the drug is discontinued. Stimulation of drug metabolism may produce an apparent condition of drug tolerance. Thus, patients treated chronically with barbiturates metabolize the drugs more rapidly than do nonexposed persons.

Many drugs are inducers in animals, but species differences are important and each drug must be assessed in man. For example, benzodiazepines are good inducers in rats, but induction is of no clinical importance in man. Among psychotropic drugs known to induce their own metabolism are phenobarbitone and other barbiturates; glutethimide, meprobamate, chlorpromazine, and imipramine; and the anticonvulsants phenytoin and primidone. Caffeine, ethanol, cigarette smoking, adrenal steroids, and sex hormones are also capable of induction.

Induction can be quite marked, resulting in a 50% reduction in plasma concentrations of the drugs. Response to enzyme inducers is partly genetically controlled.

Another example of genetically determined differences in drug metabolism is acetylation. Isoniazid is metabolized mainly by acetylation: about half the population acetylate rapidly, the other half slowly. Higher concentrations of unmetabolized drug are maintained in the slow metabolizers, with greater chance of side effects, but clinical response seems less affected.

EXCRETION

Each day 190 litres of plasma water are filtered through the glomeruli, all but 1.5 litres being reabsorbed. Only drug dissolved in free (ie, unbound) plasma water can be filtered, and lipid-soluble nonionized drugs will be reabsorbed because they diffuse back into the tubules.

This resorption cannot occur with lipid-insoluble (water-soluble) drugs, which, along with their metabolites, are therefore cleared from the plasma. The pH of the urine is an important factor influencing the rate of drug excretion. Thus, it is the nonionized form of the drug that tends to diffuse back across the tubule cells and out of the urine. Weak acids tend to be excreted in alkaline urine because they form ions, whereas weak bases remain in acidic urine. For example, amphetamine, a weak base, is excreted rapidly in urine of low pH but slowly and erratically in alkaline urine. Acidification of the urine with ammonium chloride therefore hastens the excretion of amphetamine in cases of overdose. Conversely, barbiturates, being weak acids, are excreted more rapidly if the urine is made alkaline by administering bicarbonate.

Drugs can also be excreted by the liver cells into the bile, where they can then be reabsorbed from the intestine, a process that forms the enterohepatic cycle.

TIME COURSE OF DRUG ACTION

Drug absorption proceeds either at a constant rate independent of the amount of drug to be absorbed or at a diminishing rate proportional to the amount of drug still to be absorbed. The first rate is called zero-order kinetics, and the latter rate is known as first-order. Constant-rate absorption occurs when a continuous infusion is given and may be approximated by some sustained-release preparations taken orally, whereby absorption is more rapid than dissolution. Otherwise, absorption usually follows first-order kinetics.

Drug elimination follows similar rules. Elimination refers to all the processes, metabolic and excretory, that act to lower the concentration of drug in the body. Usually, the rate of elimination follows first-order kinetics; that is, the rate of elimination is proportional to the concentration in the body so that less and less is excreted per unit time. If the elimination mechanism is saturated, however, zero-order kinetics will exist, the rate of elimination being constant.

Figure 4-3. Model concentration-time relationship for two hypothetical drugs with the same concentration rise after each dose but with different elimination rates. (Data from Curry SH: *Drug Disposition and Pharmacokinetics.* London, Blackwell, 1977.)

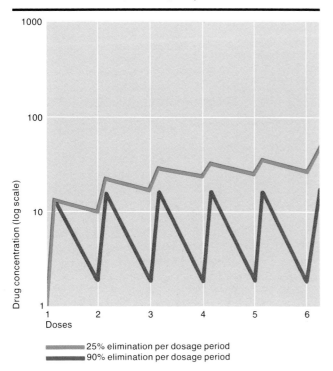

25% elimination per dosage period
90% elimination per dosage period

An example of zero-order kinetics is the elimination of ethanol. The rate in man is essentially constant at about 10 ml/hour. The constant rate is probably due to finite amounts of coenzymes necessary for elimination. Thus, four "whiskies" (120 ml of 45% ethanol) will take about five hours to be eliminated.

Most elimination mechanisms are first order and follow an exponential course (Figure 4-3). The time required for bodily concentrations to fall to half the initial levels is called the half-life. The half-life usually estimated is that of the drug in the plasma, as this body fluid is readily available. The biological half-life is the time needed for the total amount of drug in the body to decline by half. A third half-life is also important, namely, the time during which the pharmacological effect falls by half. This is relevant to drugs such as MAO inhibitors and reserpine whose effects long outlast their presence in the body. It is also a useful concept in studying drugs that have active metabolites, all with differing plasma half-lives, in that the overall pharmacological effect is considered. In the case of such drugs, the metabolites with the longest half-lives tend to accumulate.

The main implications of the plasma half-life are:
1. Dosage intervals can be up to two thirds of the half-life without fluctuations becoming too great. Many psychotropic drugs, eg, amitriptyline and diazepam, have half-lives sufficiently long for once-daily dosage.
2. It takes four to five half-lives for a steady-state concentration to build up in the body, ie, a state in which the amount of drug eliminated per unit of time equals that given. Thus, such levels will be attained only slowly in the case of drugs with long half-lives.
3. Doubling the dose does not double plasma concentrations, because the rate of metabolism also increases.

THE YOUNG, THE OLD, AND THE PHYSICALLY ILL

The lactating mother is likely to secrete lipophilic drugs into the milk. This is known to occur with diazepam, which has been reported to have appreciable effects on the baby. Similarly, lipophilic drugs would be expected to reach the fetus in utero.

The microsomal enzymes that metabolize drugs are not fully active until about eight weeks after birth. Hence neonates metabolize most drugs slowly. Conjugation to form glucuronides is less deficient. Furthermore, especially in the premature infant, the blood-brain barrier is immature so that centrally acting drugs penetrate the brain readily and have enhanced effects. Finally, renal excretion mechanisms may be impaired. Thus, babies in the first weeks of life, especially the newborn, are usually very sensitive to psychotropic drugs.

Adults and children metabolize drugs similarly, but smaller doses must be used in children, especially prepubertal children, because of their smaller size.

The elderly, like the newborn, are particularly sensitive to psychotropic drugs. The effects of the patient's age on pharmacokinetic mechanisms are many, and they vary from drug to drug. In some cases, the drug distribution is altered; in others, hepatic metabolism is slowed; and with other drugs, renal clearance seems impaired. Differences from effects in young persons can be substantial. For example, the plasma half-life of diazepam in hours is on average about the same as the age of the patient in years.

Patients with liver disease are unduly sensitive to most psychotropic drugs. However, hydroxylation is more impaired than conjugation. Protein binding may also be affected because of hypoalbuminemia.

Renal disease may impair excretion, especially of lithium.

DRUG INTERACTIONS

Drug interactions can occur at the metabolic level (pharmacokinetic interaction) or at the site of action (pharmacodynamic interaction). The former includes competition for plasma albumin binding sites, but no important example concerning psychotropic drugs is known. Enzyme induction interactions are very important. The concurrent administration of phenobarbitone with chlorpromazine or nortriptyline produces liver enzyme induction, more rapid metabolism of the psychotropic drugs, and a drop in plasma concentrations. Other barbiturates also induce enzymes and counteract other psychotropic drugs. Antiparkinsonian drugs such as orphenadrine are powerful liver inducers and should not be given routinely with antipsychotic medication. Enzyme induction by alcohol partly explains the tolerance that alcoholics have to alcohol and the cross-tolerance they have to barbiturates; cellular changes are also an important factor. Phenytoin is also a powerful enzyme inducer and can interact with other drugs.

Relatively weak inducing agents may compete for the metabolizing enzymes more than they induce those enzymes. Thus, chlorpromazine and amitriptyline given together result in plasma concentrations of each that are higher than what would be attained by the individual drugs given alone.

RELATIONSHIP BETWEEN PLASMA CONCENTRATIONS AND THERAPEUTIC EFFECT

Many investigators have expected that estimation of plasma concentrations of drugs would result in greater precision in therapy, inasmuch as clinical response should relate more closely to plasma concentrations than to dose. It has been hoped that the incidence of poor or absent response might be cut by monitoring plasma concentrations. However, there are several reservations and limitations:

1. The drugs would need to have a reversible action, because irreversible effects would not be related to plasma levels once initially adequate levels were attained.
2. Tolerance at receptor sites would not be important, otherwise plasma concentrations would not bear a constant relation to receptor effects.
3. The concentration of unbound drug in plasma should reflect the concentration at the receptor sites (this is impossible to confirm in man).
4. The drug must be distributed simply, without active transport mechanisms.
5. The chemical measured would have to be the active drug, preferably without active metabolites.
6. The time of venipuncture for plasma would need to be carefully standardized.

Lithium concentrations are routinely monitored because there is a narrow range between therapeutic and toxic levels of the drug. Measurement of plasma concentrations by chemical methods is rather slow and expensive, but rapid and inexpensive bioassays are being developed. Unfortunately, as will be detailed in the chapters on individual drugs, correlations between plasma concentrations and therapeutic responses are tenuous in most instances.

FURTHER READING

Curry SH: *Drug Disposition and Pharmacokinetics* (ed 2). London, Blackwell, 1977.

Mayer SE, Melmon KL, Gilman AG: General principles: Introduction; the dynamics of drug absorption, distribution, and elimination, in Goodman LS, Gilman A (eds): *The Pharmacological Basis of Therapeutics* (ed 6). New York, Macmillan, 1980, pp 1-55.

Goldstein A, Aronow L, Kalman SM: *Principles of Drug Action: The Basis of Pharmacology.* New York, John Wiley, 1974.

Lader M: Clinical Psychopharmacology, in Granville-Grossman K (ed): *Recent Advances in Clinical Psychiatry.* Edinburgh, Churchill Livingstone, 1975.

Porter R, Rivers J, Whelan J (eds): *Drug Concentrations in Neuropsychiatry: CIBA Foundation Symposium 74.* Amsterdam, Excerpta Medica, 1980.

Schoolar JC, Claghorn JL (eds): *The Kinetics of Psychiatric Drugs.* New York, Brunner/Mazel, 1979.

Werry JS: Principles of use of psychotropic drugs in children. *Drugs 18:* 392-397, 1979.

Antipsychotic Drugs

INTRODUCTION

The term *antipsychotic drug* is preferable to the expressions *major tranquilizer*, *antischizophrenic agent*, and *neuroleptic*, because it indicates the type of clinical action of these drugs—more than a tranquilizing effect but less than a specific antischizophrenic action. The term *neuroleptic*, although popular in continental Europe, is less appropriate, since it refers to the extrapyramidal effects and not to the therapeutic actions.

The primary chemical group of antipsychotic agents is the phenothiazine group (Figure 5-1). The thioxanthenes, the phenylbutylpiperidines (butyrophenones), and several other chemical structures with antipsychotic activity have also been introduced as drugs (Figure 5-2). The phenothiazines themselves can be divided into three subclasses on the basis of the side chain: the aliphatic compounds such as chlorpromazine, the piperidine compounds such as thioridazine, and the piperazine group, which includes fluphenazine, trifluoperazine, and perphenazine. All three main chemical groups of antipsychotic agents have the common property of blocking dopaminergic receptors. Reserpine and tetrabenazine also have antipsychotic actions but interfere with dopaminergic transmission by depleting the nerve endings of neurotransmitter vesicles.

The antipsychotic drugs have wide uses outside psychiatry. They are useful for the treatment of vomiting and vertigo and to potentiate the analgesics. In psychiatry, their main uses are (a) to tranquilize disturbed patients whatever the underlying pathology, but most commonly those with acute schizophrenia, mania, or brain damage; (b) as maintenance therapy to prevent acute relapses in the chronic schizophrenic patient; (c) as maintenance therapy to suppress psychotic phenomena in chronic paranoid patients; and (d) in low dosage, as antianxiety agents in selected neurotic patients. Despite some claims, these drugs are not unequivocally "antischizophrenic," and any drug-related improvement in prognosis for such patients has been modest. Many difficulties attend the use of the antipsychotic drugs, but new drugs and improved formulations of older ones are providing steady but unspectacular progress.

HISTORY

The parent antipsychotic compound, phenothiazine, was used as an anthelminthic in animals; a derivative, promethazine, is a powerful antihistaminic with sedative properties.

In 1950, the closely related compound chlorpromazine was synthesized in France and found to have very powerful sedative properties, inducing "artificial hibernation" with retention of consciousness, marked indifference to surroundings, and hypothermia. This so-called *lobotomie pharmacologique* led to the trial of chlorpromazine in 1952 by Delay and his colleagues, first in manic and then in other patients. The effects on schizophrenia were described a short time later. The vast array of pharmacological actions indicated a novel profile of effects.

Other phenothiazines, including increasingly potent compounds, were synthesized and introduced. In the mid-1960s, fluphenazine was formulated in an oily medium to be administered by intramuscular injection once every two to four weeks. This preparation is popular in many countries as maintenance therapy.

About the same time as the introduction of chlorpromazine, interest focused on the antipsychotic properties of rauwolfia root, a traditional remedy in India. Reserpine, the principal alkaloid, was isolated and introduced as an antihypertensive agent and as a tranquilizer. It was displaced by the phenothiazines because its therapeutic effects were preceded by a phase of increased disturbance and because it was suspected of being prone to induce depressive illnesses.

The thioxanthenes, closely related chemically to the phenothiazines, were introduced in the 1960s; the butyrophenones, discovered in the search for better analgesics, have also been available for many years.

PHARMACOKINETICS
Metabolites

The prototypal drug chlorpromazine has received the most attention despite the difficult technical problems of measuring it in biological fluids. Another complication with studying chlorpromazine is its metabolic complexity (see Figure 5-3). More than 150 metabolites have been hypothesized, of which about 75 have been detected in blood or urine. If all the metabolites were psychotropically inactive, the complexity of the breakdown pathways would be irrelevant; however, both clinical and experimental evidence indicates that several derivatives have psychotropic effects in man and animals. The most important metabolite is 7-hydroxychlorpromazine; by contrast, chlorpromazine sulfoxide, another important metabolite, is inactive: drug responders tend to have high concentrations of 7-hydroxychlorpromazine and low levels of the sulfoxide.

52

Figure 5-1. Formulae of some phenothiazines.

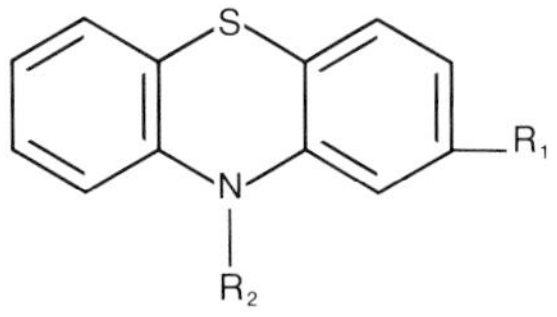

Phenothiazine nucleus

	R₁	R₂
Aliphatic		
Promazine	$-H$	$-(CH_2)_3-N\big<{}^{CH_3}_{CH_3}$
Chlorpromazine	$-Cl$	$-(CH_2)_3-N\big<{}^{CH_3}_{CH_3}$
Trifluopromazine	$-CF_3$	$-(CH_2)_3-N\big<{}^{CH_3}_{CH_3}$
Piperidine		
Thioridazine	$-SCH_3$	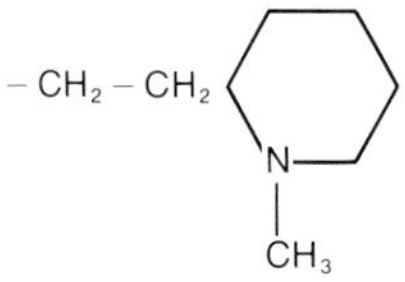 $-CH_2-CH_2$ (N-methylpiperidine)
Mesoridazine	$-\overset{O}{\overset{\|}{S}}CH_3$	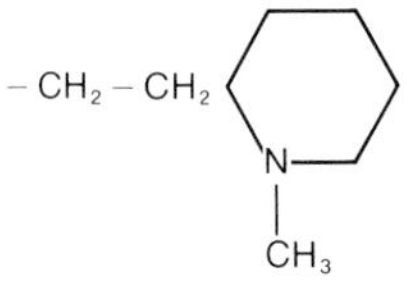 $-CH_2-CH_2$ (N-methylpiperidine)
Piperazine		
Prochlorperazine	$-Cl$	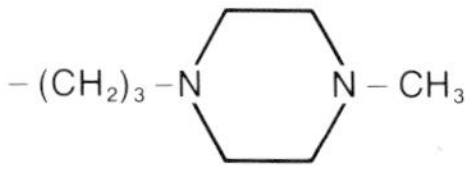 $-(CH_2)_3-N\underset{}{\bigcirc}N-CH_3$
Trifluoperazine	$-CF_3$	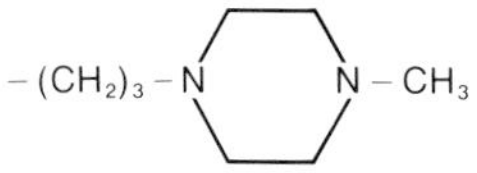 $-(CH_2)_3-N\underset{}{\bigcirc}N-CH_3$
Perphenazine	$-Cl$	$-(CH_2)_3-N\underset{}{\bigcirc}N-CH_2-CH_2OH$
Fluphenazine	$-CF_3$	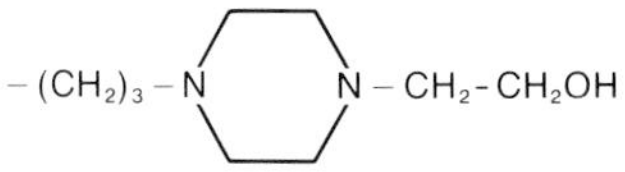 $-(CH_2)_3-N\underset{}{\bigcirc}N-CH_2-CH_2OH$
Thiopropazate	$-Cl$	$-(CH_2)_3-N\underset{}{\bigcirc}N-CH_2-CH_2-O-\overset{O}{\overset{\|}{C}}-CH_3$

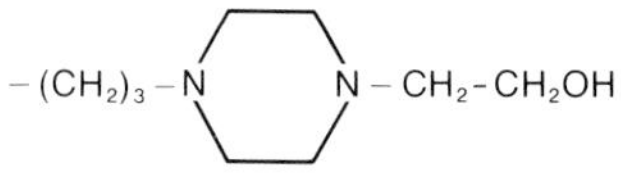

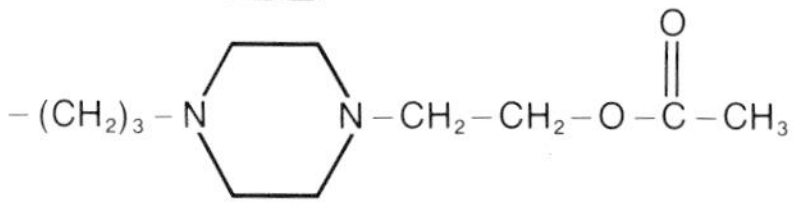

53

Figure 5-2. Some nonphenothiazine anti-psychotic drugs.

Thioxanthenes

Chlorprothixene

Thiothixene

Flupenthixol

Butyrophenones (Phenylbutylpiperidines)

Haloperidol

Diphenylbutylpiperidines

Pimozide

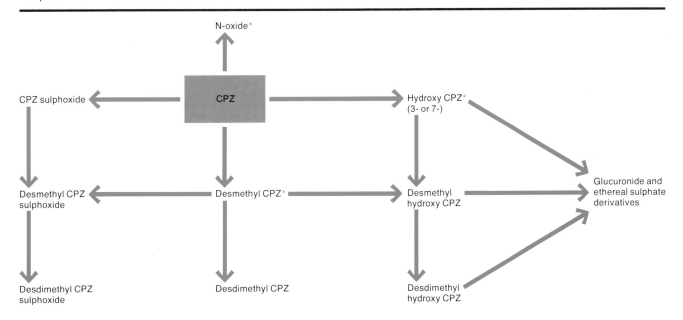

Figure 5-3. Major metabolic pathways of chlorpromazine.

N-oxide*

CPZ sulphoxide ← CPZ → Hydroxy CPZ* (3- or 7-)

Desmethyl CPZ sulphoxide ← Desmethyl CPZ* → Desmethyl hydroxy CPZ

Desdimethyl CPZ sulphoxide

Desdimethyl CPZ

Desdimethyl hydroxy CPZ

Glucuronide and ethereal sulphate derivatives

*active metabolites

The metabolism of other phenothiazines is possibly a little less complex. Butyrophenones such as haloperidol and thioxanthenes such as flupenthixol are believed to be metabolized to inactive metabolites only.

Absorption and metabolism

Being lipophilic, antipsychotic drugs are generally well absorbed, mainly from the jejunum. However, chlorpromazine is metabolized to a substantial extent (more than 75% on average) on passage through the gut wall and liver (Figure 5-4). This first-pass metabolism is even greater in the case of fluphenazine. Both chlorpromazine and fluphenazine injected intramuscularly avoid this metabolic breakdown and are consequently much more potent given by injection. The obviation of first-pass metabolism provides some rationale for the effectiveness of the long-acting depot antipsychotic medications in relatively low dosage. Haloperidol and pimozide undergo less first-pass metabolism than does chlorpromazine.

Plasma concentration and clinical response

Because chlorpromazine has a plasma half-life of about eight hours, plasma concentrations show substantial fluctuations with each dose. When the drug is given in single high doses for tranquilization, plasma concentrations are high, but both low and high (greater than 500 ng/ml) concentrations may be associated with a poor response. With very high concentrations, a toxic drug psychosis may occur.

At the end of a month, plasma concentrations of chlorpromazine varied twelvefold in 32 patients maintained on a dosage of 100 mg three times a day. Correlations with clinical response were weak but positive. In 86 chronic schizophrenic patients, global ratings of improvement were not related to plasma chlorpromazine concentrations. Nor have useful correlations been found in studies of butaperazine or thioridazine.

By contrast, some relationship has been established between clinical effects and parkinsonian side effects. The latter are uncommon at plasma chlorpromazine concentrations less than 50 ng/ml but are common at concentrations much above.

On fixed dosage, plasma concentrations of chlorpromazine rise over the first week but then fall during the next five to eight weeks to a sustained low level. Despite the decrease, which is attributable to induction of liver enzymes, clinical improvement is usually maintained.

When chlorpromazine is discontinued, the drug rapidly disappears from the plasma, as would be expected because of its short half-life. However, the drug persists in lipid tissues in the brain and body for some time, metabolites being excreted in the urine for some months. Clinical deterioration is usually also delayed.

Drug interactions

Besides accelerating its own metabolism by inducing liver enzymes, chlorpromazine can accelerate the metabolism of other drugs, and reciprocally its own metabolism will be increased. Drugs that can interact in this way include phenobarbitone and other barbiturates, but also, more important, several of the antiparkinsonian drugs such as orphenadrine and trihexyphenidyl. In one study, the addition of either phenobarbitone (50 mg every 8h) or orphenadrine (100 mg every 8h) about halved the chlorpromazine concentration in patients maintained on 100 mg every 8h of chlorpromazine. Orphenadrine also had a direct anticholinergic action, and the antiparkinsonian actions are due more to that action than to the drug's effect of decreasing neuroleptic concentrations. Cigarette smoking has also been implicated in inducing liver enzymes, resulting in a decline in chlorpromazine concentrations.

By contrast, some drugs interact with chlorpromazine to increase plasma concentrations by competing for the liver enzymes. The tricyclic antidepressants imipramine, amitriptyline, and nortriptyline all compete in this way with chlorpromazine and may potentiate its actions. However, in one unpublished study, this potentiation led to an intensification of psychosis, with confusional features probably due to drug toxicity.

PHARMACOLOGY

Biochemical pharmacology

Interest has focused on the ability of all antipsychotic compounds to block dopamine receptors. Animal studies using a wide variety of models and systems have demonstrated this property, and tests have been devised to screen new compounds. An in vitro model is the dopamine-stimulated adenylate cyclase system. Enzyme preparations from the basal ganglia can be stimulated by dopamine, and the increased activity can be blocked by antipsychotic drugs. Drug potencies for blocking this stimulation tend to correlate with clinical activity except that the butyrophenones tend to be less potent on the biochemical system than would be expected.

55

Figure 5-4. Modes of administration of chlorpromazine.

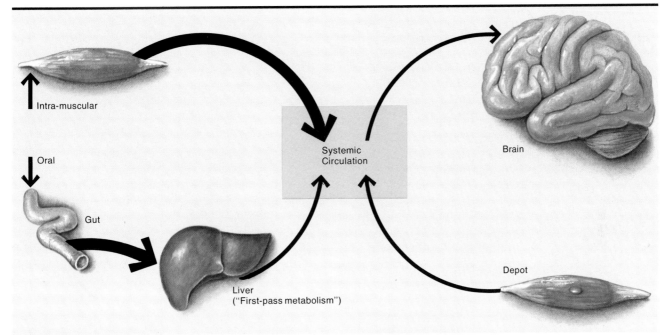

An even more direct method is to assess the affinity of antipsychotic drugs for the dopamine receptor through the use of radioactively labelled standard drugs such as haloperidol or spiroperidol. The ability of an antipsychotic agent to interfere with this binding (ie, presumably to interact directly with the receptor) seems to correlate with its clinical potency. Another method is to estimate the affinities of antipsychotic drugs for muscarinic cholinergic receptors in the brain. The affinity varies widely; haloperidol has low affinity, chlorpromazine moderate, and thioridazine is about as good at blocking cholinergic receptors as dopaminergic ones. This seems to correlate with the propensity of the antipsychotic drugs to induce extrapyramidal effects: thioridazine, blocking both receptors, produces little or none; chlorpromazine, a moderate amount; and haloperidol, predominantly a dopamine antagonist, a great deal. However, haloperidol does have some anticholinergic activity, which may explain why extrapyramidal effects may disappear at very high dosage levels. This, however, is not good routine prescribing practice.

An alternative explanation for the differences in the propensities of the antipsychotic drugs to induce extrapyramidal syndromes is that these drugs vary in their affinities for the populations of dopamine receptors in various parts of the brain. There is some evidence, direct and indirect, to support this view, which also suggests the possibility of developing new drugs that would act preferentially on mesolimbic and mesocortical dopamine receptors.

In man, antipsychotic drugs increase concentrations of the major metabolite of dopamine, homovanillic acid (HVA), in the cerebrospinal fluid. The increase is attributed to a blockade of dopamine receptors, with a compensatory increased synthesis and release of dopamine in the presynaptic neuron. However, this elevation of dopamine turnover returns to normal after three weeks or so, despite continuing medication. Such studies emphasize the importance of seeking long-term biochemical mechanisms in drug action.

Other actions
The anticholinergic actions account for dry mouth, constipation, and blurring of vision, whereas alpha-adrenergic blocking effects lead to vasodilatation, tachycardia, and postural hypotension. An extensive range of other pharmacological actions varies widely among the members of this group but includes antihistaminic, antiserotonin, neuromuscular-

blocking, quinidine-like, and allergy-inducing properties.

The secondary psychotropic actions are relevant to prescribing choices: some antipsychotic drugs such as chlorpromazine are sedative, and others such as trifluoperazine are somewhat stimulant. Little is known of the pharmacology of these actions, which in animals tend to correlate with the ability to potentiate narcotic and hypnotic properties such as hexobarbitone-induced sleeping time.

Behavioural pharmacology

A vast literature has accrued on this subject, but how relevant it is to clinical actions remains unclear. Thus, chlorpromazine reduces motor activity without affecting motor power or coordination, and treated animals maintain unnatural postures – so-called catalepsy. Chlorpromazine has a taming effect, and conditioned responses are more disrupted by antipsychotic drugs than are unconditioned responses. Sham rage provoked by stimulation of the amygdala is prevented.

Many such test results are difficult to interpret, but others are more directly related to dopaminergically mediated functions. These include amphetamine stereotypies and toxicity, apomorphine-induced vomiting, and circling behaviour after lesions in the basal ganglia. Even so, one must be cautious in extrapolating such results to clinical antipsychotic actions.

Human pharmacology

In normal subjects, the detectable effects of the antipsychotic drugs are the secondary psychotropic actions, sedative or stimulant, and the wide range of autonomic effects. It is difficult on single-dose administration to detect differences between chlorpromazine and a barbiturate, but on repeated dosing, tolerance occurs to chlorpromazine but not to the barbiturate. Ability to sustain attention seems more impaired than does ability to perform cognitive tasks.

Antipsychotic drugs slow the EEG patterns of normal subjects, particularly increasing theta waves. The piperazine derivatives such as fluphenazine increase alpha activity as well. Paroxysmal activity may be induced, together with an increased likelihood of convulsions.

CLINICAL EFFECTS
Tranquilization
The first important psychiatric use for chlorpromazine was to reduce severe agitation, psychomotor excitement, or dis-

turbed behaviour from whatever cause. Before chlorpromazine was available, bromides, barbiturates, paraldehyde, and opiates had been used. Complications, however, included a phase of increased excitation due to removal of inhibition, marked torpor or even coma, toxic confusional psychoses with overactivity and aggression, and marked withdrawal phenomena. Chlorpromazine was quickly recognized to be devoid of these drawbacks and able to tranquilize without impairing consciousness.

The introduction of chlorpromazine to treat disturbed patients resulted in marked general improvement as shown by fewer assaults on staff, less use of restraints, and so on. Despite murmurs of distaste for this "chemical straitjacket," the use of antipsychotic medication in this nonspecific way has become widely established.

Symptomatic tranquilization is indicated in patients with:

a schizophrenia – restlessness, excitement, paranoid tension, panic, aggressive outbursts, stereotyped and bizarre, noisy and destructive behaviour

b affective disorders – manic and hypomanic states; agitated and paranoid features

c acute symptomatic psychoses – states of intoxication, delirium, and hallucinosis

d chronic symptomatic psychoses – restlessness, confusion, violent outbursts, noisy and destructive behaviour

e psychoneurotic and personality disorders when severe tension or aggression occurs.

These features have been called target symptoms, a term that emphasizes the drug effects on symptoms irrespective of diagnosis.

Acute schizophrenia
The use of these drugs to treat acute schizophrenia has become their main indication. Some controversy concerns the specificity of these drugs. Few dispute the contention that these drugs are antipsychotic, that is, that they lessen psychotic symptoms such as thought disorder, paranoid features, delusions, and hallucinations. However, claims that they are antischizophrenic have met with more opposition. Such claims were based primarily on the observation that the phenothiazines improved the primary core or "process" symptoms such as thought disorder at least as much as they did the secondary symptoms such as hallucinations and emotional flattening. However, the relative prognostic importance of these various symptoms is not firmly established, so effec-

tiveness against primary symptoms may be open to other less optimistic interpretations such as a general dampening of all abnormal symptoms and signs. Furthermore, 25 years' experience with these drugs demonstrates that they do not "cure" schizophrenia, at least the severer forms in young adults. Rather, the drugs curb the progress of the condition by cutting short the acute, initial attack and subsequent relapses and, as discussed later, by delaying relapse when the drugs are taken as maintenance therapy. Both the personal and social sequels of the acute exacerbations are attenuated in most cases. In some, however, the course is inexorably deteriorating, such unfortunates becoming our "new chronics."

In patients with paranoid schizophrenia of later onset, symptom suppression with these drugs is often complete as long as medication continues. These patients preserve their mental faculties, and their delusional systems are usually encapsulated. In particular, monosymptomatic hypochondrial delusions, such as those of infestation, are suppressed.

The effectiveness of antipsychotic medication has been established in a long series of large-scale controlled trials. First, the superiority of the phenothiazines over placebo or phenobarbitone was quantified. In one study, 12 weeks of phenothiazine treatment was associated with improvement in ratings of belligerence, resistiveness, thinking disturbances, perceptual distortion, paranoid ideas, and withdrawal.

The large trial carried out in the early 1960s by the American National Institute of Mental Health studied 463 newly admitted, acutely schizophrenic patients, each of whom was treated with one of three phenothiazines in flexible dosage or with a placebo (Figure 5-5). About 75% of the patients given active drug were much improved after six weeks as compared with only 25% of those given placebos. Thirteen areas of psychopathology were rated significantly more improved by drug than by placebo; ineffective social participation, confusion, poor standards of self-care, hebephrenic symptoms, agitation and tension, slowed speech, incoherent speech, irritability, indifference to environment, hostility, auditory hallucinations, ideas of persecution, and disorientation. The improvement was not confined to symptoms related to overactivity but was seen across the spectrum.

A large-scale comparison of five treatment regimens in acute schizophrenia showed that drug therapy alone was almost as effective as drugs plus psychotherapy and that both treatments were more effective than either psychotherapy alone or concomitant with routine ward care (dignified by

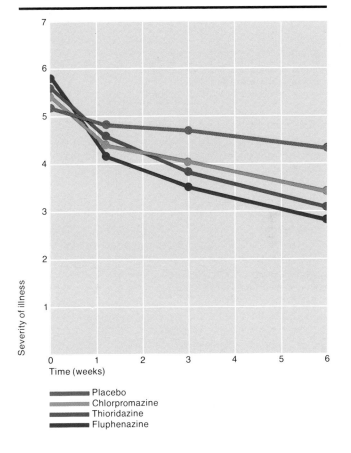

Figure 5-5. Effect of phenothiazines on severity of acute schizophrenia.(Data from National Institute of Mental Health, Psychopharmacology Service Center Collaborative Study Group: Phenothiazine treatment in acute schizophrenia. *Arch Gen Psychiatry 10*:246-261, 1964.)

the term "milieu therapy"). The fifth treatment, electroconvulsive therapy, was more effective than psychotherapy but less so than drug therapy. The psychotherapy was administered by trainee therapists, but even experienced practitioners are wary of making excessive claims in the treatment of acute schizophrenic patients.

From many studies of this sort, it seems that the most helpful single therapeutic step in managing acutely ill schizophrenic patients is the administration of adequate but not excessive doses of antipsychotic medication. However, this must be combined with a supportive environment, sympathetic nursing, and appropriate social measures.

Prevention of relapse

The term "maintenance therapy" has been widely applied to the long-term drug treatment of schizophrenic patients who are in remission and living in the community. Antipsychotic medication suppresses chronic symptoms such as hallucinations and delusions and also prevents, at least in part, socially disastrous acute relapses.

Assessment of maintenance therapy entails such measures as rehospitalization rate and assessments of residual symptom severity, social functioning, and adjustment at work. More than 20 controlled studies concur in concluding that patients taking antipsychotic medication are much less likely to relapse than those maintained on placebo. For example, in one study in the United States, more than 80% of schizophrenic patients maintained on drugs were able to remain outside hospital for 18 months or so, whereas half of a control group given placebo relapsed. Similarly, a British study found that during the course of a year about a third of patients treated with phenothiazines relapsed as compared with 80% given placebos. Patients who had a first attack with acute onset of illness incorporating depressive features and who had a previously healthy personality had a good prognosis even with placebo "therapy," according to the study, and should not be entered routinely into a maintenance program. Furthermore, patients admitted to the study covered the middle range of prognosis: those with a better outlook did well without drugs, and those excluded from the trial because of a poor prognosis relapsed despite drug maintenance.

One problem is that of drug compliance. Do patients relapse because they stop taking their medication regularly, or do they relapse and then cease medication? Perhaps a bit of both applies.

The value of social work to continued medication is complex. In one study, social-work intervention comprised counselling intended to help the patient adjust to his "major role" as wage-earner or homemaker. After two years, 80% of placebo-treated and half the drug-treated patients had relapsed. Social intervention had little effect on drug-placebo differences but did reduce later relapse in patients who remained six months or more in the community. Drug therapy plus social work was effective in these patients, who were presumably of intermediate prognosis. Early relapse was associated with previously poor adjustment, longer and more severe illnesses, social instability after discharge, poor interpersonal relationships, and poor medication compliance.

The Social Psychiatry Unit in London have investigated those factors in the patients' homes that govern relapse (Table 5-1). From an interview with the closest relative at the time of the schizophrenic patient's index admission, the patient's home environment was categorized as high or low in "Expressed Emotion" (EE), depending on the number of hostile, critical, or emotionally overcharged comments made by relatives. During nine months the relapse rate among patients discharged to high-EE homes was 51%, but it was only 13% in those in low-EE homes. Patients who spent more than 35 hours per week with their high-EE relatives had a much higher relapse rate (69%) than did those who spent less than 35 hours in close contact (28%). Regular antipsychotic medication gave further protection. Thus, patients in high-EE environments, in close contact with their relatives, and without medication had a 92% relapse rate. Conversely, those in such a household with less than 35 hours per week contact and who also took their drugs had the same chance of relapse as those in low-EE homes: 13%. Drugs made no demonstrable difference to patients in low-EE homes.

Life events also seem important and tend to cluster in the three weeks immediately before relapse. Drug maintenance therapy often seems relatively ineffective in preventing such event-related relapses, especially when the life events are major.

Long-stay patients

Despite some studies that fail to show any significant advantage of drug over placebo, there is general agreement that some useful effects can be obtained in the chronically ill patient, although much less than in the acute patient. Hallucinations, delusions, anxiety, tension, and restlessness are

Figure 5-1. Relapses among schizophrenic patients nine months after hospital discharge. (Data from Vaughn CE, Leff JP: The influence of family and social factors on the course of psychiatric illness. *Br J Psychiatry 129*:125-137, 1976.)

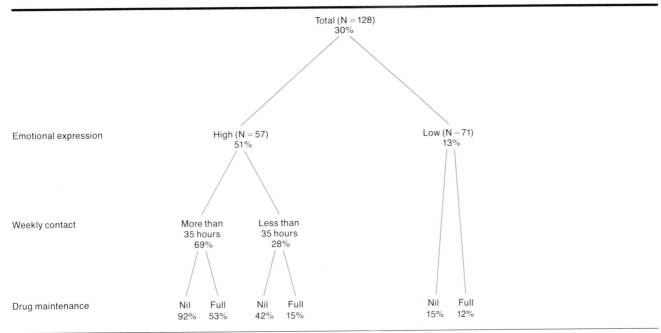

particularly amenable to amelioration by drugs. Indeed, it has been suggested that other symptoms such as apathy and social withdrawal—so-called negative symptoms—are refractory to drugs.

The emphasis is now on the use of antipsychotic drugs to facilitate occupational and social rehabilitation programs. Intensive occupational therapy is equal to chlorpromazine treatment alone in improving work and social functioning, at least initially; however, the combination of drug plus "total-push mobilization" gives the best chance of rehabilitation. Without drugs, constant supervision is needed to prevent relapse.

Recent studies in which computer-assisted tomography ("CAT scans") was used have confirmed that some chronic schizophrenic patients have definite pathological brain changes, ventricular enlargement in particular. Such patients seem particularly unresponsive to antipsychotic medication.

Unwanted Effects

Many of the wide range of unwanted effects of the antipsychotic drugs are fairly minor: feelings of slowness, sluggishness and heaviness, weakness or faintness, and anticholinergic effects such as dry mouth and blurred vision. Other unwanted effects are mediated by dopamine receptor blockade, the most important of which are the motor disorders.

Extrapyramidal effects: The earliest effect is acute dystonia, which is particularly likely to occur in males and in children and is commonest as an effect of the butyrophenones and piperazine phenothiazines. The diverse and often bizarre features include retrocollis, torticollis, tongue protrusion, dysarthria, facial grimacing, opisthotonus, and scoliosis. Misdiagnoses include tetany, tetanus, or even hysteria. A few doses or even a single dose of drug may be sufficient to induce the condition, which usually responds promptly to the parenteral administration of an antiparkinsonian agent or diazepam.

Akathisia is an uncontrollable physical and psychological restlessness characterized by fidgetting and pacing. It usually occurs within the first two weeks of treatment and may be mistaken for increasing psychotic tension. Antiparkinsonian agents are often ineffective but a benzodiazepine may help. Usually the dose of antipsychotic drug needs to be reduced.

Figure 5-6. Dopamine-acetylcholine balance
in parkinsonism.

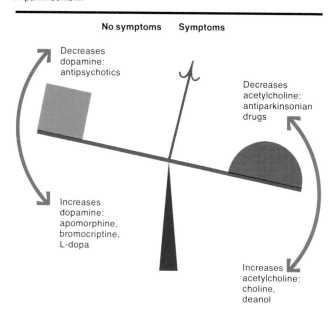

The commonest extrapyramidal effect is akinesia with weakness in those muscles used in repetitive actions such as walking (see Figure 5-6). The akinesia also affects fine-movement control, so that handwriting becomes smaller, a sign that is quite useful as an indicator of extrapyramidal effects. More-severely affected patients show loss of associated movements: rigidity, coarse tremor, stooped posture, festinant gait, and even excessive salivation and seborrhoea, all of which are signs of drug-induced parkinsonism. Women, especially the elderly, are more commonly affected. The condition supervenes within a few weeks of treatment initiation and often lessens or disappears within a month or two. The incidence of parkinsonism is about 15% to 25% among patients being treated with moderate doses of chlorpromazine (600 mg/day).

Less common reactions include akinetic mutism and catatonic reactions. These tend to occur with high doses of the potent antipsychotic drugs as do withdrawal dyskinesias when high doses are discontinued. These acute choreoathetoid reactions, which last a few days, may result from a rebound increase in the activity of previously blocked dopaminergic extrapyramidal pathways. For all these reasons, high-dose therapy as advocated by some is not without its particular dangers.

Antiparkinsonian medication: Drugs for the treatment of parkinsonism should not be used routinely with antipsychotic medication. There is no evidence for any prophylactic effect against extrapyramidal syndromes; instead, the anticholinergic effects can summate to produce severe constipation or ileus, urinary hesitancy or retention, intolerably dry mouth, and blurring of vision. The most dangerous interactive complication is a toxic psychosis. As mentioned earlier, the antiparkinsonian drug can induce drug-metabolizing enzymes in the liver, resulting in decreased plasma antipsychotic drug concentrations. Tardive dyskinesia may be more likely to occur eventually with the combination treatment. Thus, even if parkinsonism supervenes, it is better to try a modest reduction in antipsychotic drug dosage before resorting to anticholinergic drugs. With depot neuroleptics, a judicious choice of dose and dosage interval usually minimizes the problem. If antiparkinsonian medication is absolutely necessary, it can usually be restricted to the week after injection of the antipsychotic drugs.

Tardive dyskinesia: Because this condition is now regarded as a serious constraint to the long-term use of antipsychotic medication, it requires careful consideration. Tardive dyskinesia comprises involuntary repetitive, tic-like, or choreoathetoid movements that typically affect the orofacial region but often the trunk, limb, and respiratory muscles instead or as well. Among the earliest signs are an inability to keep the tongue extruded and a quivering of the tongue and floor of the mouth. The orobuccal masticatory movements are more common in the elderly, and limb movements are more common in the young.

Age, length of hospital stay, brain damage, and neuroleptic usage are all implicated in the aetiology of tardive dyskinesia, but in a complex way. Otherwise healthy elderly people who have never taken neuroleptic drugs may display spontaneous sucking and pouting movements ("schnauzkrampf"). However, drug-related dyskinesias can occur in young patients after relatively little antipsychotic medication. It must be assumed that sufficient drug for a sufficient time will result in tardive dyskinesia in most patients. The reported incidence ranges from 3% to more than 50%, the variation depending on the type of patient, prescribing habits of the psychiatrist, and care with which the syndrome is sought. In-patients maintained on long-acting depot neuroleptic therapy are especially likely to show the syndrome. In some patients, the condition worsens or becomes apparent only when the neuroleptic is discontinued. In about half of patients with tardive dyskinesia the condition persists after the neuroleptic is stopped. The syndrome typically takes several years to supervene but has been reported to occur after a few months of treatment.

The usual hypothesis for the pharmacological basis of the syndrome is the development of sustained hyperactivity of the dopaminergic systems in the basal ganglia, perhaps as a form of denervation supersensitivity, the "denervation" being the chronic blockade of dopamine receptors (Figure 5-7). This suggestion explains the observations that:

1. Most cases of tardive dyskinesia are preceded by drug-induced parkinsonism, confirming the dopamine-blockade theory.
2. Stopping the neuroleptic worsens the condition by uncovering more receptors.
3. Anticholinergic drugs, including the antiparkinsonian agents, unmask or worsen the condition by tipping the cholinergic dopaminergic balance in the basal ganglia towards even more dopaminergic preponderance. Indeed, it has been suggested that routine administration of anti-

Figure 5-7. Dopamine-acetylcholine balance in tardive dyskinesia.

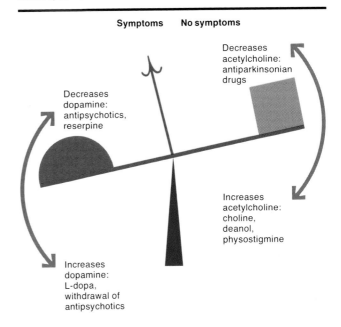

62

parkinsonian drugs predisposes the patient to tardive dyskinesia.

4. Patients with idiopathic parkinsonism often develop dyskinesias after prolonged treatment with L-dopa, which again increases dopaminergic influences.

5. L-dopa, amphetamine, and apomorphine may all exacerbate the dyskinesia; physostigmine with its cholinergic effects ameliorates it temporarily.

Tardive dyskinesia can be mild and trivial but often progresses to an embarrassing and distressful severity. The patient may find dressing and feeding difficult. Many treatments have been advocated but none are satisfactory:

1. The antipsychotic drug can be reinstituted or the dose raised, but this merely postpones the dyskinesia, which will eventually recur as "supersensitivity" increases.

2. Antiparkinsonian medication makes the patient's condition worse.

3. Dopamine-depleting agents such as reserpine and tetrabenazine may be effective for a time, but eventually the condition recurs because of increased supersensitivity due to the lack of dopamine.

4. Cholinergic drugs such as physostigmine (an acetylcholinesterase inhibitor) are temporarily effective, but administration of the precursor, choline, or of the cholinergic drug deanol, seems ineffective.

5. Sodium valproate or a benzodiazepine enhance inhibitory actions in the brain but are relatively ineffective. Any improvement might be due to a nonspecific sedative action.

6. Lithium diminishes the release of dopamine but again has been disappointing in practice.

All these treatments are either temporary in effect or unsatisfactory. It has been suggested that the supersensitivity can be reversed directly by treating the patient for a few weeks with L-dopa. This increases dopamine concentrations in the basal ganglia, making the dyskinesia worse but reversing the supersensitivity. It is claimed that withdrawal of the L-dopa is followed by cure of the dyskinesia.

However, so long as treatment remains ineffective or unestablished, it is best to avoid the condition by reserving long-term antipsychotic medication for those who really need it. Regular review of dosage and treatment duration is essential. Drug "holidays," (eg, discontinuation of drugs one month in every six) might be worth considering on theoretical grounds in an attempt to prevent supersensitivity but could jeopardize the schizophrenic patient's clinical status.

Other unwanted effects: A long list of side effects of antipsychotic medication has been catalogued over the years. Changes in incidence have occurred; for example, cholestatic jaundice is now relatively uncommon so that routine liver tests are superfluous.

As well as the extrapyramidal disorders, hyperprolactinaemia is a direct consequence of antipsychotic medication and can be associated with amenorrhoea and galactorrhoea in women and with gynaecomastia and loss of libido in men. The suggestion that the likelihood of breast cancer is increased is not supported by clear data, nor is there evidence of teratogenicity. Weight gain is common and may be significant. Its mechanism is unclear but may reflect hypothalamic effects, perhaps of an antiserotonin nature.

Another long-term side effect, mainly with chlorpromazine and other low-potency compounds, is the accumulation of drugs and their metabolites and pigments in the cornea, lens, and skin. This leads to a purple-gray discoloration, especially in sunny climates, but vision is not usually impaired. The retinal degeneration that can follow high doses (more than 800 mg/day) of thioridazine is a separate but serious phenomenon.

Phenothiazines, in particular thioridazine, cause ECG changes indicative of prolonged ventricular repolarization (prolongation of Q-T interval and T-wave blunting), presumably by shifting potassium into the intracellular compartment. Arrhythmias are more likely and may underlie the instances of sudden death reported to occur among patients treated with phenothiazines. Nevertheless, the condition is rare and its significance difficult to establish.

A large number of unwanted effects is attributable to the autonomic effects of the drugs, especially of chlorpromazine and even more especially of thioridazine. The alpha-adrenergic blocking effects produce vasodilatation in muscle blood vessels, postural hypotension, and a reflex tachycardia. Anticholinergic effects include dry mouth, blurred vision, urinary hesitancy, and constipation. Paralytic ileus and retention of urine have been documented. Inhibition of ejaculation may occur.

The induction of depression by antipsychotic medication is controversial. Irrespective of medication, schizophrenic patients often have affective swings: suicide is at least 50 times more common among schizophrenic patients than among the general population. It is thus difficult to disentangle any association with antipsychotic medication.

Among rare adverse reactions are cholestatic jaundice and agranulocytosis.

Overdosage of antipsychotic medication is not usually life-endangering except in children. The two main problems are cardiac arrhythmias and parkinsonian rigidity of the respiratory muscles. Bizarre neurological syndromes may occur, especially in children.

USE OF ANTIPSYCHOTIC DRUGS
Choice of drug
Most of the antipsychotic drugs currently available in the United Kingdom and United States are listed in Table 5-2. The large number of drugs precludes firm recommendations regarding differential indications, and the number of possible controlled comparisons on which to base such conclusions runs into the hundreds; nor can any one practitioner gain sufficient personal experience with more than a few compounds. Furthermore, the newer antipsychotic drugs have not been attended by claims for greatly enhanced effectiveness, fewer side effects, and so on, as have some newer antidepressants. Consequently, contrasts among the various antipsychotic agents are not impressive. The major alternative is the use of long-acting injectable preparations.

In considering the effectiveness of the various antipsychotic drugs, one must face the problem of the criteria for effectiveness. These include behavioural variables such as aggression, agitation, and slowing; social variables such as coping in the community and work adjustment; psychopathological states such as hallucinations, delusions, and thought disorders; and administrative factors, including length of hospital stay and discharge rate. Antipsychotic drugs do not differ appreciably or significantly among themselves with respect to their overall clinical effectiveness, although some patients respond to one drug and not to another. Supposedly, the aliphatic phenothiazines (eg, chlorpromazine) are more effective against the "positive" symptoms of schizophrenia, such as overactivity, as compared with the piperazine compounds (eg, trifluoperazine and the butyrophenones), which are said to be more useful in combatting the "negative" symptoms such as social withdrawal. Systematically controlled evaluations of differential drug response, however, provide no support for this widely held notion.

The significant differences among antipsychotic drugs are in their unwanted effects. Chlorpromazine and thioridazine are soporific, whereas trifluoperazine, prochlorperazine, and

Table 5-2. Some antipsychotic agents.

Phenothiazines (Aliphatic side-chain)	**Thioxanthenes**	**Indoles**
Chlorpromazine	Chlorprothixene	Oxypertine
Laevopromazine	Clopenthixol	Molindone
Trifluopromazine	Flupenthixol	
Alimemazine	Thiothixene	**Substituted Benzamides**
		Sulpiride
(Piperidine side-chain)	**Azepines**	**Amine depletors**
Thioridazine	Loxapine	Reserpine
Mesoridazine	Clozapine	Tetrabenazine
Mepazine		
Piperacetazine	**Thiazines**	
Pericyazine	Prothipendyl	
(Piperazine side-chain)	**Acridanes**	
Prochlorperazine	Chlomacran	
Trifluoperazine		
Butaperazine	**Butyrophenones (Phenylbutylpiperidines)**	
Fluphenazine	Droperidol	
Perphenazine	Haloperidol	
Acetophenazine	Benperidol	
Thiopropazate	Trifluperidol	
Thioproperazine	Spiroperidol	
Carphenazine		
Dixyrazine	**Diphenylbutylpiperidines**	
Perazine	Penfluridol	
	Pimozide	
	Fluspirilene	

haloperidol are much less so. More distinctly, thioridazine is almost devoid of extrapyramidal effects, chlorpromazine has a modest incidence, and the piperazine high-potency phenothiazines and the butyrophenones have high incidences. Conversely, anticholinergic effects are common with thioridazine, present with chlorpromazine, and minor or negligible with the other compounds.

Dosage

To attain adequate drug concentrations in the patient in a psychopathological crisis, an intramuscular dose of, say, 100 mg of chlorpromazine or 5 mg of haloperidol is necessary. However, as unwanted effects may be troublesome after such a loading dose, in less urgent circumstances a build-up of oral medication is preferable. The practitioner "titrates" the dose for the individual patient to obtain the optimal response – maximal therapeutic effect with minimal side effects. The dosage varies widely from patient to patient and even from country to country. Because the time-course of the antipsychotic effect is rather slow, dosage changes should be relatively infrequent to permit rational assessment of drug effect.

Moderate dosage, ie, equivalent to 400 mg per day of chlorpromazine, is on average more effective than lower dosages, particularly in acutely ill schizophrenic patients. However, it is doubtful whether the routine use of high doses (more than 600 mg per day of chlorpromazine equivalent) has any benefits over lower doses, and unwanted effects can be severe. However, occasional patients may respond only to high doses. Very high doses are not justified. There is no support for the view that definite extrapyramidal effects are essential for a clinical response.

Although the plasma half-lives of some phenothiazines are relatively short, once-a-day dosage seems perfectly adequate in most cases. Chlorpromazine given as one dose at night often exerts useful hypnotic effects.

Long-acting preparations

Long-acting injectable (depot) neuroleptics have made much more impact in the United Kingdom than in the United States, presumably reflecting different health-care systems for the chronic ambulatory schizophrenic patient. Fluphenazine decanoate and fluphenazine enanthate are available in the United States and the United Kingdom, and flupenthixol decanoate and clopenthixol decanoate are also available in the United Kingdom. These drugs are administered by depot injection into the gluteal muscles once every two to four weeks. The formulation with a long-chain fatty acid makes the drug highly lipophilic; it dissolves in the fatty tissues of the muscle and is released very slowly.

The rationale for the use of these drugs is threefold:

1. By depot injection into muscle, the drug can be absorbed into the systemic circulation without running the gauntlet of first-pass metabolism in the liver, as is the case with oral administration. Some patients are rapid metabolizers of phenothiazines and are greatly benefitted by a switch to a depot formulation.

2. Drug defaulting can be minimized. The main reasons for failure to adhere to the prescribed regimen are unpleasant side effects (real or expected), the patients' attitudes to the use of drugs in their illness, and problems of communication between patient and practitioner. With the injectable drugs, the prescriber knows whether or not the drug is being administered.

3. The use of depot neuroleptics is often attended by the institution of a specially organized clinic with adequate social support in the community. Such a system can reduce drug defaulting from about a third to less than a sixth of patients. Vigorous steps can be taken if social crises supervene or if the patients are reacting adversely to home, social, or work circumstances.

The depot neuroleptics often help individual patients who have responded poorly to oral medication, and they also improve the overall prognosis to some extent. Most patients treated with placebos relapse during the course of a year (Table 5-3), but only about 10% of patients treated with depot neuroleptics relapse in that time. For those treated with orally administered drug, the figure is about 35%. However, over the longer term, the prognosis is somewhat poorer. It is still unclear whether the injectable drugs are superior to oral medication only in those patients who are drug defaulters and who metabolize the drugs rapidly. Depot neuroleptic drugs often have little influence on the chronic symptoms yet lessen social withdrawal and buffer the patient from stressful influences.

Of the drugs available (in the United Kingdom), flupenthixol seems to be associated with less depression of mood than does fluphenazine. This contention remains controversial, as does the whole question of antipsychotic medication and the incidence of depression.

Table 5-3. Relapse rate over ensuing year of 74 schizophrenic patients discharged from hospital and maintained on either fluphenazine decanoate or placebo injections. (Data from Hirsch SR, Gaind R, Rohde PD, et al: Outpatient maintenance of chronic schizophrenic patients with long-acting fluphenazine: Double-blind placebo trial. Report to the Medical Research Council Committee on Clinical Trials in Psychiatry. *Br Med J 1*:633-637, 1973.)

	Number of Patients	Relapse	No Relapse
Active medication	36	3	33
Placebo	38	25	13
		$p < 0.001$	

The Young, the Old, and the Physically Ill

Antipsychotic medication is sometimes used to control hyperactive and explosive behaviour in children with autism. Social withdrawal and apathy may also be lessened. Chlorpromazine and thioridazine tend to make the child drowsy; conversely, extrapyramidal reactions may be troublesome with the piperazine phenothiazines or the butyrophenones. Thiothixene, flupenthixol, and pericyazine have been advocated. Other indications for antipsychotic medication include psychotic behaviour associated with mental handicaps and organic brain damage. Haloperidol is often effective in tiqueurs and in adolescents with Gilles de la Tourette syndrome. The danger of tardive dyskinesia must be borne in mind constantly, however, during treatment.

The elderly are more prone to develop parkinsonism during treatment with antipsychotic medication than are the young. Thioridazine is often favoured but it may induce excessive drowsiness or anticholinergic effects. Thus, the optimal medication can be arrived at only by trial-and-error. Whatever drug is tried, low initial dosage is essential, especially in the physically frail and wasted.

In physically ill patients as well, especially those with organic brain disease or liver damage, any antipsychotic medication must be given cautiously and in low initial doses. Because many antipsychotic drugs lower the convulsive threshold, particular care is necessary in epileptic patients. Monitoring of the ECG is needed in patients with cardiac conditions, especially with abnormalities of conduction.

THE DOPAMINE HYPOTHESIS OF SCHIZOPHRENIA

This hypothesis, which stems from the effects of dopamine agonists and antagonists on behaviour, states that dopaminergic activity is excessive in schizophrenia. The various lines of evidence will be briefly reviewed.

1. *Type of action of antipsychotic drugs.* Although all these drugs can interfere with dopaminergic transmission, it is not clear whether any specific antischizophrenic properties can be claimed. Thus, dopamine block should not necessarily be equated with antischizophrenic actions.

2. *Model psychoses.* Many chemical substances can induce a psychotic state. Whereas the anticholinergic drugs in overdose are associated with clouding of consciousness, the psychotomimetics such as lysergic acid and mescaline affect

consciousness much less (see also Chapter 9). Amphetamine provides the best model state: repeated high doses induce a paranoid psychosis usually indistinguishable from schizophrenia. The only somewhat atypical features are orofacial movements and stereotyped behaviour. In schizophrenic patients with active symptoms of psychopathology, amphetamine or methylphenidate markedly exacerbate the symptoms but have little effect in remitted patients. Of amphetamine's various actions, its dopamine-releasing properties are most deeply implicated in inducing psychosis. Thus, the psychosis is prevented or reversed by haloperidol but not by adrenergic-blocking agents, and HVA concentrations in cerebrospinal fluid are increased after amphetamine administration.

3. *Dopamine manipulations in schizophrenia.* As discussed in Chapter 2, alpha-methyl-paratyrosine blocks dopamine synthesis. Administration of this compound does not consistently improve the mental state of schizophrenics, but it apparently permits the use of a lower dose of antipsychotic medication. Conversely, L-dopa can exacerbate schizophrenic symptoms, especially motor activity.

4. *Dopamine levels in schizophrenia.* Dopamine turnover, estimated as a measure of cerebrospinal fluid HVA, is inconsistently altered in schizophrenic patients but tends to be elevated in those with excessive motor activity. Prolactin concentrations, which should be low if dopamine activity was abnormally high in the tuberoinfundibular pathway, are normal in schizophrenic patients. Similarly, if nigrostriatal activity is excessive, parkinsonism and schizophrenia should be mutually exclusive, but they are not. Finally, postmortem studies of brains of schizophrenic patients have not shown any clear-cut dopamine excess, especially when the effects of medication with phenothiazines are taken into account.

5. *Dopamine receptors.* An alternative suggestion is that the overactivity is secondary not to excessive dopamine but to abnormally sensitive receptors. Dopamine-sensitive adenylate cyclase levels are normal in schizophrenic brains, but there is some evidence of increased numbers of dopamine receptors when assessed by the spiroperidol-binding technique. Whether the patient had taken drugs confuses the issue, but this line of research is currently most interesting.

In general, the evidence is suggestive but far from compelling that dopaminergic activity is excessive in schizophrenic patients. Of course, the abnormality might be highly localized but, if so, it seems to affect particular motor mechanisms and systems mediating the direction of motor responses. That a symptomatic remedy acts on certain mechanisms suggests only that those mechanisms are somehow involved in the symptom expression, not that they are causal in the illness. The example of the anticholinergic drugs in the treatment of parkinsonism demonstrates the need for caution in interpreting drug actions.

FURTHER READING

Bowers B: Thioridazine: Central dopamine turnover and clinical effects of antipsychotic drugs. *Clin Pharmacol Ther 17*:73-78, 1974.

Casey DE: Managing tardive dyskinesia. *J Clin Psychiatry 39*:748-753, 1978.

Casey JF, Lasky JJ, Klett CJ, Hollister LE: Treatment of schizophrenic reactions with phenothiazine derivatives. *Am J Psychiatry 117*:97-105, 1960.

Creese I, Burt DR, Snyder SH: Dopamine receptor binding predicts clinical and pharmacological potencies of antischizophrenic drugs. *Science 192*: 481-483, 1976.

Curry SH, Marshall JHL, Davis JM, Janowsky DS: Chlorpromazine plasma level and effects. *Arch Gen Psychiatry 22*:289-296, 1970.

Davis JM: Overview: Maintenance therapy in schizophrenia. I. Schizophrenia. *Am J Psychiatry 132*:1237-1245, 1975.

DeWied D, DeJong W: Drug effects and hypothalamic-anterior pituitary function. *Ann Rev Pharmacol 14*:389-412, 1974.

Freyhan FA: Therapeutic implications of differential effects of new phenothiazine compounds. *Am J Psychiatry 115*:577-585, 1959.

Gardos G, Cole JO, Orzack MH: The importance of dosage in antipsychotic drug administration – a review of dose-response studies. *Psychopharmacologia 29*:221-230, 1973.

Johnson DAW: Practical considerations in the use of depot neuroleptics for the treatment of schizophrenia. *Br J Hosp Med 17*:546-558, 1977.

Jørgensen OS: The psychopharmacological treatment of psychotic children: A review. *Acta Psychiatr Scand 59*:229-238, 1979.

Loga S, Curry S, Lader M: Interactions of orphenadrine and phenobarbitone with chlorpromazine: Plasma concentrations and effects in man. *Br J Clin Pharmacol 2*:197-208, 1975.

May PRA: *Treatment of Schizophrenia: A Comparative Study of Five Treatment Methods.* New York, Science House, 1968.

Prien RF, Klett JC: An appraisal of the long-term use of tranquillizing medication with hospitalized chronic schizophrenics: A review of the drug discontinuation literature. *Schizophr Bull 5*:64-73, 1972.

Snyder SH, Banerjee SP, Yamamura HI, Greenberg D: Drugs, neurotransmitters and schizophrenia. *Science 184*:1243-1253, 1974.

Tarsy D, Baldessarini RJ: The pathophysiologic basis of tardive dyskinesia. *Biol Psychiatry 12*:431-450, 1977.

Vaughn CE, Leff JP: The influence of family and social factors on the course of psychiatric illness. *Br J Psychiatry 129*:125-137, 1976.

Wyatt RJ, Torgow JS: A comparison of the equivalent clinical potencies of neuroleptics as used to treat schizophrenia and affective disorders. *J Psychiatr Res 13*:91-98, 1976.

Antidepressant Drugs

INTRODUCTION

The term *antidepressant* is the one most widely used to denote drugs that combat depression, but it is open to the criticism that it implies some actions against depressants, an unfortunate misconception. *Antidepressive* is also used with less confusion, but the term *antidepression drugs* (which might be most apposite) is not extant. Other terms such as *thymoleptic* and *mood elevators* are ambiguous.

In this chapter, the two major groups of antidepressants are discussed: (a) the tricyclic and related compounds, which are believed to act by blocking amine re-uptake, and (b) the monoamine oxidase inhibitors, which, by definition, block the widespread enzyme monoamine oxidase (MAO). The term *tricyclic antidepressant* is most unsatisfactory. Some drugs of similar action are tetracyclic, bicyclic, or monocyclic. The term *monoamine re-uptake inhibitor* has been suggested and has much to commend it because it avoids the mistaken emphasis on chemical structure. Even so, some drugs in this class may increase amine neurotransmitter concentrations in the synaptic cleft by other means.

The antidepressants were discovered by accident, and their mode of action still poses many questions. Nevertheless, perhaps more than any other class of psychotropic drug, they have stimulated scientific interest in the mechanisms of mental illness. The important and still-dominant amine hypotheses of depression and mania stem directly from juxtaposition of the clinical and biochemical actions of the monoamine oxidase inhibitors, with extra emphasis when the biochemical effects of the uptake-inhibiting antidepressants became clear. A vast amount of research effort has been expended in both laboratory and clinical experiments to elucidate the mode of action of the antidepressants in the hope that such knowledge would unlock the secret of the biological concomitants of depression.

Indeed, at times the amine hypothesis has been so vigorously promoted that its basis in psychopharmacology has seemed forgotten. New antidepressants have been sought not in terms of clinical effects or even animal behavioural tests, but as to whether the amine changes predicted by the hypothesis have been induced. The circularity of this approach is evident and has threatened at times to stifle innovation. Luckily, some atypical compounds have survived this developmental ordeal and have led to some rethinking of the various amine hypotheses. In particular, the long-term effects of antidepressants have been reevaluated.

On a more practical level, the nagging problem has been the incomplete response to antidepressant therapy. In controlled trials, about 33% of depressed patients show a satisfactory response to placebo, and another 33% respond to the drug. Why the remaining third do not respond is still unclear, although a pharmacokinetic explanation is becoming increasingly favoured.

One particular problem has been the concept of depressive illness. Symptoms are many and varied, differentiation from anxiety and schizophrenia is not clear, and diagnostic habits differ from clinic to clinic. The classification of depressive illnesses is contentious, with both dimensional and dichotomous models being put forward. Depressive symptoms occur in other psychiatric conditions and must be distinguished from depressive syndromes and illnesses. For these reasons, among others, the interpretation of drug trials is often difficult, and conclusions must be limited.

As far as the biological aspects of depression are concerned, two typologies seem useful. One is based on the immediate clinical picture and refers to whether any retardation or agitation is discernible in the patient. The other concerns the natural history of the condition in patients with repeated episodes. If only depressive phases occur, the condition is said to be "unipolar"; if manic episodes also occur, the illness is termed "bipolar." Even so problems arise. A patient can have several depressive illnesses and be regarded as unipolar and then belatedly show a manic phase and have to be reclassified. Also, the more careful the history, the more likely to be elicited is a minor elevation of mood preceding a depressive illness. Operational criteria for an episode such as admission to hospital are also suspect, as social factors also operate.

A second problem is the high relapse rate in treating depressed patients when antidepressant medication is withdrawn. The widespread realization of this limitation has led to the realistic appraisal of the antidepressants as symptom suppressant rather than as providing a fundamental cure. That is, these drugs render the patient less depressed or induce a normal mood while natural remission takes place.

MONOAMINE RE-UPTAKE INHIBITORS (TRICYCLICS AND OTHERS)

History

Iminodibenzyl, the parent compound of imipramine, was first synthesized at the end of the last century. In the late

1940s, during the search for antihistaminic compounds, various iminodibenzyl derivatives were developed. They were usually sedative, but because the antihistamine activity was insufficient, they were shelved. The discovery of the antipsychotic properties of the phenothiazines led to a reexamination of the psychotropic profile of the iminodibenzyls, but they appeared devoid of antipsychotic activity. However, Professor Roland Kuhn, convinced that an antidepressant drug should be as feasible as an antipsychotic, tried one or two compounds in depressed patients. The iminodibenzyl analogue of promazine, coded G22355 and now known as imipramine, proved active. In Zurich in 1957, after having studied more than 100 depressed patients, Kuhn reported on the antidepressant activity of imipramine. He also published full reports that year and the next. Most of what we now know of the clinical actions of the tricyclic antidepressants is adumbrated in those reports.

Three limitations became quickly apparent: not all patients responded, there were many troublesome side effects, and response was often delayed for two weeks or more. The search began for drugs that were improvements over imipramine. The major rival, amitriptyline, was introduced in 1961 and is currently the most widely prescribed antidepressant in many countries. The desmethylated derivatives desipramine and nortriptyline were introduced under the assumption that they were the active derivatives of imipramine and amitriptyline, respectively, and should accordingly act more rapidly. They do not.

Other tricyclic compounds were introduced, varying mostly in either central ring structure or side chain (see Figure 6-1). More recently, tetracyclic, bicyclic, and monocyclic compounds have been developed and marketed with claims that they are more effective and have a wider spectrum of action, fewer side effects, or more rapid action. The continuing popularity of amitriptyline and imipramine suggests some scepticism regarding these claims.

Despite reservations and disappointments regarding the utility of these drugs, they are standard therapy for depressed patients. Electroconvulsive therapy is now reserved for the severely ill, especially patients with psychomotor retardation, and for those who have responded well to electroconvulsive therapy in the past. After a few years of hesitancy, family physicians now use the tricyclic antidepressants extensively.

Figure 6-1. Formulae of some antidepressants.

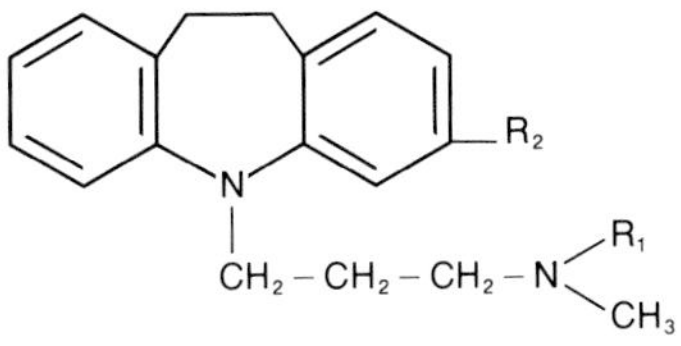

$R_1 = CH_3$	$R_2 = H$	Imipramine
$R_1 = H$	$R_2 = H$	Desipramine
$R_1 = CH_3$	$R_2 = Cl$	Clomipramine

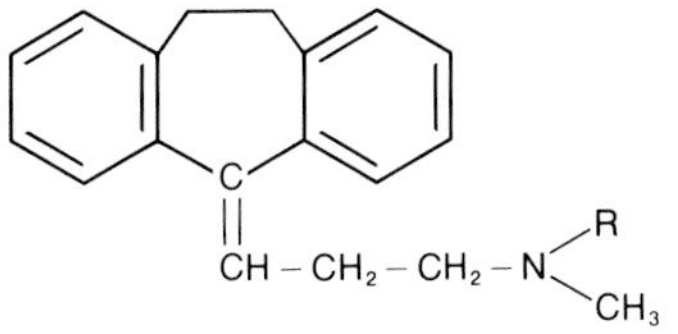

$R = CH_3$	Amitriptyline
$R = H$	Nortriptyline

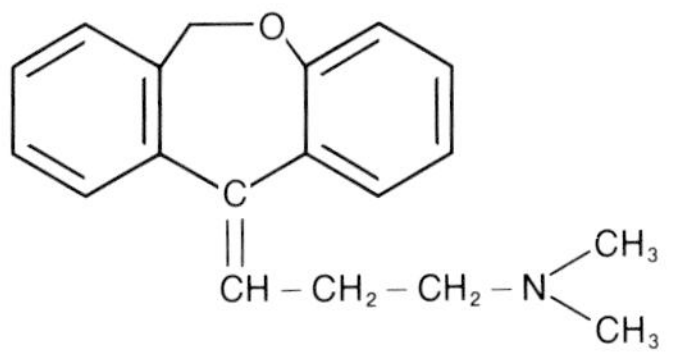

Doxepin

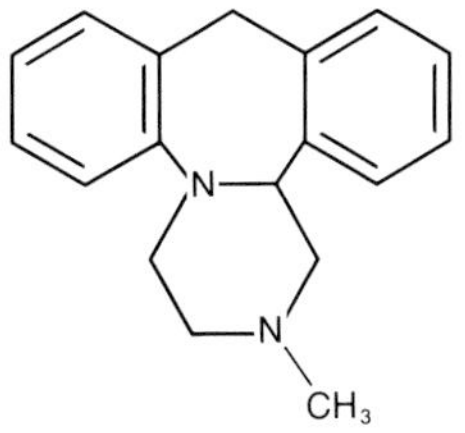

Mianserin

Figure 6-2. Main metabolic pathways of imipramine.

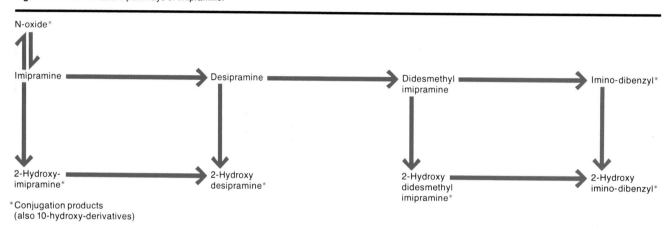

*Conjugation products
(also 10-hydroxy-derivatives)

Figure 6-3. Main metabolic pathways of amitriptyline.

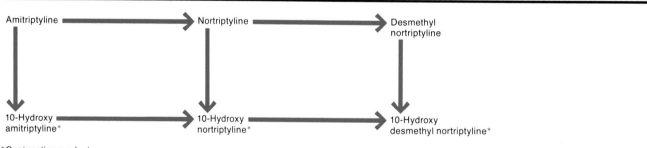

*Conjugation products

Pharmacokinetics

Absorption and metabolism: Imipramine and amitriptyline are rapidly absorbed and extensively metabolized. Absorption is usually complete within ten hours of oral ingestion, and maximal plasma concentrations are attained after one to two hours. Absorption after intramuscular injection is rather slower.

Imipramine rapidly passes into the brain, where high concentrations are attained especially in the neocortex, paleocortex, hippocampus, and thalamus. At least 97% of the drug is bound intracellularly, so the concentration at synaptic receptors is presumed to be low.

Tricyclic antidepressants are extensively metabolized in the liver, and only minute amounts of unchanged drug are excreted. In human beings, imipramine is metabolized in four main routes (Figure 6-2):

1. N-desmethylation of the side chain, producing the active metabolite desipramine
2. N-oxidation of the side chain
3. Hydroxylation in position 2 (and probably other positions) of the ring system
4. Glucuronide formation.

Amitriptyline undergoes essentially similar transformation; N-desmethylation of the side chain to produce nortriptyline, and 10-hydroxylation of ring system are particularly important (Figure 6-3). Between 25% and 75% of these drugs are metabolized first-pass through the liver after oral administration. Of the various metabolites, only the desmethyl and perhaps the hydroxy derivatives are psychotropically active to any degree.

Plasma concentrations and clinical response: The pharmacokinetics of nortriptyline have been worked out in greater detail than have those of amitriptyline or imipramine. Treatment with standard doses results in up to thirtyfold differences among patients with respect to "steady-state" plasma concentrations. Even so, these levels can be determined from the kinetics of a single test dose so that at least theoretically it is possible to plan an appropriate dosage schedule. Studies of twins and families show a marked genetic influence on metabolism, plasma binding, and distribution constants.

Plasma concentrations of nortriptyline correlate with effects such as inhibition of noradrenaline uptake into the iris in rats and reduction of the tyramine pressor response. Unwanted effects, including subjective complaints and impairment of visual accommodation, also correlate with plasma concentrations. The relationship of plasma concentration to clinical response is more contentious. Several groups of workers, mainly in Scandinavia, have presented evidence that both low and high concentrations of plasma nortriptyline are associated with an absent or incomplete clinical response. In patients whose plasma concentrations are above the optimum (50 to 150 ng/ml), reduction in dosage is followed by a prompt recovery. However, various workers have arrived at somewhat different optimal plasma concentration ranges (the "therapeutic window"), and yet others have found no such relationship with clinical response. Nevertheless, evidence of a curvilinear relation between clinical response and plasma concentrations has been presented for other desmethylated compounds, protriptyline and desipramine. There is probably sufficient evidence now to advise that dosages of nortriptyline be adjusted to yield plasma concentrations of about 125 ng/ml for optimal response.

Claims had been made for a straight-line relationship between persistent response to amitriptyline and high concentrations of the drug. The most recent studies, however, have failed to confirm such a relationship for either amitriptyline or imipramine. Anyway, such an effect would be difficult to explain because nortriptyline and desipramine build up during long-term treatment with amitriptyline and imipramine, respectively, to form about half of the active substance in the body. Thus, treatment with amitriptyline is essentially treatment with a mixture of the parent drug and its derivative, nortriptyline. In practice, the dosage of amitriptyline should be tailored to produce levels of amitriptyline plus nortriptyline up to 250 ng/ml to encourage response in the hitherto unresponsive patient.

Drug interactions: The pharmacodynamic interactions are discussed later. Because the tricyclic antidepressants are extensively metabolized in the liver, both induction and competition can occur. Induction occurs to a moderate extent with imipramine and probably other tricyclics. Barbiturates, but not benzodiazepines, enhance this liver microsomal enzyme induction and can thereby reduce plasma concentrations of the tricyclic compound, sometimes to zero. Conversely, phenothiazines and tricyclic antidepressants may mutually compete so that plasma concentrations of both are elevated. This may improve clinical response but could lead to excessive anticholinergic activity, including a toxic psychosis.

72

Pharmacology

Biochemical pharmacology: For some time the mechanism of action of the tricyclic antidepressants was unclear, but their clinical effects are now believed to be related to their activity in blocking the re-uptake into the presynaptic vesicles of 5-hydroxytryptamine (serotonin), noradrenaline, and probably dopamine. These active uptake pumps are located in the cell membranes. As well as having central actions, most tricyclics can block the uptake of noradrenaline from the peripheral circulation into noradrenergic sympathetic nerves. Similarly, uptake of 5-hydroxytryptamine by blood platelets can be blocked. By this blockade of uptake and inactivation, imipramine potentiates the effects of nerve stimulation or locally applied catecholamines on such adrenergic structures as vas deferens, spleen, cardiac muscle, and nictitating membrane. At high doses the effects of catecholamines are reduced, possibly by postsynaptic blockade.

When rats are injected with reserpine, a characteristic sedation is produced. Pretreatment with a tricyclic antidepressant results in amines being released and being potentiated by the antidepressant. This is widely used as a screening test.

The tertiary amine tricyclics such as chlorimipramine and amitriptyline tend to inhibit 5-hydroxytryptamine uptake more than noradrenaline uptake; the secondary amine derivatives such as desipramine and nortriptyline tend to do the reverse. However, whereas clinical potencies tend to be fairly similar, in vitro uptake tests show differences of at least a thousandfold among drugs. Moreover, some drugs that are antidepressant clinically are very poor uptake inhibitors; conversely, some powerful uptake inhibitors such as cocaine are limited in antidepressive usefulness. Finally, when the drugs are taken chronically, uptake effects and amine dispositions are modified by compensatory mechanisms so that variable changes are produced. For all these reasons, uptake inhibition as the sole mode of action is unlikely. Presynaptic and postsynaptic receptor blockade may be an alternative or additional mode of action.

The blockade of uptake results in the potentiation of amine effects such as the increase in pressor concentrations that occurs after adrenaline administration. Other drugs, the indirectly acting sympathomimetics, are taken up into the presynaptic neuron to cause the release of noradrenaline. The effects of these amines, such as tyramine, are therefore blocked. Similarly, some antihypertensive agents, namely, bethanidine, guanethidine, debrisoquine, and clonidine, also rely on the noradrenaline-uptake pump to reach their sites of action. Again, their effects are blocked or attenuated by tricyclic antidepressants, so that the blood pressure may rise alarmingly.

Many of the tricyclics, amitriptyline and imipramine in particular, have definite anticholinergic actions. Other properties resemble those of chlorpromazine and include antihistaminic and hypothermic effects.

Site of main action: Unlike the antipsychotic drugs, whose pharmacological effects can be related to specific pathways, the antidepressants' sites of action are unclear. Peripheral effects as mentioned above are important, but central effects have been poorly correlated with specific pathways. It is unknown whether the antidepressant effects are mediated mainly through noradrenergic, serotonergic, or even dopaminergic pathways – or some combination of these. The powerful anticholinergic properties of some antidepressants have led to speculation about the role of a central atropine-like action in the antidepressant effects. Some apparently effective antidepressants are only weakly anticholinergic, however. Moreover, anticholinergic agents such as atropine are not useful antidepressants.

The enhancement of psychomotor activity with the tricyclics, especially protriptyline and nortriptyline, has been attributed to increased central noradrenergic activity, presumably of the projection bundles (see Chapter 3), and the mood elevation has been regarded as a sign of increased 5-hydroxytryptamine concentrations, but all this remains speculative.

Behavioural pharmacology: Low doses of imipramine produce little behavioural impairment, and only high doses diminish activity. In many tests, even those sensitive to small doses of other psychotropic agents, the uptake-inhibitor antidepressants have no specific effects, and only secondary effects such as sedation are detected. Only when other drugs are used concomitantly are specific effects noted, such as reversal of reserpine effects and potentiation of amphetamine.

Human pharmacology: The re-uptake inhibitors produce EEG desynchronization and increased theta activity and may activate epileptic discharges. The EEG changes are said to be characteristic of antidepressants, but some anticholinergic effects are not dissimilar. REM sleep is suppressed.

Studies of cognitive, psychomotor, and affective changes in normal human beings have indicated little except mild sedative effects with imipramine and amitriptyline. Nausea, which also impairs performance, is often induced.

Anticholinergic activity, the pharmacological effect easiest to detect, produces mydriasis, tachycardia, decreased salivation and sweating, and disturbances of accommodation. Attenuation of the pressor response after tyramine infusion reflects the degree of blockade of noradrenaline uptake. The monoamine re-uptake inhibitor antidepressants vary greatly in their pharmacological profiles.

Clinical Effects

Kuhn described the clinical effects of imipramine in some detail. He regarded the main indication as "simple endogenous depression," every added complication lessening the chances of an adequate response. Depression of a severe degree, with gross retardation or marked agitation and with paranoid delusions and auditory hallucinations of self-blame, guilt, and worthlessness, usually responds better to a short course of electroconvulsive therapy. Depression associated with early dementia may be relieved by tricyclic drugs, but depression in schizophrenic patients may be unresponsive. Rapidly cycling manic-depressive illnesses and atypical episodic psychoses with affective components are often refractory to the tricyclic antidepressants.

Response to the tricyclic antidepressants is often delayed for two weeks or more. However, it is customary to initiate treatment at a modest dosage such as 75 mg/day of amitriptyline, either at night or in divided doses during the day. With the relatively long half-life of these drugs, steady-state concentrations are not attained for about a week (four to five times the half-life of 24-36 hours). The dose is then usually doubled and, again, a week elapses before the new level (which one hopes is now therapeutic) is attained. Therefore, the first two weeks of the latent period between initiation of therapy and eventual response is explicable in pharmacokinetic terms. Nevertheless, it is possible that a true pharmacodynamic lag period must elapse, a possibility suggesting that response depends not on the initial biochemical changes but rather on compensatory mechanisms.

The response, if and when it occurs, is disjointed in that not all depressive features respond simultaneously. Often, the first symptom to subside is that of insomnia — the patient falls asleep readily and does not awaken until morning.

A few days later, an increase in psychomotor activity is apparent. Typically, the patient begins attending to routine tasks and completing them. Memory and concentration improve. Lastly, the depressed mood starts to lift. Diurnal variation is often pronounced; patients feel better in the evening, especially if they have completed a satisfactory day. Variations from day to day are also usually significant, and patients must be warned that occasionally they may feel so depressed for two or three days that they despair of ever feeling better. The patient should be encouraged to take a longer-term view, assessing his progress week by week.

Some patients initially feel much worse on tricyclic antidepressants, especially the more sedative ones; some patients may stop taking the drug, and the physician might mistakenly conclude that he is dealing with a treatment-refractory patient.

Controlled clinical trials generally concur in proving the partial effectiveness of these drugs. However, as mentioned earlier, placebo response may be appreciable. One estimate is that about 15% of chronically depressed inpatients and outpatients improve substantially with placebo alone; the figure for acutely ill patients is about 45%. About 70% improve with imipramine therapy.

Many attempts have been made to identify those patients who are not likely to respond to imipramine and to identify those factors that prevent response. Age, sex, and education seem not to affect outcome, whereas a higher socioeconomic level is associated with a better response. Few previous episodes, brief duration, and insidious onset signify a favourable outcome, as does the absence of clear precipitating factors. Improvement is greater in patients with physiological signs such as early waking, anorexia, weight loss, and psychomotor disturbance and is less in those with neurotic, hysterical, or hypochondriacal personality traits.

The pharmacokinetic factors have been outlined earlier.

Imipramine may help schizophrenic symptoms such as lack of drive, social withdrawal, and depression, but it may exacerbate hostility, delusions, hallucinations, and agitation. It is generally combined with antipsychotic medication in this context.

Generalized anxiety states do not respond well to tricyclic antidepressants, although any associated depression may be relieved. Controlled trials have demonstrated their usefulness in phobic anxiety, especially in patients whose attacks come "out of the blue" and who were previously normal.

Nocturnal enuresis in children can be alleviated by imipramine and probably by other drugs of this class as well. However, relapse occurs if the drug is withdrawn, so it should be reserved for short-term use in special circumstances such as the child staying away from home or living in a household under severe temporary social strain.

Maintenance therapy: The consensus among clinicians is that the antidepressants hold the depressive symptoms and features at bay until natural remission occurs. In other words, the therapy is not "curative" in reversing the pathogenesis of the condition. Natural remission is estimated to occur within two years in about 90% of patients with moderate or severe depression.

The strongest evidence for this concept of the therapeutic type of action of the antidepressants comes from the high relapse rate following discontinuation of drug therapy. In one typical trial, 92 patients with a primary depressive illness who had responded to amitriptyline or imipramine were allocated randomly to either continuing active medication or receiving a placebo. Of those receiving active treatment, 22% relapsed; of those receiving placebo, 50% relapsed. In a similar six-month trial, female neurotic depressive patients who had responded to amitriptyline were allocated to one of three groups: continuation therapy with amitriptyline 100 to 150 mg daily, placebo treatment, or no drug. Further, each group was subdivided into those given psychotherapy and those who were not. Of those maintained on placebo or not given drugs, 40% relapsed; of those on drugs, only 15%. Social adjustment but not incidence of relapse was improved by psychotherapy. Adverse life events were more common among those who relapsed. A year later most patients were symptom free, but 70% had received further advice or treatment.

Unwanted Effects: These antidepressant drugs have a wide range of pharmacological actions that are reflected by a host of unwanted effects. The tricyclics vary in their side effects, but the general pattern is similar. Unwanted effects are often overestimated because many of them closely mimic naturally occurring somatic symptoms in depressed patients. Dry mouth and constipation are prime examples. The unwanted effects are very common at the initiation of therapy but usually lessen as treatment is continued. Occasionally, a side effect persists indefinitely.

Central effects: The tricyclic drugs can be divided roughly into those with marked sedative actions (eg, amitriptyline, dothiepin, doxepin, and mianserin), those less sedative (eg, imipramine and dibenzepin), and those that are somewhat stimulant in effect (eg, desipramine, nortriptyline, and especially, protriptyline). With the latter group, insomnia is common if the drug is taken during the evening. These secondary psychotropic effects can be used to advantage. For example, a sedative tricyclic can be given as one dose at night to exert a useful hypnotic action.

A fine, rapid tremor of the extremities can occur with the tricyclic drugs, and ataxia and parkinsonism have been reported to occur in patients treated with imipramine or amitriptyline at doses greater than 300 mg/day. Hypomania or mania may be precipitated in patients with bipolar illness, although it is difficult to be sure that this is not a spontaneous switch. Psychotic features in schizophrenic patients may be made worse. Central anticholinergic effects presumably account for the occasional toxic psychosis, because the psychosis can be reversed by the administration of physostigmine. Visual phenomena, heightened perceptions and illusions especially, are not uncommon in patients treated with high dosages. Most tricyclic drugs lower the convulsive threshold, thus increasing the probability of convulsions, which are most likely to occur in patients with preexisting brain damage.

Weight gain of 3 kg or more can occur during treatment. It is associated with carbohydrate craving and may be related to hypothalamic actions of the tricyclics, perhaps to 5-hydroxytryptamine mechanisms.

Peripheral autonomic effects: These include dry mouth, loss of visual accommodation, pupillary dilatation, constipation, postural hypotension, and hesitancy of micturition. More-extreme effects comprise palpitations, episodes of profuse sweating, urinary retention, decreased sexual performance, aggravation or precipitation of glaucoma, and, rarely, paralytic ileus.

Cardiovascular effects: Tachycardia and hypotension are common, as are changes in cardiac conduction. The electrocardiogram may show lengthened PR and QT intervals, depressed ST segments, and flattened T waves, Bundle-branch block and ventricular arrhythmias may also be found. Patients with heart disease are particularly susceptible, and cardiac failure may supervene. Some studies suggest association between amitriptyline therapy and sudden death among patients with a history of cardiac trouble, whereas in other studies the association is too tenuous to be significant. Impaired myocardial contractility is believed to occur after many years of tricyclic use. Further surveys are needed.

The cardiotoxic effects of the tricyclics are hardly surprising inasmuch as their concentrations can be 40 to 100 times greater in cardiac muscle than in plasma. The mechanism of the toxicity is probably related to excessive concentrations of noradrenaline in the cardiac muscle.

Other effects: Mild cholestatic jaundice of the chlorpromazine type may occur, as may allergic skin reactions. Agranulocytosis is rare. Some teratogenic effects in animals subjected to very high doses of tricyclics have been documented, but no excess of fetal abnormalities has been proved to be associated with maternal use of the drugs in therapeutic doses. Nevertheless, administration in pregnancy must be very carefully considered, the risk to the fetus being weighed against the mother's distress.

Overdosage: Overdoses of tricyclic drugs produce restlessness, agitation, and delirium. Convulsions, coma, and death may supervene. Cardiac effects are particularly troublesome, and cardiac irregularities are very common. Since tricyclic drugs are highly bound to plasma and tissue proteins, forced diuresis and dialysis are of no use. Severe anticholinergic effects can be reversed by slow infusion of physostigmine.

Similar Drugs

More than 15 tricyclic-type drugs are currently marketed in the United Kingdom and about half that number in the United States. Unlike the neuroleptic drugs, among which similarities outweigh dissimilarities within broad groups, the antidepressants are claimed to represent a range of differential actions. The deficiencies of the early tricyclics were identified as their being effective in only about two thirds of the patients, delayed in onset of action, accompanied by numerous troublesome side effects, toxic in overdose, cardiotoxic, and associated with problems of patient compliance. Most of the newly introduced drugs have been claimed to possess advantages over the standard compounds, imipramine and amitriptyline. Very recently, the biochemistry of the drugs has been invoked despite the lack of clear proof that re-uptake blockade of one amine neurotransmitter or another underlies the clinical action. The various compounds of this type will now be briefly discussed. They are listed according to their chemical structure.

Dibenzapines: *Desipramine* is the desmethylated metabolite of imipramine. When it was found to be psychotropically active, researchers hoped that desipramine would also be faster acting than the parent compound. The pharmacology of desipramine resembles that of imipramine, but it is less potent in general. As with most secondary amines of its class, it is a more potent noradrenaline re-uptake inhibitor than its parent tertiary amine, but it has much less effect on 5-hydroxytryptamine. Clinically, its speed of action is indistinguishable from that of imipramine, and possibly it is marginally less efficacious. It is more stimulant than imipramine.

Trimipramine is interesting chemically in that it has two stereoisomeric forms depending on the configuration at the point of branching in the side chain. In animals, the laevorotatory form is mainly sedative and the dextro form is stimulant. The clinical form is racemic, and the drug is more sedative than imipramine. Uptake mechanisms are hardly affected by trimipramine. It is favoured by the cognoscenti for combination with the monoamine inhibitors (but see page 82).

Cycloheptadienes and cycloheptatrienes: *Amitriptyline*, in many countries the most widely prescribed tricyclic, is marginally more effective than imipramine. It is powerfully sedative and anxiolytic and has marked anticholinergic effects. It is often used as the standard in comparative clinical trials. *Nortriptyline*, the desmethylated metabolite of amitriptyline, is an effective antidepressant but is less sedative. It has been extensively evaluated pharmacokinetically (see page 71).

Protriptyline is the most stimulant of the tricyclic drugs, sometimes producing restlessness and insomnia. It is more potent than most of its congeners. The relationship between plasma concentration and clinical response seems curvilinear, as with nortriptyline; both low and high plasma concentrations are associated with lack of response.

Butriptyline is a sedative compound similar in its clinical actions to amitriptyline. Its cardiotoxicity is appreciable at higher dose levels.

Other tricyclic antidepressants: *Dibenzepin* resembles imipramine very closely and perhaps has a slightly more rapid onset of action. *Doxepin* is more akin to amitriptyline and has pronounced sedative properties. Its anxiolytic actions are comparable to those of the benzodiazepines. One noteworthy property of doxepin is its paucity of cardiotoxic effects even at high dosage or overdosage levels. *Dothiepin* is the thio analogue of amitriptyline, which it closely resembles in most respects.

Iprindole is an interesting antidepressant in that it seems almost devoid of effect on uptake mechanisms. It has minimal anticholinergic and antihistaminic actions, weak antagonism against reserpine, does not block the actions of indirectly acting sympathomimetic agents, and does not alter REM sleep. It has few side effects except for a relatively high incidence of jaundice, and, although its clinical effectiveness has been questioned, some antidepressant activity has been established.

Among other tricyclics are *melitracen, dimethacrin*, and *noxiptilin*. They resemble imipramine in their actions but are more sedative.

Other related antidepressant drugs: *Maprotilene* is related to the anxiolytic compound benzoctamine. It does not block 5-hydroxytryptamine uptake. It closely resembles the standard tricyclic drugs in efficacy, speed of onset of action, and side effects.

Mianserin, a tetracyclic compound, was originally discovered in the search for 5-hydroxytryptamine antagonists, and it has pharmacological properties uncharacteristic of the tricyclic drugs. It has no central anticholinergic activity, it is only weakly antagonistic to reserpine, and it does not potentiate the central actions of amphetamine. In the brain, mianserin impairs the uptake of noradrenaline and 5-hydroxytryptamine, but uptake of the latter into platelets is not affected. Clinically, it is equivalent to imipramine and amitriptyline but has fewer side effects other than drowsiness. It seems devoid of cardiotoxicity and safer than other antidepressants in overdosage.

Nomifensine powerfully inhibits the re-uptake of noradrenaline and also dopamine. Clinically it resembles imipramine. The dopaminergic activity suggests that it might be especially useful in idiopathic parkinsonian patients with depression, but conversely it is not indicated in the depressed schizophrenic patient. Unlike most drugs of the tricyclic type it has a relatively short plasma half-life (about five hours), so multiple daily dosage is necessary. Nomifensine is apparently the least likely of all antidepressants to lower the convulsive threshold and may be the treatment of choice in depressed epileptic patients.

Viloxazine, an oxazine derivative related to the beta-blockers, has many of the pharmacological actions of imipramine, with minimal antagonism of acetylcholine and histamine. It has a short half-life and is associated with troublesome side effects such as nausea and vomiting.

Choice of drug
To summarize, the choice of drug rests broadly on the following considerations:
1. The type of depressive illness. It has been proposed that secondary amines such as desipramine, nortriptyline, and protriptyline, which act preferentially on noradrenergic systems, should be more effective in increasing psychomotor activity and drive, whereas the tertiary amines such as imipramine and amitriptyline, which preferentially block 5-hydroxytryptamine re-uptake, have a greater effect on mood. However, it must be remembered that the tertiary amines are metabolized to secondary amines so that the former have a comprehensive profile of action lacking in the latter. Nevertheless, clinical demonstration of such differential effects is not conclusive, although it is established practice to use a sedative tricyclic such as amitriptyline for the agitated depressive and a more stimulant drug for the retarded patient.
2. The side effects. Anticholinergic effects among the drugs vary widely. Amitriptyline is powerfully anticholinergic, whereas other drugs such as mianserin are almost free from such effects. It has been suggested that general clinical efficacy depends partly on anticholinergic actions, but there is no firm evidence either way. In prescribing a specific tricyclic drug for an individual patient, the physician should consider the drug's relative cardiotoxicity and sedative properties and its potential for interacting with concomitantly administered drugs such as antihypertensive drugs and sympathomimetic compounds. The risk of suicidal overdosage may suggest the use of the less toxic drugs such as mianserin and nomifensine.
3. The speed of action. There seems little to choose among these drugs.
4. The convenience of dosage. Once-nightly dosage is preferred by some patients; others prefer "little and often."

The Young, the Old, and the Physically Ill
The delineation of a true depressive syndrome in children has remained elusive, so the value of antidepressants in children is unestablished. Tricyclic drugs such as imipramine are useful in the *temporary* symptomatic treatment of enuresis. Tricyclic antidepressants are often taken in accidental overdosage by young children and seem particularly toxic.

Affective disorders, particularly depression, are common in old age. Tricyclic antidepressants should be initiated at lower doses than in younger patients and the dosage cautiously increased. Some elderly patients may require full dosage. Side effects are often more troublesome in the elderly, especially anticholinergic effects such as constipation and hesitancy of micturition. Hypotensive episodes are common.

Patients with liver or kidney disease need careful evaluation before, and monitoring during, tricyclic antidepressant treatment. Patients with cardiac disorders are also at risk, so once-nightly dosage regimens are best avoided. Antihypertensive medication must be reviewed.

MONOAMINE OXIDASE INHIBITORS
History
The monoamine oxidase inhibitors (MAOIs) were developed and their therapeutic effects discovered contemporaneously with imipramine. The development of MAOIs followed the pattern so common with the modern generation of psychotropic drugs; namely, the accidental stumbling onto important therapeutic actions in psychiatry during a program of research into drugs for another therapeutic purpose.

The first MAOI, iproniazid, was synthesized by Fox at Roche Laboratories, together with isoniazid. Both drugs were used for the treatment of tuberculosis, and the latter has remained a mainstay of therapy for many years. Central effects were noted with both drugs, iproniazid in particular inducing euphoria and overactivity. The drugs were therefore tested in psychiatric patients, mainly those with schizophrenia. One placebo-controlled study showed that iproniazid could increase the activity of schizophrenic patients, but when most trials yielded unimpressive results, interest waned.

However, it has been shown that iproniazid but not isoniazid is a potent inhibitor of the widespread enzyme monoamine oxidase. It was hypothesized that mental stimulation resulted from the increased concentrations of brain amines induced by monoamine oxidase inhibition. This attractive hypothesis rekindled interest in iproniazid, and further evaluations followed. Unfortunately, the earliest clinical studies were overenthusiastic and led to the widespread uncritical use of the drug.

One immediate outcome was that the toxicity, especially with respect to the liver, became quickly apparent and led to a violent swing away from the drug. It was withdrawn from the market in the United States but not the United Kingdom.

Other MAOIs, including nonhydrazine derivatives devoid of hepatotoxicity, were introduced. Even so, drug and dietary restrictions are irksome. The MAOIs have never recovered their initial popularity and have been eclipsed by imipramine and related drugs. However, the MAOIs have always had their devotees, particularly in the United Kingdom, who claim that there is a limited but valuable niche for these drugs in the treatment of particular types of patients. Recently, controlled trials have evaluated these claims and demonstrated some efficacy, and the MAOIs are slowly regaining a therapeutic role. Nevertheless, especially in the United States, many clinicians never use them.

Pharmacokinetics
MAOIs belong to various chemical classes (Figure 6-4), so their pharmacokinetics are rather varied.

Iproniazid is well absorbed and rapidly distributed. After intraperitoneal administration to rats, it reaches maximal brain concentrations within 20 minutes. By 24 hours, none is detectable in the brain. There is evidence that the active principle is not iproniazid itself but a metabolite, probably isopropylhydrazine. Alkylhydrazines are known to be more toxic than hydrazine itself. The enzyme monoamine oxidase is irreversibly inhibited by iproniazid; in other words, it is actually destroyed. It takes 7 to 14 days for resynthesis to predrug levels. The action of iproniazid can be prevented by preadministration of harmaline, a reversible MAOI, presumably by protecting the vulnerable site on the MAO molecule. Little is known of the breakdown pathways of iproniazid, but isonicotinic acid is an intermediate metabolite.

Isocarboxazid was one of the first MAOIs developed to avoid the toxicity of iproniazid. It is rapidly absorbed and is metabolized by hydrolysis to benzylhydrazine and then changed to hippuric acid, which is excreted in the urine. *Nialamide* is excreted partly unchanged and partly metabolized to hippuric and benzoic acids.

Phenelzine has been more extensively evaluated with respect to its pharmacokinetics. It is a widely used hydrazine MAOI, but because it has less inhibitory activity than iproniazid in the liver and more in the brain, it was expected to be less hepatotoxic. A major route of metabolism is acetylation by hepatic acetyl transferase. The rate of acetylation is genetically determined and is bimodally distributed in the population: persons are either slow or fast "acetylators." Slow acetylators seem to develop more unwanted effects with

Figure 6-4. Formulae of some MAOIs.

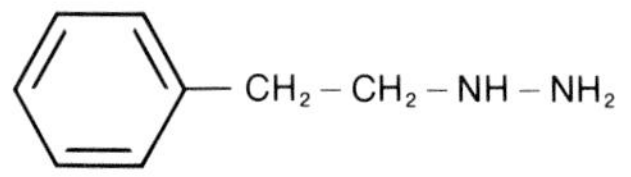

$C_6H_5-CH_2-CH_2-NH-NH_2$	**Phenelzine**
$C_6H_5-CH_2-NH-NH-\underset{\overset{\displaystyle O}{\|}}{C}-C=C-CH$ (with N, O, CH_3 ring)	**Isocarboxazid**
$C_6H_5-CH-CH-NH_2$ with CH_2	**Tranylcypromine**
$N-C_6H_4-\underset{\overset{\displaystyle O}{\|}}{C}-NH-NH-CH(CH_3)_2$	**Iproniazid**
$N-C_6H_4-\underset{\overset{\displaystyle O}{\|}}{C}-NH-NH-(CH_2)_2-\underset{\overset{\displaystyle O}{\|}}{C}-NH-CH_2-C_6H_5$	**Nialamide**

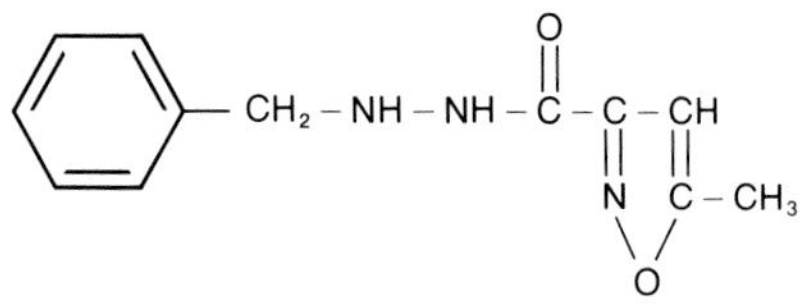

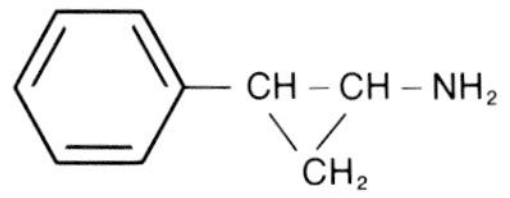

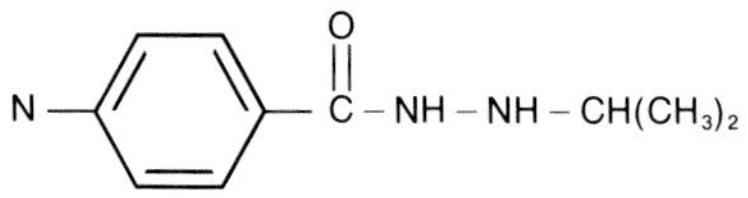

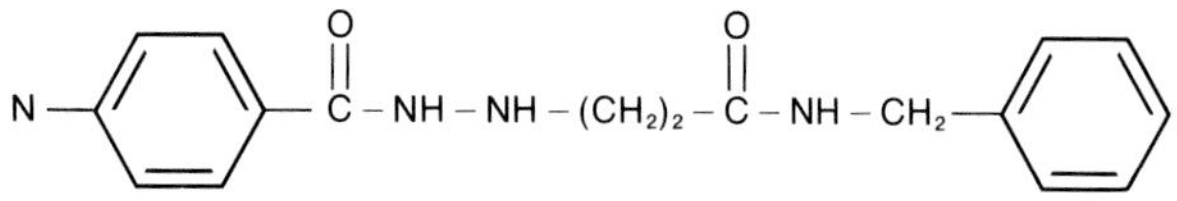

phenelzine than do fast acetylators. Also, the rate but not the eventual degree of monoamine oxidase inhibition and clinical response is marginally greater in the slow acetylators.

Tranylcypromine, a nonhydrazine MAOI, is rapidly absorbed and almost entirely metabolized and eliminated within 24 hours.

Pharmacology

Biochemical pharmacology: Monoamine oxidase is an enzyme or group of related enzymes widely distributed throughout the body. In the cell it is localized in the outer membrane of the mitochondria, where by oxidative deamination it serves to inactivate aromatic amines including 5-hydroxytryptamine, dopamine, and noradrenaline. Brain monoamine oxidase is obviously difficult to study in human beings, and much has been inferred from indirect methods such as urinary amine excretion and from monoamine oxidase activity in accessible tissues such as blood platelets. The enzyme activity of monoamine oxidase is influenced by many factors such as age, hormones, stress, and a variety of diseases. Its relationship to depression is unclear (see later).

Monoamine oxidase exists in a number of forms with various substrate and inhibitor specificities and various mechanisms of distribution in body tissues. Type A oxidatively deaminates 5-hydroxytryptamine and noradrenaline but not phenylethylamine; it is preferentially inhibited by the MAOI clorgyline. Type B has reverse specificity and is preferentially inhibited by the MAOI deprenyl. Tyramine is oxidized by both types. Such selective inhibition should provide the basis for the development of drugs that would inhibit brain monoamine oxidase while leaving the detoxifying enzymes in the gut and liver unchanged. So far this has not been achieved in man despite in vitro and preclinical pointers.

The monoamine oxidases are inhibited by a wide, heterogeneous group of compounds, and it is a matter of nomenclature which drugs are excluded from the MAOI category. In practice, many drugs such as dexamphetamine, ephedrine, diphenhydramine, cocaine, and procaine that show *in vitro* inhibition at supratherapeutic concentrations are not regarded as exerting any useful therapeutic action by virtue of their monoamine oxidase inhibitory properties. Some of the tricyclic antidepressants also have MAOI properties at high concentration. Many other drugs possess monoamine oxidase inhibitory properties to some extent; many but not all of these drugs possess a hydrazine (-NH-NH-) linkage.

Inhibition of monoamine oxidase leads to the build-up in the tissues, including the brain, of many aromatic amines normally present in only minute amounts. These include the monoamines active in neurotransmission and the exogenous amines such as tyramine. Deaminated products such as 5-hydroxyindole acetic acid are decreased in concentration whereas the concentrations of conjugated and methylated products such as normetanephrine, produced extraneuronally by catechol-o-methyltransferase, are increased in tissues, CSF, plasma, and urine.

Relationship to clinical response: Since monoamine oxidase concentrations in most tissues are excessive, fairly extensive inhibition is required before amine disposition is altered. Something of the order of 80% inhibition has been found necessary in animal experiments before brain monoamines alter in concentration. In clinical studies, platelet monoamine oxidase has been used as the index of drug effect. In one study of 62 depressed outpatients treated with a fixed effective dose of phenelzine (60 mg/day), two thirds of patients with monoamine oxidase inhibition greater than 80% at four weeks responded favourably to the drug. In the patients with less than 80% inhibition, only 44% responded. However, the situation is obviously not simple, with the placebo response in this trial running at one third. Thus, partial inhibition is associated with response in another one sixth of the patients, and putatively adequate inhibition is associated with response in only another one quarter of the patients.

Time course of inhibition: A further complication is that monoamine oxidase inhibition, at least as monitored by blood platelets, is fairly rapid, often within a few doses of the MAOI drug, yet clinical response may be delayed for two to four weeks or even longer. This delay has led to an alternative suggestion for the biochemical actions deemed most relevant to the clinical response: When monoamine oxidase is inhibited, pathways of degradation for amines that normally are only of secondary importance become the main routes of catabolism. As a consequence, there is an accumulation of amines that are present normally in only trace amounts. Tyramine is metabolized to octopamine, a neurotransmitter in lower orders of animals. In mammals it acts as a pseudo-transmitter, displacing noradrenaline from its presynaptic storage vesicles but acting as a very indifferent adrenergic transmitter when released. This hypothesis would explain the hypotensive actions of the MAOIs (one is marketed solely as an antihypertensive agent) in terms of interference with noradrenergic transmission. The hypothesis would attribute the therapeutic actions of the MAOIs in the brain to decreased rather than increased monoaminergic transmission.

Animal pharmacology: The pharmacology of the MAOIs can be conveniently divided into those effects that are secondary to monoamine oxidase inhibition and those attributable to other actions. Certain criteria should be observed if the effect is to be regarded as due to MAO inhibition:

1. The action after even one dose should be prolonged, because the monoamine oxidase inhibition is irreversible.
2. The onset of action should be a little delayed, because it takes time for the amines to accumulate.
3. The actions should be prevented by harmaline, a reversible monoamine oxidase inhibitor that competes for the enzyme sites.

A single dose of iproniazid has little if any physiological or behavioural effect, but on repeated dosage in some species such as the rabbit, overactivity and sympathomimetic signs appear. The effects can be related to increases in brain noradrenaline concentrations. Only in massive doses do most MAOIs activate the EEG.

Premedication with iproniazid can prevent reserpine-induced signs such as inactivity, ptosis, miosis, and hypothermia. However, unlike amphetamine and tranylcypromine, it cannot reverse these signs once established.

The effects of some exogenous amines are potentiated by iproniazid and other MAOIs. Tryptamine, an excellent substrate for MAO, induces convulsions in mice. This effect is enhanced by iproniazid pretreatment. The pressor effects of tyramine and the hyperthermic actions of 5-hydroxytryptophan and L-dopa are potentiated. However, the effects of adrenaline and noradrenaline are not markedly potentiated, because other mechanisms operate for their inactivation.

The hypotensive actions of the MAOIs are probably mediated by interference with noradrenergic transmission, perhaps by the mechanism outlined earlier. These drugs have some ganglion-blocking action but probably insufficient to account for their hypotensive actions. Blockade of re-uptake of amine neurotransmitters is another property that is probably unimportant at normal clinical concentrations.

Tranylcypromine is atypical both in its monoamine oxidase inhibition and in its possession of amphetamine-like properties. Monoamine oxidase inhibition is quicker in onset and offset than with iproniazid, suggesting a different mode of monoamine oxidase inhibition. It is more effective against type B monoamine oxidase. In addition, in animals it increases spontaneous activity, produces toxicity in aggregated mice, induces hypersensitivity to external stimuli, and results in sympathomimetic effects. EEG activation is produced at moderate doses. Like amphetamine, tranylcypromine releases noradrenaline from its storage vesicles and inhibits its re-uptake.

Human pharmacology: Most MAOIs show very few effects in normal subjects, although postmortem studies of MAOI-treated patients have confirmed that amine concentrations in the brain are generally elevated. A slight euphoria may be detected with iproniazid and phenelzine, although drowsiness is often reported. Tranylcypromine is more clearly stimulant at higher doses.

Clinical Effects

The first batch of uncontrolled trials led to a wave of uncritical enthusiasm for the MAOIs. Clinical experience showed that depressive symptoms often did not improve for two to four weeks after starting therapy. However, controlled trials, especially those evaluating treatment of inpatients, were unable to confirm any therapeutic effects. One trial found iproniazid no better than psychotherapy or even placebo in patients with the symptom of depression. Another recorded that 26 of 50 depressed patients responded to iproniazid, 150 to 400 mg daily for two to four weeks, but only 12 relapsed when placebos were substituted for the drug. In a more favourable study, 50% of drug-treated patients improved, as compared with a placebo rate of only 11%. Nevertheless, some signs of depression were particularly responsive to MAOIs – restlessness and depressive speech content were reduced in one study. In another, increased motor and verbal activity and quicker reaction times were produced without much change in mood, a form of "psychic energizing."

Some advocates of the MAOIs have stressed that the drugs are useful in only certain types of depressed patients. In one retrospective study of iproniazid response, it was suggested that those who improved were more often diagnosed as suffering from "anxiety hysteria with secondary atypical depression," were more likely to have shown signs of phobic and hysterical conversion, had had a poor response to electroconvulsive therapy, and, when treated with MAOIs, showed improvement within a week. Recently, iproniazid has been shown to be as effective as behaviour therapy in the management of severe agoraphobia.

Isocarboxazid and nialamide have been disappointing clinically, but phenelzine has been used in several clinical trials and is now regarded as the standard MAOI. Most comparative trials show it to be superior to placebo but not as efficacious as imipramine in inpatients. However, at higher dosage (more than 45 mg/day), its effectiveness in certain types of patients becomes apparent. Phobic patients particularly seem to benefit, as do patients with symptoms of irritability, somatic anxiety, and hypochondriasis. However, cases of classical "endogenous" depression may also respond, so that the indications for treatment are by no means clear. One criterion said to be useful is that depressed patients who oversleep rather than complain of poor sleep will respond to MAOI therapy. Tranylcypromine is also an effective MAOI, proving superior to placebo and equal to imipramine in a few trials.

Unwanted Effects

The monoamine oxidase inhibitors have a wide range of unwanted effects, many of which are predictable from their pharmacological effects.

CNS effects include mood elevation and even a hypomanic reaction, although it is difficult to ascribe this with certainty to a drug effect when it occurs in a patient known to have manic-depressive illness. Toxic psychoses may occur and schizophrenic symptoms may be reactivated. Phenelzine tends to produce drowsiness, and tranylcypromine tends to produce insomnia; irritability, restlessness, and overactivity may supervene. Other effects include muscle jerking and tremors, and, like isoniazid, iproniazid can produce pyridoxine-reversible peripheral neuropathy. Convulsions may be precipitated in susceptible persons.

Autonomic effects are variable but include orthostatic hypotension, warm extremities with reduced sweating, dry mouth, constipation, delay in micturition, impotence, delayed ejaculation, and dizziness. Only the hypotension is of much practical significance, and it may be quite troublesome in the elderly. Blood pressure should be monitored from the start of treatment.

An uncommon but serious reaction to hydrazine MAOIs is *hepatocellular jaundice*. The clinical syndrome closely resembles viral hepatitis, with the development of jaundice, diffuse cellular damage, increased serum concentrations of liver enzymes, and bile stasis. The mortality rate is 20% to 25%. Hepatocellular jaundice is presumably not related to MAO inhibition, as it does not occur with the nonhydrazine drugs.

Miscellaneous effects include headache, exacerbation of migraine, and ankle oedema. Blood dyscrasias and skin reactions are rare. The amphetamine-like stimulant properties of tranylcypromine have led to similar abuse on occasion.

Dietary interactions constitute the best-known untoward effect. The syndrome takes the form of a severe headache with a hypertensive crisis. The headache is severe and sudden, usually occipital in site. Vomiting, chest pain, hyperpyrexia, and restlessness are common. The attack usually subsides within a few hours, but subarachnoid haemorrhage and death may supervene. The syndrome can occur with any of the MAOIs but has been documented most frequently with tranylcypromine. A great many foods have been recorded as being implicated in a dietary reaction, a recent one being caviar! However, serious reactions are unlikely if the patient avoids meat and yeast extracts, red wine, matured cheese, and food that is clearly not fresh. With these precautions, the incidence of serious side effects is small but by no means negligible.

The mechanism of the interaction mainly involves tyramine, but tyrosine, L-dopa (in broad bean pods), histamine, dopamine, and phenylethylamine have also been implicated. Tyramine is formed by the decarboxylation of the amino acid tyrosine and is present in many fermented foods. Normally it is oxidatively deaminated by monoamine oxidase in the gut wall and liver, and it is thus detoxified and prevented from entering the systemic circulation. When monoamine oxidase inhibition is induced, tyramine is no longer detoxified but enters the circulation. Thence it is taken up into noradrenergic nerve endings. These already contain a surfeit of noradrenaline consequent on the monoamine oxidase inhibition. The tyramine releases large quantities of noradrenaline, which *inter alia* constricts blood vessels in muscle by an alpha-adrenoceptor action, thereby producing the severe hypertension. The treatment of the hypertensive crisis is to block the alpha-adrenoceptors by parenteral administration of phentolamine. If phentolamine is not readily available, chlorpromazine, with its useful alpha-adrenoceptor blocking actions, should be given by intramuscular injection. The blood pressure must be monitored and the drug dose repeated as necessary. Sometimes overshoot occurs and the blood pressure drops too much. Pressor agents should not be added, but the foot of the patient's bed should be raised.

Drug *interactions* are very important. Any indirectly acting sympathomimetic agent can cause a hypertensive reaction, the mechanism being that described above for tyramine. Examples of such agents are ephedrine, amphetamine, phenylephrine, and phenylpropanolamine, which are common constituents of cough medicines and nasal decongestants. Adrenaline and noradrenaline are potentiated to some extent, but because they are not good substrates for monoamine oxidase, the interaction is not as serious as with, say, tyramine. Other drugs are potentiated by mechanisms that are somewhat obscure. Alcohol, ether, the barbiturates, pethidine, morphine, cocaine, procaine, and insulin can all be involved in dangerous and even fatal interactions. The most likely explanation is that the MAOIs also inhibit a wide range of enzymes, including L-aromatic amino acid decarboxylase; oxidases of diamine, methylamine, and choline; and some nonspecific microsomal enzymes. The latter are required in the breakdown of many drugs that will thus be potentiated. However, several mechanisms, central and peripheral, probably also operate.

The dietary and drug interactions are so common, important, and dangerous that the patient and a responsible relative must be carefully apprised of the risks. The patient should also carry a reminder card listing foods and drugs to avoid and alerting medical attendants in case treatment is required for an accident or another illness. Anesthetists must be warned if a patient requiring an operation is taking an MAOI.

Overdose with the MAOIs can produce agitation, hyperpyrexia, hyperreflexia, hallucinations, convulsions, and changes in blood pressure. The effects come on in a few hours. Conservative, supportive management with chlorpromazine as necessary is indicated.

Choice of MAOI

This is severely restricted by the availability of drugs in various countries. Far fewer are marketed in the United States than in the United Kingdom. Moreover, because of the problems of unwanted effects and the limited use of the drugs, there has been much less commercial interest in introducing new members of the class.

Comparative trials and crude success rates reported suggest that iproniazid and phenelzine are the most effective among the hydrazine derivatives, with tranylcypromine at least as effective as these. However, clinical usage is more dependent on side effects than on main effects. Phenelzine is the safest of the MAOIs and should be chosen by those with limited experience in the use of these drugs. Tranylcypromine sometimes is effective when the others have failed, but it is more likely to be associated with unwanted effects, euphoria, and perhaps dependence.

The Young, The Old, and The Physically Ill

The safety and efficacy of MAOIs in children are not established; use of the drugs in children should be avoided. In the elderly, MAOIs are sometimes effective when tricyclic medication has failed to improve the patient. The dose should be regulated cautiously with respect to initial level and the rate at which it is increased, because hypotension is a troublesome, unwanted effect.

MAOIs are generally not recommended for use in physically ill patients because of interactions with other medications.

Tricyclics and MAOIs combined

Few topics are more controversial in psychopharmacological practice than the use of combined antidepressant therapy. In the early 1960s some deaths were reported of patients treated with a tricyclic antidepressant and an MAOI simultaneously, leading most practitioners to avoid prescribing such combinations. Regulatory authorities such as the FDA in the United States came out strongly against this form of therapy, and manufacturers of both tricyclic and MAOI drugs state categorically in their drug information that the combination is dangerous and should be avoided.

The pharmacological logic behind the combination is that the MAOI increases the concentration of neurotransmitter amines in the presynaptic neurons. Once released these amines cannot be taken back because of the tricyclic blockade of uptake. Thus, the increased concentrations of amines stay in the synaptic cleft and exert a prolonged action. That such potentiation can be extremely powerful is evidenced by the untoward reactions, sometimes fatal, that can occur. The main signs are fulminating hyperpyrexia (up to 43 C), restlessness, agitation, hypertension, and later, hypotension, convulsions, and coma.

Despite this, some experienced practitioners, mainly in the United Kingdom, assert that the combination is clinically more effective than either component alone, especially in atypical depressed patients and those refractory to more conventional therapy. Furthermore, untoward reactions are rare, provided that both drugs are chosen carefully and started simultaneously. The safest tricyclic is stated to be trimipramine; doxepin and prothiadin are also said to be safe but are less frequently used. Amitriptyline and imipramine are less safe, and the secondary amines desipramine, nortriptyline, and protriptyline are dangerous. For some unexplained reason clomipramine seems especially dangerous. Of the MAOIs, phenelzine and isocarboxazid are safest, and tranylcypromine is more dangerous. An especially hazardous practice is to stop the MAOI and then to commence treatment with a tricyclic antidepressant within the ensuing two or even three weeks.

The pharmacology of the toxic interaction is that of excessive central and peripheral concentrations of amines, noradrenaline in particular. Why the various members of the two classes should vary so much in their combined toxicity has not been systematically evaluated.

In one large-scale clinical trial of unselected depressed outpatients, combination treatment was *inferior* to either the tricyclic or the MAOI antidepressants alone. Side effects were not troublesome. So long as the therapeutic and pharmacological status of the combined drugs remains unclear, the wise clinician will avoid prescribing the combination unless he has had experience in their use, believes he can spot the patient likely to respond, and is confident that his instructions will be followed to the letter.

L-TRYPTOPHAN

L-tryptophan is the precursor of 5-hydroxytryptamine, as tyrosine is of dopamine and noradrenaline. The feasibility of increasing central transmitter function by administering large doses of precursor was demonstrated by the effective use of L-dopa in the treatment of parkinsonism. The therapeutic ratio between wanted and unwanted effects was increased by the simultaneous administration of a dopa-decarboxylase inhibitor that was unable to penetrate to the brain, thus acting only peripherally and preventing the excessive accumulation of catecholamines outside the brain. However, as the following account shows, the effects of L-tryptophan in affective disorders have been far less dramatic.

Absorption, distribution, and metabolism

L-tryptophan is an essential amino acid, the daily requirement in a normal diet being about 0.5 gm. Only a small fraction is used to synthesize 5-hydroxytryptamine. L-tryptophan is carried into the brain and into serotonergic neurons by active transport mechanisms shared by other neutral amino acids such as tyrosine, leucine, methionine, and phenylalanine. The excessive concentration of any one amino acid competitively interferes with the uptake of the others, so that excessive L-tryptophan can result in relative deficits in the brain of other amino acids.

In blood, L-tryptophan is the only amino acid to be bound to plasma albumin, from which it can be released by unesterified fatty acids. In turn, these are released by stress, which can thus modify tryptophan disposition. The concentration of free amino acid determines the uptake into the brain and then into the neurons, and finally it governs the rate of synthesis of 5-hydroxytryptamine.

In man, L-tryptophan is rapidly and completely absorbed from the intestine, and blood concentrations reach their peak in one to two hours. Distribution to tissues and brain is rapid.

The amount of dietary tryptophan affects brain 5-hydroxytryptamine concentrations. Animals fed a tryptophan-free diet develop a deficit in brain 5-hydroxytryptamine, which is rectified by the addition of the amino acid to the diet. In man, ingestion of large amounts of tryptophan leads to an increase in metabolites in the cerebrospinal fluid within four to six hours. However, the 5-hydroxytryptamine formed may be metabolized by monoamine oxidase before it can become functionally active in the neuron, because pretreatment with an MAOI results in much more behavioural change than with the tryptophan loading alone.

Tryptophan is also metabolized to tryptamine and is used in protein synthesis, but the major metabolic pathway is by disruption of the indole ring by the liver enzyme tryptophan pyrrolase to form kynurenine and, eventually, nicotinic acid. The activity of this enzyme can be enhanced by adrenocortical steroids and oestrogens, stress, and by induction effects of L-tryptophan itself. This diverts tryptophan away from the 5-hydroxytryptamine pathway and could conceivably be operative in the pathophysiology of some affective disorders. There is some diurnal variation in the activity of tryptophan pyrrolase, which is maximal at 06.00 hours and minimal at 20.00 hours. Tryptophan blood concentrations are maximal at about 20.00 hours.

A number of cofactors are essential in the metabolism of tryptophan and may become deficient on prolonged administration of large doses of the drug. Among these are ascorbic acid, which is the cofactor in the 5-hydroxylation, and pyridoxal-5-phosphate, which is the cofactor in the decarboxylation of 5-hydroxytryptophan and also at several steps in the kynurenine-to-nicotinic-acid pathway. The effects of vitamin deficiency or supplementation are thus complex, but in most earlier clinical studies supplements of pyridoxine and ascorbic acid had been used.

Effects in normal persons
Large doses of L-tryptophan have little effect in normal persons. An intravenous dose that increased free plasma concentrations fortyfold produced some drowsiness and slowing of the EEG but little change in objective performance tests. Euphoria, disinhibition, and increased sexual awareness have been noted.

Tryptophan is claimed to have hypnotic effects in doses greater than about 2 gm. It increases total sleep time by prolonging non-REM phases without affecting REM time. Both on administration and on withdrawal, tryptophan only minimally alters the pattern of sleep.

Clinical Effects
The evidence for a 5-hydroxytryptamine deficit of some sort in depressed patients is outlined later. Here we are concerned with the empirical demonstration of its usefulness in depressed patients. However, the pharmacokinetics of tryptophan in depressed patients have been shown not to differ from those in normal control subjects.

The first use of tryptophan was in conjunction with MAOIs. The assertion that the combination is more effective than the MAOI alone has been confirmed by controlled trials. However, the claim that tryptophan on its own was as effective as ECT in the treatment of hospitalized depressed patients has not been upheld. In a number of controlled comparisons, tryptophan seemed about as effective as imipramine or amitriptyline in mildly or moderately depressed patients; in one trial in general practice, tryptophan was superior to placebo.

There is some evidence that tryptophan may ameliorate symptoms in manic and hypomanic patients. Used in conjunction with an MAOI in schizophrenic patients, tryptophan produces minor increases in motor activity and sociability.

The MAOIs are potentiated by L-tryptophan both biochemically and clinically. Similarly, the clinical effects of tricyclic drugs that block the uptake of 5-hydroxytryptamine may be enhanced by tryptophan. In summary, the therapeutic effects of tryptophan are most firmly established when it is used as an adjunct to an MAOI; its use in combination with a tricyclic antidepressant or on its own is more controversial.

Unwanted Effects
The most common unwanted effects of L-tryptophan are mild drowsiness, nausea, anorexia, and epigastric fullness, but these usually abate as treatment continues. Some preparations leave an unpleasant taste in the mouth. The drug is safe in overdosage.

The combination of tryptophan with an MAOI may increase MAO inhibitory side effects such as headache and blurring of vision, so the dosage should be cautious. An intoxication-like syndrome has also been reported.

One potential danger is the carcinogenicity of the kynurenine derivatives. The organ most susceptible is the bladder, in which the concentrations are at their highest. Studies with animals suggest that the long-term effects of high, sustained doses of tryptophan should be carefully appraised and the risks weighed against the potential benefits of the drug, whose efficacy is still controversial.

5-HYDROXYTRYPTOPHAN
The biochemical and theoretical aspects of this 5-hydroxytryptamine precursor are summarized later. Its therapeutic value remains unestablished.

ANTIPSYCHOTIC DRUGS
Antidepressant effects have been detected with several antipsychotic drugs, among which are chlorpromazine, thioridazine, and, more recently, flupenthixol. Some of this apparent therapeutic effect is perhaps attributable to antipsychotic actions in agitated or paranoid patients or to an anxiolytic effect in the less ill. However, in addition, genuine antidepressant properties seem to be present for some antipsychotic drugs. Why some drugs apparently possess particular activity of this sort is a mystery. Further clinical trials are needed before the true value of such therapy is established, but it already has a place in the patient "resistant" to tricyclic antidepressants and to MAOIs. However, the dangers of tardive dyskinesia on prolonged usage must be remembered.

Amine Hypotheses
of Affective Disorders
The observation that certain drugs normalize mood and also alter brain amine concentrations led to two important hypotheses regarding the pathophysiology of affective disorders. One hypothesis concentrated on noradrenaline and the other on 5-hydroxytryptamine, and the two formulations

are known as the catecholamine and the indoleamine hypotheses, respectively. Although the biochemistry of affective disorders is still mainly unknown, these two hypotheses have spawned so much research, both basic and applied, that they deserve review.

The catecholamine hypothesis: This hypothesis proposes that at least some depressions are associated with an absolute or relative deficiency of catecholamines, particularly noradrenaline, at functionally important adrenergic receptor sites in the brain. Conversely, mania might be associated with an excess of catecholamines. This theory was regarded from the start as an oversimplification of a very complex biochemical state, but it was thought useful as a first approximation. Moreover, the hypothesized functional deficiency of noradrenaline at receptors was deemed to result from a decrease in synthesis, and impairment of noradrenaline binding and storage, increased intracellular release and deamination of noradrenaline, or from a decrease in receptor sensitivity; each type of deficiency perhaps was related to a specific clinical subtype of depression.

Several lines of evidence can be adduced to support or refute the hypothesis. Among the more important is assessment of noradrenaline turnover and breakdown. It is believed that methoxy-hydroxyphenyl-glycol (MHPG) is the primary metabolite of noradrenaline in the brain (see page 21) and furthermore that the bulk of urinary MHPG is derived from brain. Urinary concentrations of MHPG tend to decrease in bipolar patients as they become depressed and to rise during manic phases. Treatment with tricyclic drugs tends to have variable effects on MHPG excretion. Clinical features of retardation, agitation, and anxiety do not seem to be related to MHPG excretion in a predictable way. Patients with unipolar depression show less consistent alterations in urinary MHPG during their illnesses.

One study claimed that depressed patients who excreted relatively low concentrations of MHPG before treatment with imipramine responded better than did those patients who excrete higher concentrations, but the claim has not been uniformly confirmed. Conversely, patients who excrete high concentrations of MHPG are claimed to respond better to amitriptyline.

Both free and conjugated MHPG are detectable in the cerebrospinal fluid but do not provide as useful a measure as do the acid metabolites of other amines. Several studies have shown a poor correlation between cerebrospinal fluid and urinary MHPG variables. There are no consistent abnormalities of cerebrospinal fluid MHPG in depressed or manic patients.

Some interest has also been shown in the role of dopamine in affective disorders, more as a factor associated with the subtype of depression than as a primary abnormality. Homovanillic acid (HVA), the deaminated O-methylated metabolite of dopamine (see page 22), can be detected in cerebrospinal fluid, and its concentration rises when its egress is prevented by probenecid. In general, homovanillic acid concentrations are lower than normal in depressed patients, perhaps more so in unipolar than in bipolar patients, and particularly in retarded patients. Hypomanic patients also have somewhat decreased concentrations of homovanillic acid in the cerebrospinal fluid, whereas manic patients have elevated concentrations, which have been attributed to the excessive motor activity.

Studies of catecholamine concentrations in the brains of patients who committed suicide have not been very helpful. Some studies show that dopamine and noradrenaline concentrations were low in these persons who were presumably depressed before death; in other studies the concentrations were normal or marginally raised.

The concentrations of catecholamine-synthesizing enzymes in the brains of patients who committed suicide were not consistently altered. Other enzyme studies have been concerned with plasma dopamine-β-hydroxylase and platelet monoamine oxidase in depressed persons. Despite interesting claims of abnormalities that would result in lowered catecholamine values, no consistent replications have appeared.

Drug studies: Two linchpins of the amine hypotheses of affective disorders are:
1. Reserpine depletes the brain of amines and is associated clinically with the precipitation of depression (or perhaps more accurately, psychomotor retardation) in a few susceptible people.
2. The antidepressants, both the tricyclic and the MAOIs, are associated with increased amine concentrations in the brain.

However, indoleamines as well as catecholamines are affected, so these lines of evidence do not clearly support one or the other hypothesis. Alpha-methyl-para-tyrosine (AMPT) is a potent, competitive inhibitor of tyrosine hydroxylase, the rate-limiting enzyme in catecholamine synthesis (page 18). It reduces brain catecholamine levels in animals and urinary catecholamine excretion in man. Depression is induced or worsened by the drug, and mania is improved. Both dopamine and noradrenaline concentrations are lowered by AMPT, but fusaric acid inhibits dopamine-β-hydroxylase and thus lowers noradrenaline concentrations only. Its effects in manic patients are inconsistent.

The corollary treatment would be to increase the concentration of amines by loading with precursors. L-dopa, with or without a peripheral dopa decarboxylase inhibitor, does not ameliorate depression except perhaps in patients with psychomotor retardation. Other patients became more psychotic or angry, and some with bipolar illnesses became hypomanic.

It can be seen that the catecholamine hypothesis of affective disorders is not consistently supported as any simple formulation. Three areas deserve further study and evaluation. The relationship of noradrenaline and dopamine disposition to psychomotor retardation is interesting. Similarly, bipolar illnesses form a subgroup in which catecholamines appear especially relevant. Finally, reports that noradrenergic receptors are supersensitive in depressed patients deserve study.

The indoleamine hypothesis: This hypothesis centres on the role of 5-hydroxytryptamine in affective disorders, postulating a deficiency in depression and an excess in mania. As with the catecholamine hypothesis, the nature of the 5-hydroxytryptamine abnormality is presumed to stem from several mechanisms related to synthesis, storage, release, breakdown, and receptor sensitivity.

Metabolite studies have concentrated on estimations of 5-hydroxyindoleacetic acid (5-HIAA, see page 26) in the cerebrospinal fluid. Most studies have found a decrease of about a third in such concentrations in depressed patients. One study claimed a bimodal distribution, levels being either normal or markedly reduced, but this is not a general finding. Unipolar but not bipolar depressed patients had low concentrations in those studies that categorized the patients in such a manner. Manic patients show no consistent abnormality.

Reduced concentrations of 5-hydroxytryptamine in platelets and reduced rates of uptake of 5-hydroxytryptamine into platelets have been reported in some studies but not in others. Prior drug administration may have obscured the issue, and seasonal variations are marked.

Postmortem studies have also been a focus of interest. 5-HIAA concentrations seemed low in a couple of studies of persons who had committed suicide, but this apparent difference from normal disappeared when the time from death to necropsy was taken into account. Nor are 5-hydroxytryptamine concentrations consistently abnormal in depressed patients who have committed suicide, provided that the numerous factors such as age, sex, mode of death, and previous drug treatment are accounted for.

Drug studies: The use of tryptophan in depression was discussed earlier. Some investigators have searched for abnormalities in tryptophan concentrations, free and bound, in the plasma of patients with affective disorders. Free plasma tryptophan concentrations, observed to be abnormally low in a group of unipolar depressed women, increased as the patients improved. Other studies, including those incorporating dietary controls, have reported less success. Manic patients in one study had normal concentrations of tryptophan, but these rose significantly after the patients' recovery.

Cerebrospinal fluid concentrations of tryptophan were low in one study of depressed patients and normal in another. Tryptophan concentrations did not correlate with 5-HIAA concentrations in the cerebrospinal fluid except after L-tryptophan administration.

As mentioned earlier, L-tryptophan is marketed as an antidepressant agent, but the evidence for its effectiveness is not compelling. It potentiates MAOIs and tricyclic antidepressants and may be useful in mildly depressed outpatients. It is not effective in the more severely ill patients. The next substance in the chain of synthesis, 5-hydroxytryptophan, can also be administered as a precursor of serotonin but may be less specific than tryptophan because it is taken up into catecholaminergic neurons, presumably then forming 5-hydroxytryptamine, which acts as a pseudotransmitter. The evidence that it is effective as an antidepressant is even less convincing than the evidence for tryptophan efficacy. Patients who seem to respond are believed to be those with low 5-HIAA concentrations in the cerebrospinal fluid.

Tryptophan hydroxylase activity is inhibited by p-chlorophenylalanine, but it also depletes catecholamines and competes with some natural amino acids for transport into brain and neurons. It does not have replicable effects on its own in patients with affective disturbances; however, it appears capable of negating the therapeutic effects of tranylcypromine and imipramine.

OVERVIEW

There are many technical problems in evaluating central amine disposition in man. Plasma values are generally a poor correlate of brain concentrations, and urinary excretion is usually at least as uninformative. Concentrations in lumbar cerebrospinal fluid may also be a relatively weak correlate of brain amine turnover, because the lumbar canal is a cul-de-sac and because many amines are found in the spinal cord and must therefore contribute to the cerebrospinal fluid values. Ventricular fluid is probably much more representative in general.

Similarly, postmortem studies need very careful control of such factors as time from death to storage and length of time in the mortuary. Moreover, the mode of death in suicide is atypical, being violent or occurring more commonly after a coma, perhaps out-of-doors. Nor does suicide necessarily indicate a terminal depressive illness.

Technical problems of estimation are still important despite the immense methodological improvements with techniques such as radioisotope labelling and gas chromatography. Nevertheless, various techniques, or even the same technique in various laboratories, may yield disparate results; sharing samples between laboratories is therefore an obvious safeguard. Recent technical developments such as positron-emission tomography may clarify these issues.

The most disturbing aspect of the accumulated mass of data on the psychobiology of depression is its lack of consistency. On average, less than half of the various studies support the amine hypotheses, perhaps half are equivocal, and a minority are inconsistent with the hypotheses. This has led to the formulation of more-complex speculations that would account for several amines. The discrepancies are presumably related to differences in diagnostic practice and failure to control for diet, activity, drug therapy, and milieu. Nevertheless, searching for biochemical correlates of retardation or agitation and categorizing patients on the basis of the type of episodes, unipolar or bipolar, seems more heuristic than does dealing with depression as an amorphous yet heterogenous mass.

It must be remembered that during the past decade, the emphasis on noradrenaline and 5-hydroxytryptamine reflects the availability of techniques purporting to assess amine neurotransmitter function in the brain. Yet there are many other such substances, less easy to study, that would repay investigation. For example, physostigmine, the acetylcho-linesterase inhibitor, transiently abolishes manic symptoms. Furthermore, unusual amines such as octopamine can, under the influence of antidepressant drugs, accumulate and affect neuronal and synaptic function.

An interesting finding in a few studies has been the persistence of some biochemical abnormalities despite attainment of normal mood. That observation raises questions concerning our concept of affective disorders. Does it solely comprise a succession of affective episodes (depressive or manic, or both) or is it really a phase of personal and biochemical vulnerability that lasts a year or two, during which time episodes may be precipitated?

Whatever the ultimate outcome concerning biochemistry and affective disorders, the discovery and introduction of the antidepressants triggered a spate of studies that has continued unabated. That the drugs improve many patients cannot be gainsaid. The drugs have many biochemical effects, however, and we still do not know which are most relevant to their therapeutic actions.

FURTHER READING

Asbert M, Thoren P, Träskman L, Bertilsson L, Ringberger V-A: Serotonin depression – a biochemical subgroup within the affective disorders? *Science 191*: 480-484, 1976.

Atkinson RM, Ditman KS: Tranylcypromine: A review. *Clin Pharmacol Ther* 6:631-655, 1965.

Avery GS: Doxepin: A review. *Drugs 1*:194-227, 1971.

Bant WP: Antihypertensive drugs and depression: A reappraisal. *Psychol Med 8*:275-283, 1978.

Bielski RJ, Friedel RO: Prediction of tricyclic antidepressant response: A critical review. *Arch Gen Psychiatry 33*:1479-1489, 1976.

Blackwell B, Marley E, Price J, Taylor DC: Hypertensive interactions between monoamine oxidase inhibitors and foodstuffs. *Br J Psychiatry 113*:349-365, 1967.

Cocco G, Agué C: Interactions between cardioactive drugs and antidepressants. *Eur J Clin Pharmacol 11*:389-393, 1977.

Coppen A, Gupta R, Montgomery S, Ghose K, Bailey J, Burns B, De Ridder JJ: Mianserin hydrochloride: A novel antidepressant. *Br J Psychiatry 129*:342-345, 1976.

Davis JM, Janowsky DS: Recent advances in the treatment of depression. *Br J Hosp Med 12*:219-228, 1974.

D'Elia G, Hanson L, Raotma H: L-tryptophan and 5-hydroxytryptophan in the treatment of depression. *Acta Psychiatr Scand 57*:239-252, 1978.

Dimascio A, Klerman GL, Prusoff B: Relative safety of amitriptyline in maintenance treatment of depression. *J Nerv Ment Dis 160*:34-41, 1975.

Dunner DL, Fieve RR: Affective disorder: Studies with amine precursors. *Am J Psychiatry 132*:180-183, 1975.

Gram LF: Metabolism of tricyclic antidepressants. A review. *Dan Med Bull 21*: 218-231, 1974.

Herrington RN, Bruce A, Johnstone EC, Lader MH: Comparative trial of L-tryptophan and ECT in severe depressive illness. *Lancet ii*:731-734, 1974.

Herrington RN, Bruce A, Johnstone EC, Lader MH: Comparative trial of L-tryptophan and amitriptyline in depressive illness. *Psychol Med 6*:673-678, 1976.

Ho BT: Monoamine oxidase inhibitors. *J Pharm Sci 61*:821-837, 1972.

Johnstone EC: The relationship between acetylator status and inhibition of monoamine oxidase, excretion of free drug and antidepressant response in depressed patients on phenelzine. *Psychopharmacologia 46*:289-294, 1976.

Kuhn R: The treatment of depressive states with G22355 (imipramine hydrochloride). *Am J Psychiatry 115*:459-464, 1958.

Maas JW: Biogenic amines and depression. *Arch Gen Psychiatry 32*:1357-1361, 1975.

Medical Research Council: Clinical trial of the treatment of depressive illness. *Br Med J 1*:831-836, 1965.

Mindham RHS, Howland C, Shepherd M: An evaluation of continuation therapy with tricyclic antidepressants in depressive illness. *Psychol Med 3*:5-17, 1973.

Morris JB, Beck AT: The efficacy of antidepressant drugs: A review of research (1958 to 1972). *Arch Gen Psychiatry 30*:667-674, 1974.

Paykel ES: Depressive typologies and response to amitriptyline. *Br J Psychiatry 120*:147-156, 1972.

Quitkin F, Rifkin A, Klein DF: Monoamine oxidase inhibitors: A review of antidepressive effectiveness. *Arch Gen Psychiatry 36*:749-760, 1979.

Risch SC, Huey LY, Janowsky DS: Plasma levels of tricyclic antidepressants and clinical efficacy: A review of the literature. *J Clin Psychiatry 40*:4-16, 58-69, 1979.

Schildkraut JJ: The current status of biological criteria for classifying the depressive disorders and predicting responses to treatment. *Psychopharmacol Bull 10*:5-25, 1974.

Schuckit M, Robins E, Feighner J: Monoamine oxidase inhibitors. Combination therapy in the treatment of depression. *Arch Gen Psychiatry 24*:509-513, 1971.

Shaw DM: The practical management of affective disorders. *Br J Psychiatry 130*:432-451, 1977.

Tyrer P: Towards rational therapy with monoamine oxidase inhibitors. *Br J Psychiatry 128*:354-360, 1976.

Welner Z: Childhood depression: An overview. *J Nerv Ment Dis 166*:588-593, 1978.

Young JPR, Hughes WC, Lader MH: A controlled comparison of flupenthixol and amitriptyline in depressed out-patients. *Br Med J 1*:1116-1118, 1976.

CHAPTER 7

Lithium

INTRODUCTION

During the 19th century, lithium salts were known to be important constituents of some spa waters to which many medicinal properties were ascribed. In the 1940s, lithium salts were used as a taste substitute for sodium chloride in cardiac patients on salt-free diets. However, severe side effects and even some deaths were reported and its use was stopped. About that time, Cade in Australia was working on the premise that mania is associated with the production of an endotoxin. He injected urine from manic patients into guinea pigs and found it to be toxic, the main agent of toxicity being urea. Uric acid seemed to increase this toxicity, and in these experiments lithium urate was chosen as a highly soluble salt. Unexpectedly, the guinea pigs were protected from urea toxicity and became "tranquillized." The responsible agent was identified as lithium. In later experiments, lithium quietened ten manic patients to whom it was administered. Because of the known toxicity of lithium, little interest was shown in it for almost a decade until reports began to emerge from various centres in Europe confirming the antimanic properties. Lithium was also then claimed to be a prophylactic, preventing not only manic attacks but also depressive and perhaps schizoaffective attacks. Various other indications such as alcoholism, epilepsy, and thyrotoxicosis were put forward in a flurry of poorly substantiated claims for lithium. Even now, when several large-scale trials have been published, controversy continues about its true therapeutic role.

PHARMACOKINETICS

Lithium taken by mouth is well absorbed from the intestine; less than 1% appears in the faeces. Routinely formulated lithium salts tend to be associated with sharp peaks in serum concentrations, so sustained-release preparations have been introduced. These vary in their bioavailability: some produce disappointingly low serum concentration curves, presumably because of incomplete release of the lithium ion from the complex. Each preparation should be judged on the absorption curves provided by the manufacturer.

Distribution into body tissues is a little delayed. Peak lithium concentrations in rat brain are not attained until 24 hours after injection. In man, particularly high levels are reached in certain brain regions such as the pons.

Concentrations in human serum decline with a biphasic course, rapidly during the first six hours and then a slower elimination during the ensuing 24 hours. Lithium is not bound to plasma proteins. It is excreted by the kidney, less than half of an administered dose being cleared in 24 hours. Inevitably, very high lithium concentrations are sustained in parts of the kidney. Lithium excretion is linked to sodium balance in the body. If sodium intake is lowered, as with a salt-restricted or eccentric diet, blood pressure drops, lithium excretion is reduced, and toxicity can supervene. The thiazide diuretics increase sodium excretion without affecting lithium, therefore toxicity may result from their use.

Serum lithium estimations

Because of the low therapeutic index of lithium, toxic concentrations can be reached easily and with unexpected rapidity. It is essential clinical practice to monitor serum lithium concentrations at appropriate intervals. Monitoring is particularly important when treatment is being initiated or dosage regimens changed. A typical schedule comprises the testing of samples obtained on the 7th, 14th, 21st, and 28th days of treatment and thereafter at intervals of three to six weeks, depending on the reliability of the patient and the variability of his lithium concentrations. The blood sample must be taken at the same time of day each time: the optimal time is just before the dose after the longest interval between doses during the 24 hours – usually the early morning dose. The usual range aimed at is 0.8 to 1.4 mmol/litre. No therapeutic advantage attends concentrations greater than 1.5 mmol/litre, and toxicity generally occurs at concentrations greater than 2 mmol/litre. Erythrocyte lithium concentrations, either in absolute terms or relative to serum concentrations, are claimed to provide a better estimate of body concentrations than do measurements of serum lithium alone, but this point is still disputed.

Lithium estimations must not be used as a blind substitute for clinical observation. Some patients lose their affective swings despite serum concentrations less than 0.5 mmol/litre; others show signs of incipient toxicity at concentrations of only 1 mmol/litre. Notwithstanding this lack of high correlation, elevated serum lithium concentrations should not be disregarded simply because no clinical toxicity is apparent. There is no justification for keeping the concentrations greater than 2 mmol/litre, especially in view of the difficulties of predicting long-term toxicity.

Toxicity (see page 92) may still occur even when serum lithium is being measured regularly but infrequently. The patient and his relatives should be warned of the possibility, unlikely though it is. Nevertheless, estimating lithium concentrations reminds the patient that he is being treated with a powerful medication that must not be used in a cavalier fashion. It also detects the patient who is defaulting with his medication.

PHARMACOLOGY
Biochemical Pharmacology
Lithium, a cation, substitutes for other body-fluid cations, including sodium, potassium, calcium, and magnesium. Not surprisingly, a wide range of neurophysiological, neurochemical, and biophysical processes are altered. It is unlikely that any one action of lithium could be singled out as the mechanism for its clinical effects.

Unlike the other cations, lithium is fairly equally distributed between extracellular and intracellular body compartments. Lithium is transported into cells mainly by diffusion, but it is transported out only slowly by the sodium pump. Cation disposition is abnormal in affective disorders and is partly normalized by lithium administration. It is not clear whether the normalization is a direct pharmacological action of lithium or whether it reflects return towards normal of the abnormalities associated with affective disorders.

Many neurotransmitter functions are altered by lithium. Acetylcholine synthesis and release are depressed. Lithium interferes with the calcium that is necessary for the exocytosis of presynaptic vesicles, thereby diminishing the release of many neurotransmitters, including the monoamines. Reuptake of released amines is believed to be accelerated. Less neurotransmitter is thus available in the synaptic cleft.

Another effect of lithium is to interfere with energy processes in the cell by an action on cyclic AMP. Together with electrolyte and neurotransmitter changes, a very complex set of actions is attributable to lithium, and the effect is made even more convoluted by the inevitable compensating processes set in train. For these reasons, the mode of action of lithium (or, more realistically, the major modes of action) remains uncertain.

Human pharmacology
In normal persons, lithium produces mild subjective feelings of lassitude, lethargy, and inability to concentrate. Restlessness and anxiety are sometimes reported. Some decrease in memory function can be detected and is often a complaint of lithium-treated patients. Slow waves in the EEG increase.

CLINICAL USE
Lithium preparations are used routinely to treat manic and hypomanic patients and to prevent attacks in patients with recurrent affective disorders. These attacks comprise both manic and depressive episodes in bipolar patients, episodes of mania in the recurrently manic patients, and depressive attacks in the unipolar patient. The efficacy of lithium in preventing schizoaffective psychoses is more controversial. Other conditions in which lithium treatment has been claimed effective include the depressive illnesses, aggressive behaviour, schizophrenia, epilepsy, alcoholism, Huntington's chorea, thyrotoxicosis, spasmodic torticollis, and premenstrual tension. Because these claims are based mainly on clinical impressions and uncontrolled trials, they remain controversial. The conditions most deserving of further study as indications for lithium are aggression and alcoholism.

Treatment of mania and hypomania
The demonstration of the effectiveness of lithium in controlling manic and hypomanic disorders was overshadowed by the advent of chlorpromazine and later of haloperidol. Together with reports of lithium toxicity, the new drugs diverted attention from lithium. Even now the relative advantages and disadvantages of lithium and the antipsychotic drugs are not clearly established.

About four fifths of manic patients respond to lithium treatment. Chlorpromazine is more effective than lithium, however, in controlling highly overactive manic patients. Moreover, control of mania is attained by chlorpromazine within a few days, whereas the therapeutic effects of lithium are often not apparent for at least a week. The delay reflects the pharmacokinetics of lithium with its slow build-up to therapeutic concentrations. Attempts to hasten the onset of action by "pushing" the lithium dosage rapidly need careful monitoring to avoid toxicity. In less ill hypomanic patients, lithium is at least as effective as chlorpromazine, has few side effects, and leaves the patient feeling less sluggish and fatigued. Controlled comparisons with haloperidol, a popular choice among clinicians for treating mania, have not been carried out.

Combinations of antipsychotic medication and lithium are commonly used. An antipsychotic drug, such as haloperidol, is instituted in high dose, perhaps parenterally, to effect initial control. Lithium is added, accumulates over the next week or so, and the antipsychotic medication can then be carefully withdrawn. Adverse reactions to the combination of haloperidol and lithium have been reported but seem exceptional.

Treatment of depression

Despite early reports of ineffectiveness, there have been continuing evaluations of lithium's use in treating episodes of depression. Some uncontrolled studies suggested that perhaps 50% of depressed patients might respond. The figure is unimpressive in view of the fluctuating course and natural remissions of depressive illnesses and the substantial placebo-response rate. Patients with endogenous depression, mainly those with bipolar illnesses, respond best but still at a lesser rate than with standard tricyclic antidepressant therapy. The improvement with lithium is often only partial, suggesting the value of combining lithium and tricyclic therapy, a topic that remains unclear and controversial.

"Prophylaxis" of affective attacks

Even more controversial have been the claims that continuing treatment with lithium prevents or aborts attacks of mania and depression. The problems of designing controlled trials to test these claims led to confusion in the early stages of study, but several large-scale trials have established the role of lithium in these circumstances.

There seems little doubt that patients maintained successfully on lithium therapy are deriving benefit. Substitution of a placebo under double-blind controlled conditions is associated with a higher relapse rate than is continuing lithium therapy. However, a cohort of patients treated with lithium for some time, say a year, is unrepresentative of patients being considered for lithium prophylaxis. Any dropouts due to toxicity or ineffectiveness of the lithium will already have occurred, so the sample is biassed heavily in favour of lithium responders.

To evaluate lithium in newly diagnosed patients or those with a history of recurrent affective disorder, controlled prospective evaluations are essential. Almost all those published demonstrate that lithium, as compared with placebo, substantially reduces the number and severity of affective episodes. For example, in one study, only 11% of the patients maintained on lithium therapy were rated as unchanged or worse during the two years before the trial as compared with 75% of the placebo patients. In this trial lithium was as effective in patients with unipolar recurrent depression as in those with both depressive and manic swings. Some other trials have confirmed the observation, yet others have indicated that prophylaxis is more effective in bipolar than in unipolar patients. In bipolar patients the manic swings are more effec-tively dampened than the depressive swings. The various controlled trials disagree with respect to schizoaffective psychoses. Some detect no prophylactic effect, whereas others claim definite effectiveness. At least some of this lack of unanimity must reflect different diagnostic practices.

Trials comparing lithium with tricyclic antidepressant maintenance therapy are relatively few. Lithium is reported to be more effective than imipramine in bipolar patients, but mainly with respect to manic and not to depressive swings. Lithium and imipramine are said to be equally effective in unipolar patients. Further trials of this type are needed.

Failure to respond to lithium is often partial, with affective episodes being attenuated but not abolished. The length of the episodes is unaltered. Among patients with bipolar depression, relapse is more likely to occur in those patients with rapidly alternating cycles of mania and depression. There is some suggestion that the relapse rate of some patients tends to increase as the years go by, whereas other patients respond with a complete cessation of attacks.

On present evidence, lithium therapy is most suitable in patients with a long history of many typical affective episodes. Any patient who has had two or more distinct manic-depressive episodes during one year or one or more separate attacks each year during the preceding two years should be evaluated and considered a candidate for lithium treatment. Patients with bipolar illnesses are more likely to respond than are patients with unipolar depression, and the more closely the patient fits the bipolar stereotype the better the chance of a good response. Some psychiatrists initiate lithium therapy very readily, but others are more reluctant and may first try maintenance with a tricyclic antidepressant, especially in unipolar patients. If a patient does not show an adequate response to lithium within the first year of treatment, the drug should be discontinued because it is invidious to expose a patient to the risks of lithium treatment without due benefit.

The term "prophylaxis" is often inappropriate since it implies the complete prevention of attacks. Complete prevention is true for some patients but in others the attacks are only attenuated to the point at which the patient can be managed as an outpatient instead of being admitted to hospital or at which he needs minimal supervision instead of regular outpatient attendance. A more appropriate description is "maintenance therapy."

Treatment schedules

Before instituting lithium therapy, the physician should perform a physical examination. Chronic renal failure, hypertension, and a history of myocardial infarctions require cautious appraisal but are not absolute contraindications. Renal and thyroid function should be tested routinely. In patients with physical illness and in the old and frail, dosage schedules must be low and carefully adjusted to keep serum lithium levels at the lower limit, 0.6-0.8 mmol/litre initially. Lithium is not appropriate therapy for children.

Dosage depends on both the severity of the illness and the particular preparation and should be governed by the serum concentrations.

UNWANTED EFFECTS

Lithium has a low therapeutic index so that mild unwanted effects are common at, or just above, normal therapeutic levels. Most of these effects are harmless and easily dealt with, but some are more serious and even life threatening and need to be treated promptly. Note that symptoms initially may be minor or even absent if the rise in lithium concentrations to toxic levels is very slow.

Neurological Effects

Mild neurological side effects are common, especially during initial treatment, and include general and muscular fatigue, lethargy, and tremor. The tremor usually begins early in treatment and may or may not resolve or lessen. It is a fine tremor and affects the hands especially. Only a small minority of patients regard it as a handicap and are reluctant to continue lithium treatment because of it. Fine movements and emotional stress make it worse. Lowering the dose or adding a small dose of a beta-adrenoceptor antagonist such as propranolol is usually sufficient to minimize the tremor.

A coarsening of the tremor or its spread to other parts of the body usually presages toxicity. Ataxia, dysarthria, incoordination, difficulty in concentration, and mild disorientation are the commonest early signs of incipient toxicity. Others include muscle twitching and fasciculations in the limbs, hands, and face, as well as nystagmus, dizziness, and visual disturbances. Severe toxicity is accompanied by restlessness, confusion, nystagmus, epileptic convulsions, delirium, and, eventually, coma and death. Muscular flaccidity or, conversely, hyperirritability and irreversible brain damage have also been reported.

Extrapyramidal syndromes occasionally occur in patients who have been treated with lithium for some time. Even when serum concentrations of lithium are maintained in the therapeutic range, epileptic seizures can occur. Possibly an underlying predisposition is being unmasked in such a case, as with chlorpromazine.

Renal Effects

More than 95% of a single dose of lithium is excreted by the kidneys. The patient's renal function must be assessed before lithium therapy is instituted: a serum creatinine measurement or urinary concentration and dilution test is usually sufficiently sensitive. Some psychiatrists rely directly on the careful monitoring of lithium concentrations.

Polyuria and polydipsia occur in 15% to 40% of patients given lithium salts, but these symptoms do not always bother the patients, who may not even mention them. Nocturia is the commonest presenting symptom. The polyuria may not supervene until after months or years of treatment. Occasionally, severe polyuria (as much as 10 litres/day) may occur, causing inconvenience, nocturia, insomnia, and, in some cases, electrolyte disturbances. The primary mechanism of the polyuria seems to be an inhibitory effect on the adenyl cyclase in the kidney, which is normally sensitive to antidiuretic hormone. The syndrome is almost always reversible so that lowering the dose is indicated.

Disturbing reports of long-term nephrotoxicity have recently appeared in the literature. A small group of patients whose renal-concentrating ability had become reduced during long-term lithium treatment were examined by renal biopsy. All showed moderate-to-severe focal fibrosis, with severe tubular atrophy and many totally sclerotic glomeruli. Further studies are currently being carried out, but it seems possible that eventual renal damage is likely even with therapeutic levels of lithium. Such a possibility must lead the prescriber to consider the use of lithium very carefully in each patient, and certainly to discontinue its use in partial responders or those who do not respond.

Endocrine Effects

Thyroid functions are altered in a complex way by lithium. Sequelae include euthyroid goitre, hypothyroidism with or without goitre, and abnormal endocrine test results. Lithium-induced goitres are usually diffuse and not large enough to be readily noticeable. The incidence is about 5%. The goitre may compensate for decreased thyroid function. The onset of hypo-thyroid symptoms is quite variable between weeks and years of starting lithium therapy. Women are much more commonly affected than men.

The patients with preexisting thyroid function at the lower limit of normal are more at risk than those with average or increased thyroid function. Thyroid function in those with initially marginal function should therefore be assessed before treatment and at regular intervals thereafter. The hypothyroid-ism, which may be confused with a retarded depression, is usually reversible on stopping lithium, but it is also easily treatable with thyroid hormone.

Lithium affects thyroid function at several sites. The main effect is to inhibit the release of thyroid hormones, which leads to a stimulation in TSH secretion, compensatory augmentation of thyroid function, and often a goitre. If the compensation is insufficient, hypothyroidism ensues.

There is some evidence that lithium administration may be associated with alterations in bone mineral metabolism, lead-ing to osteoporosis in women.

Other Effects

Benign, reversible T-wave changes occur with lithium treat-ment, perhaps because of displaced intracellular potassium. Arrhythmias, including ventricular premature contractions, tachycardia, and atrioventricular block, may occur rarely at therapeutic concentrations and more commonly at toxic levels.

Among gastrointestinal side effects are nausea, anorexia, loose stools, vomiting, and abdominal pain. The main haemo-poietic effect is a benign leucocytosis. Acneform and other rashes may occur, as may oedema. Weight gain is often noted, the mechanism being unclear.

Lithium possesses teratogenic properties in some species but is believed to be safe in human beings except that major cardiovascular anomalies in the babies seem somewhat over-represented. The risk to the baby must be weighed against the dangers of affective swings, but lithium should not be lightly instituted in the pregnant woman. If lithium therapy is main-tained in pregnant women, careful serum monitoring is neces-sary because renal clearances vary over time. Lithium passes the placenta readily, and the newborn baby may be floppy and listless. Because the drug also passes into the milk at low concentrations, breast-feeding should be discouraged.

FURTHER READING

Coppen A, Nogeura R, Bailey J, et al: Prophylactic lithium in affective dis-orders: Controlled trial. Lancet ii:275-279, 1971.

Crammer JL, Rosser RM, Crane G: Blood levels and management of lithium treatment. Br Med J 3:650-654, 1974.

Goodwin FD (ed): The lithium ion. Impact on treatment and research. Arch Gen Psychiatry 36:833-916, 1979.

Jefferson JW, Greist JH: Primer of Lithium Therapy. Baltimore, Williams & Wilkins, 1977.

Johnson FN: Lithium Research and Therapy. London, Academic Press, 1975.

Petúrsson H: Prediction of lithium response. Compr Psychiatry 20:226-241, 1979.

Prien RF, Caffey EM, Klett CJ: Comparison of lithium carbonate and chlor-promazine in the treatment of mania. Report of the Veterans Administration and National Institute of Mental Health Collaborative Study Group. Arch Gen Psychiatry 26:146-153, 1972.

Prien RF, Caffey EM, Klett CJ: Prophylactic efficacy of lithium carbonate in manic-depressive illness: Report of the Veterans Administration and National Institute of Mental Health Collaborative Study Group. Arch Gen Psychiatry 28:337-341, 1973.

Prien RF, Klett CJ, Caffey EM: Lithium carbonate and imipramine in preven-tion of affective disorders. Arch Gen Psychiatry 29:420-425, 1973.

Sedatives, Anxiolytics, and Hypnotics

INTRODUCTION

The terms used to describe these drugs, primarily barbiturates and benzodiazepines, have changed in the past decade or so. About ten years ago, the term "sedative" meant anxiety-allaying, but the term has come to imply feelings of heaviness, torpor, and drowsiness, particularly in reference to the barbiturates. In its place, "anxiolytic" has been introduced to describe the newer compounds although, as will be discussed later, the new compounds are actually similar in action to the older ones and differences in their effects are a matter of degree rather than a true qualitative difference. Furthermore, "anxiolytic" together with the term "antianxiety agent" implies a specificity against anxiety that is probably not warranted. Rather, these drugs (eg, the benzodiazepines) exert a more general antiarousal or antiemotion effect.

The distinction between anxiolytic and hypnotic is also somewhat artificial: most sedatives and anxiolytics in higher dosage given at night have sleep-inducing actions, and many hypnotics in divided doses during the day are useful anxiolytics.

Sedatives and hypnotics are the most widely used of all drugs and their history is very long. Alcohol, various alkaloids, and simple organic chemicals such as chloral and paraldehyde have been, and in many instances still are, extensively used. Bromides were popular 100 years ago but were replaced by the barbiturates, which in turn in the past decade have been ousted by the benzodiazepines in many countries. Assessment of all the innovations is difficult, especially inasmuch as nonspecific factors such as placebo response, doctor's and patient's attitudes to drug therapy, patient's expectations, and concomitant psychotherapy and other treatments are important in evaluating this group of drugs.

Although differences within class are minor, differences between drug categories are often of major clinical significance. Accordingly, this chapter is divided into subsections dealing with each class.

BARBITURATES

Barbitone and phenobarbitone were introduced early this century, followed by many congeners of which about 20 are still extant. Amylobarbitone (amobarbital), butobarbitone (butabarbital), and quinalbarbitone (secobarbital) are still widely used sedatives and hypnotics because they are inexpensive, and phenobarbitone is often prescribed for epilepsy. Despite long usage of the drugs, their mechanisms of action are unclear.

Pharmacokinetics and drug interactions

Barbiturates are readily absorbed; the rate but not the amount of absorption is decreased by a full stomach. Except for barbitone and about 25% of each dose of phenobarbitone (which are excreted unchanged), barbiturates are metabolized by liver microsomal enzymes, mainly by oxidation, to less lipophilic products that the kidney eliminates. Even quite low or infrequent doses of barbiturates can stimulate the activity of these liver enzymes. This induction results in the barbiturate being metabolized more rapidly, a possible factor in tolerance. In addition, the barbiturates may accelerate the metabolism of other drugs such as the coumarin anticoagulants, griseofulvin, steroids (including oral contraceptives), and certain other psychotropic agents (eg, chlorpromazine and amitriptyline). The effects of these drugs are thereby lessened or negated, so they should not be prescribed in combination with barbiturates.

Barbiturates vary in the rate at which they penetrate the brain, depending on their lipophilicity. Thiopentone enters rapidly and is used as an anaesthetic induction agent; barbitone crosses into the brain so slowly that it is inappropriate as a hypnotic.

Pharmacology

Barbiturates, as do the benzodiazepines, potentiate GABA-mediated inhibitory processes in the brain, providing a basis for their spinal cord muscle relaxant, anticonvulsant, and sedative actions. Unlike the benzodiazepines, the barbiturates also directly depress all neurons at slightly supratherapeutic doses, perhaps by interfering with chloride ionophore channels. The neocortex and ascending reticular system are first released from inhibitory control (inhibition of inhibition), resulting in decrease of activity (inhibition of excitation). At higher doses, depression of vital centres occurs, eg, depression of respiratory and cardiovascular reflexes. In overdose, coma and death supervene, presumably reflecting widespread neuronal depression.

Psychological functions are altered in a complex way depending on the drug, its dose, and the conditions of administration. Psychomotor performance and complex tasks are most affected, especially those involving nuances of judgment.

Barbiturate-induced sleep resembles natural sleep except that rapid-eye-movement (REM) time is reduced. Tolerance to this effect occurs on repeated dosing, and, when the barbiturate is withdrawn, rebound occurs with an increase in

REM sleep that is associated with complaints of nightmares and broken sleep. Most hypnotic barbiturates are sufficiently prolonged in action to leave residual or "hangover" effects the next day.

EEG changes with the barbiturates consist typically of increased fast-wave activity with spindles of waxing and waning activity.

Clinical use

Many clinicians have stopped using barbiturates as hypnotics and sedatives except to cut short severe panic attacks, confining their use to service as anticonvulsants.

Clinical trials have shown that the barbiturates have sedative and hypnotic properties. However, they generally compare poorly with the benzodiazepines, being less effective with more side effects. As hypnotics they are effective but leave the patient feeling "drugged" the next day.

Chronic toxicity is common, resulting in drowsiness, confusion, wandering, and even psychotic features; neurological signs include nystagmus, dysarthria, and motor incoordination. Elderly patients are particularly intolerant of the barbiturates, which readily induce ataxia and confusion. The drugs are contraindicated in patients with myxoedema, myasthenia gravis, and porphyria. Liver disfunction must be gross before it affects barbiturate metabolism.

Many patients stabilized for years on barbiturates must be assumed to be covertly dependent, because withdrawal leads to anxiety, agitation, trembling, and even convulsions. Substitution of a benzodiazepine that can later be withdrawn more easily is often successful, providing the process is gradual. Even if an old person has been taking barbiturates uneventfully for many years, the case should be reviewed.

Barbiturates have been used intravenously to facilitate interviewing, although the sobriquet "truth serum" is ill advised. This technique is also helpful in (a) mobilizing the stuporous catatonic patient, (b) aiding in the diagnosis of intellectual impairment, and (c) lessening disturbing negative effects associated with previous stressful experiences ("abreaction").

Unwanted effects

It is difficult in many patients to attain satisfactory symptomatic control without oversedation. The patient typically oscillates between anxiety and torpor. Mental performance is usually impaired, and the patient should not drive or operate dangerous machinery. Alcohol powerfully potentiates barbiturate effects. Hypersensitivity reactions (especially of the skin) sometimes occur, and megaloblastic anaemia has been reported.

Overdosage

Suicidal attempts frequently involve overdoses of barbiturates, either alone or in combination with alcohol or other psychotropic drugs, particularly the tricyclic antidepressants. In many countries, suicidal attempts have increased severalfold in the past 30 years, and the barbiturates are implicated in a major part of this increase. In the United Kingdom, the incidence of barbiturate overdosage has fallen in parallel with the decrease in their prescription.

Depending on local factors such as proximity to hospital and expertise of staff, death occurs in 0.5% to 10% of cases of overdosage. Severe poisoning is likely at ten times the hypnotic dose, and twice that amount may prove fatal.

Tolerance and dependence

Tolerance to barbiturates can occur rapidly and is an effect of pharmacokinetic factors such as liver-enzyme induction as well as pharmacodynamic factors such as neuronal adaptation to chronic drug concentrations. Cross-tolerance develops to alcohol, gaseous anaesthetics, and other sedatives, including the benzodiazepines.

Psychological dependence, that is, "drug-seeking behaviour" is common. For example, patients importuning for their tablets will visit several physicians. Physical dependence may be induced by doses of 500 mg/day; intoxication may occur as evidenced by impaired mental functioning, emotional instability, and neurological signs. Abrupt discontinuation after high dosage is likely to induce convulsions and delirium. After normal dosage, withdrawal phenomena include anxiety, restlessness, agitation, tremor, muscle twitching, nausea and vomiting, orthostatic hypotension, insomnia, and weight loss.

PROPANEDIOLS

In the search for a sedative safer than the barbiturates, meprobamate was discovered and vigorously promoted. However, like the barbiturates, it tends to produce torpor, drowsiness, and oversedation. Other unwanted effects include rashes, purpura, oedema, and fever. Liver induction occurs and the drug is dangerous in overdose. It is also liable to produce dependence.

Although the use of meprobamate has waned for these various reasons, some physicians advocate using it (or its

Figure 8-1. Formulae of some benzodiazepines.

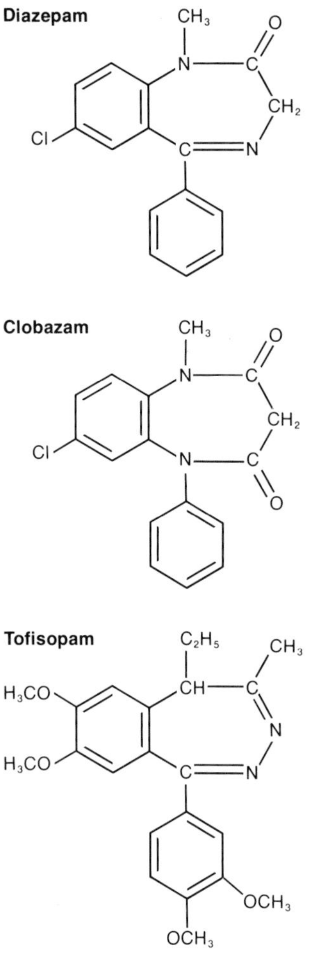

Diazepam

Clobazam

Tofisopam

derivative, tybamate) in anxious patients with excessive muscle tension because of its powerful effects on the spinal cord.

BENZODIAZEPINES

The benzodiazepines were first synthesized in the 1930s but were not systematically evaluated until 20 years later. The prototype, chlordiazepoxide, tamed animals and had muscle-relaxant and sedative properties. Given to chronic schizophrenic patients, it alleviated their anxiety without altering their psychotic features. Chlordiazepoxide was extensively evaluated in anxious patients and marketed in 1960. Since that time, several analogues – diazepam, oxazepam, medazepam, clorazepate, prazepam, nitrazepam, flurazepam, among others – have been introduced in the United Kingdom and the United States. Many other benzodiazepines have been evaluated. Diazepam is the most widely used in many countries, but prescribing preferences do vary. Nitrazepam and flurazepam were promoted as hypnotics, clonazepam as an anticonvulsant, and most of the others as daytime anxiolytics.

All the above benzodiazepines have nitrogen atoms in the 1 and 4 positions of the heterocyclic ring. Recently, a 1:5 benzodiazepine (clobazam) has been introduced, and a 3:4 compound (tofisopam) is available in France (Figure 8-1).

Pharmacokinetics

Generally, the benzodiazepines are rapidly and completely absorbed. Plasma binding is high, eg, about 98% for diazepam. The benzodiazepines are very lipophilic, and, except for oxazepam, penetration into the brain is very rapid.

The metabolic interrelationships of the benzodiazepines are complex (Figure 8-2). Medazepam is metabolized to diazepam, which in turn is N-desmethylated to N-desmethyldiazepam (sometimes called nordiazepam). Chlordiazepoxide is also partly converted to desmethyldiazepam, as is prazepam. Clorazepate is transformed in either an acid pH (such as that of the stomach) or, on absorption, to form desmethyldiazepam.

The significance of desmethyldiazepam is that it is metabolized very slowly, its plasma half-life being 72 hours or more (Figure 8-3). That of diazepam is about 36 hours, so that when the drug is administered chronically, the concentration of the desmethyl derivative soon surpasses that of diazepam itself. Desmethyldiazepam undergoes oxidation to oxazepam, which, like its 3-hydroxy analogues, lorazepam and temazepam, is fairly rapidly conjugated with glucuronic acid and excreted. Because this process is potentially much more rapid than

Figure 8-2. Metabolic pathways of some benzodiazepines.

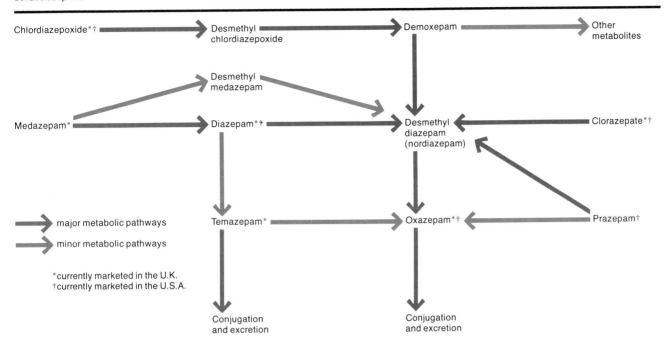

Lorazepam is a chlorinated derivative of oxazepam

Nitrazepam, flurazepam, clobazam, triazolam, and clonazepam have separate metabolic pathways.

Figure 8-3. Formula and metabolic transformation of diazepam.

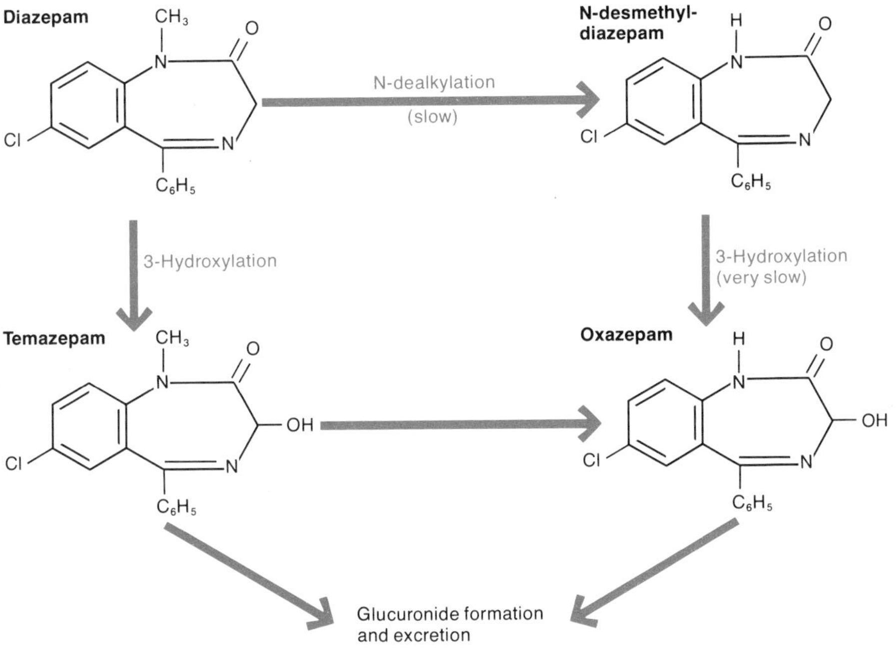

the formation of oxazepam from desmethyldiazepam, only traces of oxazepam can be detected after the administration of diazepam, medazepam, or clorazepate. The metabolism of diazepam to temazepam is by a very minor route, and temazepam is readily conjugated and excreted. Thus, the 3-hydroxy derivatives with half-lives of less than 24 hours, oxazepam, temazepam, and lorazepam, can be contrasted with the longer-acting benzodiazepines, whose main metabolite is desmethyldiazepam. Triazolam has a particularly short half-life (less than four hours). Flurazepam and nitrazepam have separate and rather complex metabolic pathways but are not short acting. In particular, the major active metabolite of flurazepam, namely, N-desalkylflurazepam, has a half-life of about 100 hours.

Because the benzodiazepines are often prescribed for lengthy periods, their long-term pharmacokinetics are important. Diazepam and desmethyldiazepam reach plateau levels after a few weeks. Diazepam concentrations may then fall somewhat without much change in the concentration of the desmethyl metabolite.

Although the benzodiazepines can induce liver enzymes in animals, induction seems of no clinical significance in man.

Correlations between plasma concentrations and clinical response have not been established.

Pharmacology

Several lines of evidence suggest that the benzodiazepines are powerful potentiators of gamma-aminobutyric acid (GABA) (see also chapter 2). They are not direct agonists that act on GABA receptors nor do they seem to inhibit the re-uptake of GABA into presynaptic nerve endings and glial cells. Enhancement of GABA activity produces muscle relaxation both by presynaptic and by postsynaptic influences; anticonvulsant effects by a general inhibiting effect, especially in centrencephalic regions; ataxia, perhaps by a cerebellar effect in high dosage; and arousal-lowering by effects on the diffuse activating systems in the brain – cholinergic, serotonergic, noradrenergic, and dopaminergic. As mentioned before, barbiturates in addition are direct depressants. The selectivity of the benzodiazepines as GABA synergists may help explain their safety in overdosage when presumably nonlethal, maximal, natural inhibition is produced.

Although this hypothesis of the GABA-enhancing action of the benzodiazepines is attractive, other neurotransmitters may also be affected. Moreover, the function with benzodiazepine receptors is puzzling. Receptors that bind diazepam strongly have been identified in various regions of mammalian brains, particularly the cerebral cortex. Furthermore, receptor occupancy for diazepam correlates with the drug's anticonvulsant effects. Other benzodiazepines compete for these receptor sites roughly in proportion to their clinical potency. However, no other drugs, not even the barbiturates, compete for these receptors, and the natural ligand has not been identified. It is not GABA, nor do benzodiazepines bind to GABA receptors. Clarification of the relationship of these highly specific benzodiazepines to GABA mechanisms is awaited.

At the physiological level, benzodiazepines depress activity in the reticular and limbic systems while leaving the cerebral cortex relatively unaffected. In conflict-avoidance studies with rats, benzodiazepines greatly reduce the suppressive effects of punishment on behaviour without reducing the general behavioural repertoire. At higher doses in man, the benzodiazepines resemble the barbiturates in impairing psychomotor and higher mental functions. Memory disturbances are particularly profound after intravenous sedation.

Clinical use

The benzodiazepines are the drug treatment of choice in the management of anxiety, insomnia, and stress-related conditions. None of the currently available compounds has any clinically significant advantages over the others. Nevertheless, some rational choice can be made to attempt to fit the patient's symptom patterns to the pharmacokinetics of the various drugs. If a patient complains of a persisting high level of anxiety, one of the desmethyldiazepam precursors such as diazepam or clorazepate is most appropriate. Patients with fluctuating anxiety may prefer to take a shorter-acting compound, eg, oxazepam, or lorazepam, when stressful circumstances supervene or are expected.

Hypnotics should induce sleep rapidly, and their effects should not persist the next day. Both flurazepam and nitrazepam are inappropriately long acting unless a persistent anxiolytic effect is welcomed the next day. Even so, diazepam given as one dose at night may be preferred. Oxazepam penetrates the brain too slowly for a dependable hypnotic effect, but both lorazepam and temazepam are appropriate. Triazolam (which is not marketed in the United States) is thought to be the shortest-acting hypnotic currently available. Lorazepam and diazepam can also be used for relaxation procedures, for preoperative medication, and for sedation during minor operations and investigations. In dentistry, the use of a benzodiazepine renders the patient calm, conscious, and cooperative but often retrospectively amnesic for the operation.

The benzodiazepines have been widely used in management of the alcohol-withdrawal syndrome. Because cross-tolerance usually exists, large doses are often needed to suppress the withdrawal syndrome. Similarly, benzodiazepines can substitute for alcohol in the chronic alcoholic, especially in those who resort to drink to quell their anxiety-phobic symptoms. In this event, the alcoholic is being converted into a chronic benzodiazepine user, but this is much less dangerous physically, and eventual withdrawal can sometimes be attained.

Diazepam has also been used in the treatment of spasticity, tetanus, and rabies. It helps relieve muscle tension in spastic patients but does so less successfully in patients with upper-motor-neuron lesions. The use of diazepam in status epilepticus is well established (see also Chapter 9).

Unwanted effects

When a benzodiazepine is taken in high doses, tiredness, drowsiness, and a profound feeling of detachment – almost as if sleepwalking – are common but can be minimized by careful adjustment of dosage. Headache, dizziness, ataxia, confusion, and disorientation are less common but may affect the elderly in particular. Marked potentiation of the effects of alcohol occurs. Other less common unwanted effects include excessive weight gain, skin rash, menstrual irregularities, impairment of sexual function, and, rarely, agranulocytosis.

Although normal subjects clearly show psychological impairment with the benzodiazepines, the situation with anxious patients is more complex. Because anxiety itself interferes with psychological performance, alleviation of the anxiety may result in improved functioning that more than cancels the direct drug-related decrement. Even at low dosages, therefore, the effects in any patient may be complicated and unpredictable.

An increase in hostility is frequently reported by patients starting a course of treatment with a benzodiazepine. Women with small children seem particularly prone to this. For some reason oxazepam is less likely to induce hostility than is either diazepam or chlordiazepoxide. The clinical significance of this phenomenon is unclear; it is a well-known sequel of imbibing alcohol and other sedatives. Adjustment of dosage up or down usually attenuates the impulses. Curiously, some benzodiazepine-treated patients report increased anxiety and perceptual disturbances, and dosage adjustment is necessary.

Because the safety of the benzodiazepines in early pregnancy is unestablished, they should be avoided unless absolutely necessary. Diazepam is known to be secreted in breast milk and may make the baby sleepy, unresponsive, and slow to feed.

Overdosage

The benzodiazepines are extremely widely prescribed, so it is not surprising that they are used in many suicidal attempts. Adults who take overdoses of benzodiazepines reportedly do not die unless they also take other psychotropic drugs or alcohol at the same time. Typically, the patient falls asleep but is rousable and wakes after 24 or 48 hours. Despite high persisting plasma concentrations of the benzodiazepine (usually desmethyldiazepam), the patient does not feel drowsy and is fit for discharge. Treatment is supportive. Stomach lavage is usually more punitive than therapeutic, and dialysis is useless because of high plasma binding.

Tolerance and dependence

Dependence, both psychological and physical, occurs with the benzodiazepines as with other drugs in this general class. Very high doses (eg, greater than 60 mg/day of diazepam) are usually necessary before marked withdrawal (characterized by convulsions and, rarely, psychosis) can be induced. Even so, in many of these instances, other drugs or alcohol had been taken as well. Abrupt discontinuation results in withdrawal phenomena such as anxiety, agitation, restlessness, insomnia, and tension, which are usually delayed for several days because of the long half-life of the major metabolite, desmethyldiazepam. Even with the normal dosage, some patients may show withdrawal effects. The fact that some patients gradually escalate the dose suggests tolerance, the increase in dose sometimes being related to particularly stressful crises.

Psychological dependence is probably common, judging by the high incidence of repeat prescriptions, but it is also mild, as the drug-seeking behaviour is much less insistent than with the barbiturates.

OTHER DRUGS
Antipsychotic drugs
Various members of this class of drug have been advocated

100

for use in small dosage as anxiolytics. Chlorpromazine, thioridazine, trifluoperazine, and haloperidol have been studied in this regard, and useful anxiolytic properties have been established. Some patients, however, find the autonomic side effects of antipsychotic agents such as thioridazine and chlorpromazine rather troublesome, especially because such effects resemble anxiety symptoms. With the low doses suggested (less than half the antipsychotic dose), acute extrapyramidal symptoms are rare. Tardive dyskinesia is also presumed to be unlikely, but the possibility cannot be entirely discounted and should be taken into consideration. These antipsychotic drugs do not induce dependence, so their main indication is in anxious patients with previous dependence on alcohol, barbiturates, or benzodiazepines. Even then, prolonged treatment should be avoided.

Tricyclic antidepressants
Several of these drugs, such as amitriptyline, doxepin, and dothiepin, have pronounced sedative effects and are the treatment of first choice in patients with anxious or agitated depression. A once-nightly schedule also provides useful hypnotic effects. Fixed combinations of antidepressants and anxiolytics cannot be recommended.

Monoamine oxidase inhibitors (MAOI)
Patients with phobic states may show a disappointing response to benzodiazepines. Administration of an MAOI may be more successful in suppressing the panic attacks, although response may be delayed for up to six weeks. The adverse effects of these drugs—the interactions with amine-rich foodstuffs and other drugs — are dangerous, and the practitioner should use MAOIs cautiously. The antiphobic effect seems unrelated to any antidepressant action.

Other sedatives and hypnotics, and alcohol
Drugs formulated primarily as hypnotics are often used as anxiolytics as well. They include chloral hydrate, paraldehyde, glutethimide, methyprylone, and methaqualone. As a rule, however, their use should be discouraged because dependence may occur and overdose is dangerous with some. Alcohol is widely used as a "nightcap," but is not a good hypnotic; it deepens sleep for the first half of the night, but broken sleep supervenes for the second half. As an anxiolytic it is effective in some persons, but at the cost of inducing disastrous dependence.

Chlormethiazole, primarily a sedative, has been used to treat alcoholic withdrawal syndromes. It has also been found useful as a hypnotic in the elderly. Occasionally, patients become dependent on chlormethiazole.

Antihistamine drugs are often sedative, a factor that limits their use. Promethazine has been used as a hypnotic and sedative in children, but it can be associated with paradoxical overexcitement.

Beta-adrenoceptor antagonists
Widespread autonomically mediated physiological changes underlie somatic symptom mechanisms in anxious patients. It is logical, therefore, to attempt to block these symptom mechanisms with appropriate drugs. Most interest has centered on the beta-adrenoceptor antagonists ("beta blockers"). In normal persons undergoing stress situations such as public speaking, musical performance, or racing-car driving, administration of a beta blocker (eg, propranolol or oxprenolol) diminishes palpitations, tremor, and other mild physical symptoms. Performance is not impaired and may even be enhanced.

In anxious patients, beta blockade reduces heart rate more than in normal subjects. Treatment with propranolol reduces autonomic symptoms such as palpitations, sweating, and diarrhea but has little effect on physical symptoms not mediated autonomically (eg, muscle tension) or on psychological symptoms (eg, worry, tension, and fear). Overall, patients with predominantly somatic symptoms often find beta-blocking agents helpful in affording symptomatic relief. By contrast, patients who complain primarily of psychological symptoms of anxiety may find beta blockade useless. Some phobic patients with somatic symptoms find symptom removal upsetting, since they lose their "signals" concerning the effect on them of phobic situations. All the evidence suggests that any anxiolytic effect of beta blockade is mediated peripherally.

Dosage should be only enough to return the pulse rate to normal. This can be as low as 30 mg/day of propranolol in divided doses and should not normally exceed 160 mg/day. Higher doses have been advocated for the treatment of schizophrenia, but there is no controlled evidence that propranolol exerts an independent antipsychotic action, although it may have some use as an adjunct to the phenothiazines. In the high doses used (greater than 500 mg/day), central actions are present together with some antiserotonin, antidopamine, and membrane-stabilizing effects.

TREATMENT OF ANXIETY

Although this book does not purport to be a textbook of therapeutics, the topics of anxiety and insomnia can be usefully related to the psychopharmacology of the individual drugs.

In the initial treatment of anxiety, a careful assessment of aetiological factors and of the patient's personality and coping stratagems is essential. Drug treatment should be regarded as appropriate only in the context of the general management of the patient. Indeed, the anxiety symptoms in many patients are self-limiting responses to stress situations that may be temporary. Accordingly, a decision to use anxiolytic therapy should be made only after careful consideration. It is bad practice to prescribe anxiolytics routinely to patients who could be better managed by explaining the mechanisms underlying alarming symptoms such as palpitations and by reassuring the patient of the malady's temporary nature.

The difficulties arise in those patients whose acute anxiety state does not resolve within a few weeks. Sometimes the severity of the anxiety precludes spontaneous remission, and vigorous treatment with an appropriate anxiolytic is necessary. Persistent anxiety occasionally masks an underlying depression. Again, use of an anxiolytic may reveal such a condition, so that careful review a week or two after commencing therapy is important.

A major quandary confronts the practitioner concerned with the patient who is chronically anxious and has major personality traits of anxiety, tension, and general neurotic symptoms. Drug therapy can alleviate the anxiety but will not alter the severe underlying predisposition. Commencing benzodiazepine therapy in some patients may be the beginning of many years of psychological reliance on these drugs. Whether or not to embark on such a course is almost a moral decision rather than a medical one. But if a patient can be seen to function better personally, socially, and at work when taking anxiolytics than when prey to his anxieties, the use of these drugs can be justified, even in the long term.

The benzodiazepines are the mainstay of symptomatic treatment. Family-practice physicians use them to combat successfully a wide range of "functional" symptoms. The factors underlying the choice of benzodiazepine are mainly pharmacokinetic and have been discussed earlier. Doses should be very flexible both in total daily amount and in schedules, because patients vary greatly in their requirements. Antipsychotic or antidepressant medication may be successful on occasion, alone or in combination with a benzodiazepine.

Careful review is essential with such combinations.

When patients complain of somatic symptoms, beta-adrenoceptor antagonists may be appropriate. These drugs can be combined quite effectively with the benzodiazepines. The patient's symptom profile should be taken into account. Those who deny psychological symptoms but stress the somatic features of their illness should have a combination with adequate doses of propranolol or a similar drug. Patients with predominantly psychological complaints need a combination, with the accent on the centrally acting benzodiazepines.

The traditional remedy for severe panic attacks is amylobarbitone (amobarbital) sodium, up to 500 mg, intravenously or intramuscularly. Diazepam and lorazepam are also available in parenteral form, the latter having a usefully short half-life. Oral medication should be instituted as soon as possible. The current oral medication should be reviewed in an attempt to lessen the frequency and severity of the panics.

TREATMENT OF INSOMNIA

The purpose of sleep remains an enigma. Complaints about loss of sleep, unsatisfying sleep, inability to fall asleep, or early awakening can be assessed only symptomatically in the vast majority of cases. Only in a few instances can the patient be referred to a sleep laboratory.

Insomnia is a common complaint, referring to both insufficient sleep and unsatisfying sleep. At times of mental and physical stress, otherwise healthy people may have bouts of sleeplessness. Other people are chronic "poor sleepers," taking longer to fall asleep, waking more often during the night, and having more stage 2 and less REM sleep than do "good sleepers." More than 10% of adults admit to sleep difficulties. the proportion increasing with age. Mild depression, anxiety, and hypochondria are common: the more pronounced the affective changes, the worse the sleep. Thus, most moderately or severely depressed patients complain of fitful sleep with early morning wakening. Perhaps 10% to 15%, by contrast, sleep longer than normal.

Treatment of insomnia must concentrate on the primary condition, be it pain, pruritus, or a psychological condition. With depressed patients, a sedative antidepressant such as amitriptyline, doxepin, or mianserin given as a large dose at night will usually obviate the need for a separate hypnotic. Similarly, some benzodiazepines have prolonged effects: one dose at night acts both as an immediate hypnotic and as an anxiolytic the next day. For occasional use, for example with travel and time-zone changes, a short-acting benzodiazepine is preferable.

A common cause of insomnia, paradoxically, is the routine administration of hypnotics. If the drug is taken intermittently or the dose is not kept constant, mild withdrawal symptoms may ensue, insomnia among them. Hypnotics should not be administered routinely to patients admitted to hospital or to those with mild physical conditions or stress responses. Many chronic users of hypnotics date their initiation to just such a well-meaning but unnecessary prescription. Nevertheless, there is no clear boundary between those whose insomnia is secondary to mild affective disturbance and those who are "poor sleepers." Each practitioner must decide where that boundary lies and whether hypnotics are justified.

THE YOUNG, THE OLD, AND THE PHYSICALLY ILL

The anxiolytics make some children worse, and there is little evidence that the drugs are useful in minor neurotic disturbances marked by disturbed sleep and anxiety. In children with situational anxiety such as school phobia, the impairment of intellectual function may outweigh any emotional benefit.

Barbiturates and benzodiazepines are tolerated less well in the elderly than in the young but are nevertheless widely used. Confusional states and paradoxical agitation are common following barbiturate use and can attend the use of benzodiazepines. Elderly people complain particularly of insomnia, but hypnotics should be used judiciously in short courses related to definite periods of stress. To avoid cumulative toxicity, short-acting benzodiazepines or a chloral derivative are preferable.

In general, glucuronide conjugation is less affected in liver disease than are oxidative processes. Consequently, in patients with liver damage, the 3-hydroxylated derivatives such as lorazepam are preferable.

SOCIAL IMPLICATIONS

Finally, what are the implications of the widespread use of anxiolytics? Both in the United States and in the United Kingdom, almost 20% of women and 10% of men have recourse to anxiolytics or hypnotics during the course of one year. About 12% of men and 5% of women use the drugs regularly for one month or more. Anxiolytics are high on the list of repeat prescriptions. Furthermore, psychotropic drug usage as a percentage of all drugs prescribed is rising steadily.

There is no doubt that patients find these drugs helpful in assuaging anxiety and ensuring sleep; family physicians are satisfied that useful symptomatic relief is obtained. Whether this extent of drug usage is something that society can tolerate without seeking to modify the economic and social roots of those symptomatic responses is a political question. Nevertheless, it is a medical duty to apprise the public of the facts concerning the extensive usage and the merits and disadvantages of these drugs.

FURTHER READING

Balter MB, Levine J, Manheimer DI: Cross-national study of the extent of anti-anxiety/sedative drug use. *N Engl J Med 290*:769-774, 1974.

Bloom FE: Neural mechanisms of benzodiazepine actions. *Am J Psychiatry 134*:669-672, 1977.

Braestrup C, Squires RF: Specific benzodiazepine receptors in rat brain characterized by high-affinity ^{3}H-diazepam binding. *Proc Natl Acad Sci (USA) 74*:3805-3809, 1977.

Curry SH, Whelpton R: Pharmacokinetics of closely related benzodiazepines. *Br J Clin Pharmacol 8* (suppl 1):15-22, 1979.

Dusken MW, Chang SS, Casper RC, Davis JM: Barbiturate-facilitated interviewing. *Biol Psychiatry 14*:421-432, 1979.

Greenblatt DJ, Shader RI: *Benzodiazepines in Clinical Practice.* New York, Raven Press, 1974.

Lader MH, Bond AJ, James DC: Clinical comparison of anxiolytic drug therapy. *Psychol Med 4:* 381-387, 1974.

Lasagna L: The role of benzodiazepines in non-psychiatric medical practice. *Am J Psychiatry 134*:656-658, 1977.

Marks J: *The Benzodiazepines: Use, Overuse, Misuse, Abuse.* Lancaster, MTP, 1978.

Oswald I: Sleep difficulties. *Br Med J 1*:557-558, 1975.

Palmer GC: Use, overuse, misuse, and abuse of benzodiazepines. *Ala J Med Sci 15*:383-392, 1978.

Rickels K: Use of antianxiety agents in anxious outpatients. *Psychopharmacology 58*:1-17, 1978.

Shader RI, Greenblatt DJ: Clinical implications of benzodiazepine pharmacokinetics. *Am J Psychiatry 134*:652-656, 1977.

Tyrer P: Towards rational therapy with monoamine oxidase inhibitors. *Br J Psychiatry 128*:354-360, 1976.

Miscellaneous Drugs

AMPHETAMINES

Drugs such as caffeine, cocaine, and ephedrine induce a sense of well-being, increase alertness, and combat fatigue. In many instances these properties have been known for thousands of years. Amphetamine is a modern synthetic drug developed in the 1920s as a substitute for ephedrine. It was widely used in World War II, and Japan was left with vast stocks that were sold openly. An epidemic of abuse followed. The lack of true antidepressant effect together with the drug's propensity to cause dependence has led to a restriction in the use of amphetamine. Nevertheless, the drug is of key importance in psychopharmacology, being relevant to the mechanisms of action of antipsychotic and antidepressant drugs.

Pharmacokinetics

Because of the high lipid solubility of its nonionized form, amphetamine is readily absorbed from the intestine and it penetrates rapidly to the brain. It is eliminated partly by renal excretion and partly by biotransformation. At usual urinary pH, about 20% to 50% of the drug is excreted unchanged, the biological half-life being 6 to 12 hours. Under acid urinary conditions, excretion is enhanced because the drug is in its ionized form and hence cannot be reabsorbed by means of the tubules. The biological half-life is thus curtailed – a fact that can be put to practical use by acidifying the urine of subjects intoxicated with amphetamine.

Amphetamine is extensively metabolized, with some quantitative differences between the D- and L-isomers. In man, the phenyl ring can be hydroxylated to form p-hydroxyamphetamine; aliphatic oxidation to yield norephedrine can also occur. Both products are biologically active. The further metabolite p-hydroxynorephedrine can be taken up by adrenergic neurons and released as a false transmitter.

Pharmacology

Amphetamine is an indirectly acting sympathomimetic agent that releases dopamine and noradrenaline from nerve terminals. It also blocks the re-uptake of catecholamines, inhibits monoamine oxidase, and acts directly on catecholamine receptors and on serotonin receptors. In the striatum, but not elsewhere, amphetamine decreases dopamine synthesis. The drug activates the diffuse projection systems both upwards to the cerebral cortex and downwards to the brain stem and spinal cord. Peripherally, sympathetic activity is increased; eg, the heart rate increases, blood vessels constrict, and bronchi dilate.

Behavioural effects comprise enhanced locomotor activity, alertness, formation of conditioned reflexes, and self-stimulation, all of which are probably mainly related to noradrenergic pathways. Stereotyped behaviours in animals – sniffing, gnawing, and running in circles – are probably mediated through dopaminergic pathways. Social factors such as aggregation influence the effects. D-amphetamine is generally more active than the L-isomer – in some instances three to ten times more active.

Amphetamine can be either counteracted or potentiated by barbiturates, depending on dose ratio and mode of administration. Although reserpine pretreatment (which depletes aminergic neurons of their neurotransmitters) prevents the peripheral effects of amphetamine, some central effects such as the stereotypies are resistant. Antipsychotic drugs prevent most effects of amphetamine by competitive antagonism at the various pertinent receptors. Tricyclic antidepressants and MAOIs potentiate amphetamine.

Effects in normal subjects

Amphetamine counteracts mental and physical fatigue, especially that associated with sustained tasks. Performance can be improved, sometimes beyond that previously achieved without the aid of amphetamine, by boosting the subject's confidence. Mood is euphoric, but dysphoric reactions are sometimes encountered. Sympathetic stimulation is apparent, together with insomnia, anorexia, and a rise in body temperature. Slow-wave and REM sleep are reduced, with a "rebound" when the drug is discontinued. EEG changes are otherwise minimal.

Clinical effects

Amphetamine in doses of 5 to 20 mg/day (half that for dexamphetamine) was widely used as a symptomatic treatment for depression before the introduction of the tricyclic antidepressants. However, controlled studies have shown amphetamine to have no appreciable effects greater than placebo in any but the most mildly ill patients. Combining amphetamine with barbiturate renders it a little more effective but still insufficient to be of much clinical significance. Amphetamine is also of little use in combatting withdrawal and inactivity in chronic schizophrenics, in whom it may intensify delusions and hallucinations.

Amphetamine and some of its derivatives, notably methylphenidate, have proved useful in the management of so-called hyperactive or hyperkinetic children, who are typically restless, quarrelsome, irritable, and inattentive. Amphetamine has somewhat paradoxical effects in children, increasing the attention span and lessening antisocial behaviour. Not all hyperkinetic children benefit: those who do are more likely to have signs of "minimal brain dysfunction," including abnormal EEGs. However, improvement may not persist despite continued treatment. There has also been a tendency, especially in the United States, to overdiagnose the condition and to administer methylphenidate to boys who are simply mischievous and unruly rather than actually brain damaged.

Side effects of amphetamine and methylphenidate in children include insomnia, tearfulness, rebound irritability, toxic psychosis, and personality change. Anorexia, weight loss, and growth inhibition may occur when methylphenidate is taken in doses greater than 0.5 mg/kg of body weight.

Amphetamine and many basically similar derivatives have been used in the treatment of obesity because of their ability to suppress appetite, but such use is unwarranted because the diminution in appetite is usually short-lived (two to four weeks) and the risk of psychological dependence is very high. Amphetamine has also been used as an adjuvant in the management of parkinsonism and epilepsy as well as to treat narcolepsy. The latter is probably the only undisputed indication, but even for that purpose it is being replaced by tricyclic antidepressants such as clomipramine.

Unwanted effects
The main unwanted effects are sympathetic overstimulation, anxiety, insomnia, and tension. After higher doses, stereotyped behaviour and transient psychotic disturbances may occur (see also page 66). Chronic consumption carries a considerable risk of psychological dependence, yet many patients are able to take low daily doses of amphetamine for years, evidently without ill effects. Withdrawal of medication is often associated with depressed mood, drowsiness, increased appetite, and REM-sleep rebound, signs that could be interpreted as indicating physical dependence. Widespread epidemics of amphetamine misuse have occurred. Middle-aged, miserable, bored, overweight housewives who take three to four tablets every day and teenagers who take many tablets for "kicks" are part of the abuse spectrum.

Other derivatives
The effects of amphetamine on central stimulation, appetite, body temperature, and autonomic activity can be independently varied by manipulative substitution on the parent phenylethylamine molecule. The most potent stimulant, methamphetamine, is obtained by substitution of a methyl group into the terminal amino group. Other effective stimulants with little autonomic activity, such as methylphenidate and pipradrol, have larger substituents in the side chain but are not useful in depression.

Some appetite suppressants, such as phenmetrazine and phentermine, also cause stimulation and have been abused. They have therefore been superseded by derivatives with less stimulant properties. Halogen substitution into the ring structure has resulted in chlorphentermine and fenfluramine. Nevertheless, some central effects remain, and use of the drugs as appetite suppressants is a practice open to debate.

HALLUCINOGENS
Of the many names for this group of compounds – psychotomimetics, hallucinogens, phantastica, psychedelics, psycholytics – none are entirely apposite. Moreover, these drugs do not form a distinct class. Under certain conditions, especially at high dosage, many of them can induce illusions, hallucinations, paranoid ideas and delusions, and mood changes. Among these are the anticholinergic drugs, antimalarial agents, corticosteroids, narcotic antagonists, cocaine, and amphetamines. Thus, hallucinogenic drugs can be arrayed on a continuum from amphetamine and the "true" hallucinogens at one end to anticholinergics and others that are less predictably psychosis-inducing. Impaired consciousness, an effect of all such drugs, becomes a relatively more important feature of each step in the continuum.

Historical background
Man has frequently resorted to drugs in his quest for unusual mental experiences. Psychoactive plants were often eaten in association with religious and mystical ceremonies, a practice that still persists in some places. In the pre-Columbian cultures of Mesoamerica, mescaline found in the Mexican dumpling cactus was used in pagan rites; it still plays a part in the rituals of certain native religious sects in the southwestern United States. In 1888, Lewin described the psychological effects of the cactus, which were brought to the attention of a wider audience in this century by Aldous Huxley.

The modern era of study was ushered in by Hofmann's accidental discovery of the powerful psychological effects of minute amounts of the ergot derivative d-lysergic acid diethyl-amide (LSD, lysergide). While preparing the compound he experienced vivid hallucinations. About 20 years of intensive research followed, directed at the theoretical implications of a "model psychosis" and at therapeutic applications. Neither line of research has fulfilled its early promise, and interest in this group of drugs has waned.

Lysergide (LSD)

LSD has a fairly short half-life in man – about three hours. Brain concentrations are two to five times higher in the hypothalamus and visual and auditory centres of the midbrain than in the cerebral cortex. In man, maximal effects occur about four hours after ingestion, at the time when bodily concentrations are no longer detectable. LSD is almost completely metabolized.

The mechanism of action of LSD is unclear. It increases the responsiveness of the brain-stem reticular system to input from sensory collaterals without altering the threshold to direct stimulation. Although 5-hydroxytryptamine mechanisms undoubtedly affect the process, LSD is not a simple 5-hydroxytryptamine antagonist. Receptors on serotonergic raphé cells are much more sensitive to LSD than are the post-synaptic serotonergic receptors, although both are equally sensitive to 5-hydroxytryptamine. LSD is therefore believed to exert its effects by inhibiting serotonergic cells directly, leading to decreased synthesis, release, and turnover of 5-hydroxytryptamine in the brain. This in turn switches on certain systems that are normally inhibited. LSD also interacts with dopaminergic systems, but the mechanisms are complex and unclear. Antagonism of LSD effects by antipsychotic agents such as chlorpromazine is probably related to both 5-hydroxytryptamine and dopamine mechanisms.

LSD produces marked sympathomimetic effects such as tachycardia, pupillary dilatation, and rise in blood pressure. Larger doses also induce piloerection, protrusion of the eyeballs, and hyperglycemia. Hyperthermia, anorexia, nausea, tremor, numbness, and muscle weakness may occur as well.

Clinical effects

Somatic symptoms appear within a few minutes after the oral ingestion of LSD. Other effects are more variable, depending on such factors as dose, time after ingestion, personality and expectations of the subject, and setting in which the drug is given. Many of the somatic features such as nausea subside before the onset of the subjective phenomena, but the autonomic effects, especially pupillary dilatation, tend to persist.

Affective changes are common. Apprehension to the extent of panic attacks is usual, and the entire experience may be overshadowed by a feeling of ineffable dread. The mood is often labile, with alternations of euphoria and depression or, more extremely, exaltation and suicidal despair. Suspicion and paranoid ideas dominate the thoughts of some LSD-treated subjects, who display withdrawn or hostile behaviour.

A rich kaleidoscope of perceptual changes may be induced, especially in the more experienced user. Subjectively, the drug taker experiences heightened perception, but objective testing usually reveals deficits. All the senses (especially vision) may be affected. The subject's sense of perspective becomes distorted so that the foreground may appear to recede. Moving objects may seem still, and motionless objects ceaselessly moving. Recurrent waves of visual illusions such as micropsia may occur or the distortion may remain for minutes at a time. Surface irregularities may become distorted so that a leather surface, for example, seems honeycombed. One or more colours appear vivid, and colour contrasts may alternate from a pleasing blend to a jarring juxtaposition.

Auditory illusions include sounds that seem either amplified or distant and muffled. Tactile illusions include the sensation of smooth objects feeling rough, and vice versa, a freezingly cold object feeling very hot, and still objects appearing to be in perpetual motion. Distortions of body image are common: limbs may feel shrunken to vestiges or swollen to elephantine proportions. A limb may feel disjointed from the body and seem to be floating around on its own. Erotic sensations are uncommon. Dissolution of ego boundaries has been reported to occur after the ingestion of large doses; the subject typically loses his sense of individuality.

Common effects are associations between sensory experiences (synaesthesiae) – colours are said to be "heard," and sounds to be "felt." Subjective time is grossly distorted, with events seeming to occur in random sequence. Time may seem suspended.

Visual hallucinations, which occur mainly after higher doses, are elaborations of visual illusions. The hallucinations tend to be rather unorganized, vivid, colourful, geometric, and patterned. More-structured hallucinations, such as seeing saints, are generally associated with religious drug-taking ceremonies. Auditory, tactile, and gustatory hallucinations are uncommon.

Vivid thoughts and associations may stream past the subject as in a reverie. This "thought-flow" experience may lead the subject to believe he is reliving his past. This distortion of awareness may become more pronounced at higher dose levels, culminating in a delirious state.

The subject's thought processes may be disrupted with indecision, distractibility, and lack of concentration. Slowness and poverty of thought or, conversely, rapid, disjointed thought may occur. Thinking becomes loose, slipshod, and illogical, and the subject may become so introspective as to refuse to talk. Ideas of persecution, influence, or grandeur may be apparent but full-blown delusions are rare. The subject usually retains insight, attributing his mental changes to the drug, but at high dose levels, insight is lost as delirium supervenes.

Medical use: LSD has been used:
1. As an abreactive agent to facilitate the release of emotional feelings.
2. To accelerate the progress of patients in psychoanalysis when they seem "blocked."
3. For regular administration in group therapy sessions to release inhibitions.
4. For the induction of a single, mind-expanding, psychedelic experience, claimed to be of therapeutic use.

Practically all psychiatric illnesses were claimed at one time or another to respond to LSD, but very few controlled clinical trials were carried out. Disillusion with the therapeutic effects has set in and very few centres still use the drug.

Nonmedical use: The medical enthusiasm for LSD was paralleled by lay claims that the transcendental and mystical aspects of its use were of great value to individuals who were not mentally ill. In the United States, the use of "acid" reached its peak in the late 1960s but has now declined. In most Western countries, LSD and other hallucinogens are subject to stringent legislation, but illicit supplies are usually available.

The decline in popularity follows a fuller recognition of the hazards and unpleasant effects of the drug. "Bad trips" often frighten the drug experimenter, and he also realizes that increased self-realization is unlikely. The general pattern is for a "trip" every few weeks or months, but the chronic users ("acid heads") take the drug once or more per week, and because tolerance develops rapidly, often in large doses. Such users may become passive and inert, unemployed, and unemployable. Their numbers are very small in most countries.

Adverse effects: A high degree of tolerance to LSD develops after a few doses. As it can be lost equally rapidly, restarting use after an interval may result in overdose.

The commonest adverse effect is a "bad trip," which resembles a toxic delirium. The patient should be nursed in a quiet environment, with support and reassurance from a friend. Phenothiazines and benzodiazepines may be helpful. These reactions are unpredictable, occurring even in chronic users.

During the phase of LSD intoxication, the subject may be a danger to himself and to others. Some bizarre crimes and accidental deaths have occurred, and profound depression may lead to suicidal attempts. Prolonged psychoses have been associated with LSD, but in some cases at least, an insidious psychosis antedated LSD use. "Flashbacks" are re-experiences of drug-induced phenomena that occur without further ingestion of the drug and can occur months after the "last trip." Their mechanism is unknown.

The association between LSD usage and chromosomal damage was never convincingly established nor is the importance of such damage fully evaluated.

Other hallucinogens

Mescaline is 3,4,5-trimethoxyphenylethylamine, one of the many alkaloids in the peyote cactus. Mescal buttons are the dried tops of these cacti. Mescaline is active in doses of 5 to 15 mg, its effects lasting 9 to 12 hours. It is more likely than LSD to induce vomiting and is therefore less popular in the so-called drug culture.

Psilocybin is a tryptamine derivative and is also found in fungi. It resembles LSD in its actions but is shorter lasting.

Bufotenine is a hallucinogenic indole derivative found in cohoba snuff and in the skin and parotid gland of the toad *Bufo marinus*.

Dimethyltryptamine, also found in cohoba snuff, induces LSD-like symptoms of shorter duration but with more-definite sympathetic effects. It occurs naturally in mammalian brain and is detectable in human plasma and urine. Urinary excretion is elevated in psychotic states, especially schizophrenia, and may be a useful marker of nonspecific psychotic intensity. Whether it can be formed in the brain in psychotomimetic amounts is unknown.

Lysergic acid monoethylamide is present in the seeds of the morning glory climbing plant. In low doses it is sedative; at higher doses it is mildly hallucinogenic.

108

Harmine, an alkaloid from a South American vine, is a mild hallucinogen but it induces marked somatic reactions, nausea, and vomiting. *Nutmeg* is also credited with these effects. *Phencyclidine* is related to pethidine and induces marked sensory blockade. Its use in anaesthesia was curtailed because many patients hallucinated after its use. It is currently widely misused as "PCP" or "angel dust."

Dimethoxymethylamphetamine (DOM) is also known as STP – "Serenity, Tranquility, and Peace." Its effects last longer than those of LSD, and it has recently been banned in many countries.

Anticholinergic drugs in high doses can induce a psychotic state accompanied by clouding of consciousness, so they are not true hallucinogens. One group of compounds, the piperidyl benzilates, are both anticholinergic and hallucinogenic, but orientation and contact with reality are usually impaired by the drugs.

A wide variety of *intoxicants* exist, among them alcohol, anaesthetics, and many organic chemical solvents. Intoxicant-induced hallucinations occur in clear consciousness only after prolonged abuse.

Marihuana is an active preparation from the easily grown plant *Cannabis sativa*. Other names include hashish, bhang, ganja, "pot," and "grass." The major active constituent is 1-Δ⁹-tetrahydrocannabinol, although there are other active alkaloids. The biochemical basis for marihuana effects is poorly understood, but the cholinergic, catecholaminergic, and serotonergic pathways are implicated.

The clinical effects range from a sense of relaxed well-being and euphoria at low doses to hallucinogenic effects at very high doses. Adverse effects include panic and dysphoric reactions and, rarely, full-blown toxic psychoses. An "amotivational syndrome" has been described as occurring among chronic users, characterized by passivity, preoccupation with drug-taking, and declining drive, ambition, and academic performance. The role of marihuana in this syndrome is unclear.

Model Psychoses

The concept of a model psychosis is an old one, being implicit in the humoral theories of affect. Many psychiatrists and psychologists have experimented with a long list of drugs, hoping by this means to gain insights into the mechanisms of mental illnesses and thereby to develop cures. Schizophrenia has been a particular focus of interest (see also page 56). The approach has always seemed fruitful, especially since the dis-

covery of the modern psychotropic drugs. However, the hallucinogens have not provided a very useful research tool, certainly not with respect to schizophrenia, because many of the fundamental phenomena of the disorder (such as thought interference, autochthonous delusions, and elaborate auditory hallucinations) are not generally induced by the drugs. Although consciousness and orientation are not formally disordered, the sensorium is not as clear as in the functional psychoses. Schizophrenic patients are able to differentiate between their usual mental phenomena and those induced by hallucinogens.

In parallel with disappointment with the therapeutic potential of the hallucinogens, there has been increasing realization that the key to schizophrenia, mania, and depression does not lie with these drugs. However, much research was triggered by the discovery and development of the hallucinogens.

COCAINE

Cocaine is an active constituent of the leaves of the South American plant *Erythroxylon coca*. Chewing the leaves produces a feeling of energy and drive, decreased fatigue and appetite, and mild euphoria. The drug was introduced in the late 19th century as a substitute for morphine but was found to have its own problems of abuse, including severe psychological dependence.

Cocaine is metabolized mainly by serum esterases. When administered intravenously, its plasma half-life is about 20 minutes, but when applied to the nasal mucosa by sniffing, peak concentrations are attained at one hour and effects wear off more slowly. Cocaine acts primarily on catecholaminergic systems, particularly by powerfully inhibiting the re-uptake of monoamines. It has little effect in releasing amines, but it is an MAOI. Dopamine is particularly affected, which may relate to the increased motor activity induced by cocaine.

OPIATES

Opiate analgesics are not strictly classifiable as psychotropic agents, but recent advances in our understanding of their mechanisms of action have thrown light on problems of narcotic dependence, which are the province of the psychiatrist. Even so, the complexity of opiate actions is already apparent, and no simple answers to dependence are likely.

Opium has been in use for several thousand years since the

days of the Sumerians. The ancient Greek and Arab physicians and later the Chinese knew of its powers. By the 19th century it was widely available in Britain and the United States as a constituent of many patent medicines, pain killers, and cough cures. Its use was widespread in society, but by the late 19th century campaigns had started to ban its use. Despite restrictions on the use and prescription of opium and related substances, opiate derivatives, heroin in particular, are widely available illicitly. Users of illegal opiates in the United States may be numbered in the hundreds of thousands; in the United Kingdom there are probably fewer than 5,000.

Opiate receptors

Opiates are fairly complex alkaloids, existing in laevo and dextrorotatory forms, only the former being active. Quite minor modifications in the molecule can lead to the production of opiate antagonists or drugs with mixed agonist-antagonist actions. All these factors favoured the possibility that the opiates bind to specific receptors in the nervous system. Specific binding has indeed been demonstrated, and the affinity of opiates for these receptors parallels their clinical potencies.

The opiate binding sites are differentially distributed in the brain, being concentrated in areas known to affect pain transmission, such as in the dorsal horn of the spinal cord and in the grey matter surrounding the fourth ventricle, the aqueduct of Sylvius, and the third ventricle. The striatum and amygdala are also rich in opiate receptors and may be concerned with motor and emotional effects of the opiates.

The existence of such specific receptors strongly suggested that an endogenous opiate-like substance must exist as the natural binding transmitter or "ligand." However, opiate antagonists have few actions of their own, so blockade of those receptors did not seem operative unless the system is activated, ie, an endogenous ligand is being produced. In 1974, Hughes and Kosterlitz in Aberdeen reported the existence of an opiate-like substance in the brain; the effects of the substance were reversible by the antagonist naloxone. Subsequently they identified two pentapeptides, which they termed "enkephalins": methionine-enkephalin (H-tyrosine-glycine-glycine-phenylalanine-methionine-OH); and leucine-enkephalin, which differs only in the substitution of leucine for methionine. The distribution of these pentapeptides parallels that of the opiate receptors.

Hughes and his colleagues noted that the methionine-enkephalin sequence occurs in the C-fragment of β-lipotropin, a pituitary peptide thought to act as a prohormone for melanocyte-stimulating hormone (MSH). Various fragments of the peptide also have opiate-like activity; all are now being termed "endorphins." The complex relationships among these various peptides are under active investigation. The enkephalins are too rapidly degraded to be of practical use as analgesics, but some endorphins produce powerful, prolonged analgesia. Synthetic derivatives are being developed and tested.

A further product of the identification of opiate receptor-rich regions of the nervous system has been the finding that quite brief electrical stimulation in these areas can provide relief of pain for several hours. Stimulation-produced analgesia can be partially reversed by naloxone and shows cross tolerance to opiates.

Tolerance to opiates develops rapidly in the course of use, and abstinence phenomena on withdrawal are also soon established. By contrast, sensitivity to antagonists tends to increase with chronic use of the agonist opiate. Pharmacokinetic factors such as more rapid metabolism do not account for tolerance. One current theory relates to the development of some form of denervation supersensitivity. By binding to the opiate receptor, opiates might result in decreased firing of the presynaptic neuron, resulting in supersensitivity of the developing receptors so that more opiate is required. On withdrawal of the opiate, supersensitivity becomes overt, with abstinence phenomena due to overactivity of the systems. Variations on this theory suggest that either the number of receptors increases or the receptors develop a higher affinity for the ligand, or that the receptor becomes differentially sensitive to antagonists as opposed to agonists. Other theories focus on the production of endorphins, which are hypothesized to increase in concentration as tolerance develops to morphine. Withdrawal of the morphine would therefore result in excessive endorphin and consequent overactivity of the systems.

Finally, the role of endorphins in emotional mechanisms is being evaluated. Claims that endorphins become altered during stress responses and in manic-depressive patients in parallel with mood need verification. Opiate antagonists and the endorphins have been tried in various psychiatric conditions, but controlled evaluations have failed to demonstrate any consistent effects.

Drugs Used in Treating Opiate Dependence

Methadone: The use of methadone directly reflects drug legislation in various countries. In the United Kingdom, heroin can be prescribed for addicts by certain designated specialists; in the United States, however, the drug cannot normally be prescribed for addicts. Management of the problem has two aims: first to help the addict stop his habit; second, and more important, to prevent the habit from spreading to other people.

In countries where maintenance heroin is legally available, the covert assumption seems to be that treatment of the individual patient is unsatisfactory but, by giving him appropriate supplies, he will not seek access to illegal sources. The approach has been fairly successful, as witnessed by the small number of addicts in the United Kingdom and the slow growth of the problem. In the United States, the legislative view has prevailed and heroin dependence is a crime. Despite draconian penalties, heroin remains available and very expensive and there are thousands of addicts.

The introduction of methadone was based on the assumption that cellular changes occur in the addict who then needs maintenance opiate. Methadone merely substitutes for the heroin. However, it is longer acting and can be given by mouth. Consequently, its action should be smoother and devoid of the "highs" that follow intravenous injection. Furthermore, the euphoriant "buzz" that follows such an injection is thought to be blocked because of prior occupancy of receptors by methadone. Nevertheless, the addict is still dependent on an opiate, albeit a safer and more convenient one. Some addicts function better on methadone, but withdrawal is still a problem. Overall, it is doubtful if maintenance with methadone has many medical, as opposed to legal, advantages.

Narcotic antagonists: These drugs occupy the opiate receptors in the central nervous system, thereby preventing narcotics from exercising their effects. Some of the earlier antagonists such as nalorphine are also partial agonists, but recently developed compounds (particularly naltrexone) are more specifically antagonist.

The use of opiate antagonists should result in heroin and other narcotics losing almost all their effect. Repeated use of heroin should not lead to dependence nor discontinuation to withdrawal syndromes. In practice, naltrexone can produce blockade for up to 24 hours. The obvious problem is motivation, and long-acting injectable forms may be necessary.

DRUGS USED IN TREATING ALCOHOLISM

The pharmacological aspects of alcohol are those of a nonspecific central nervous system depressant, and little is known of the biochemical and physiological mechanisms involved. Alcohol dependence is a large and complex topic outside the scope of this book, but some of the drugs used in treating the disorder are relevant.

Disulfiram blocks the breakdown of the intermediary compound acetaldehyde. When ethyl alcohol is given to a subject pretreated with disulfiram, the bodily concentrations of acetaldehyde rapidly increase. Within minutes the patient's face reddens, his head throbs, and a vascular-type headache occurs. Nausea, vomiting, tightness of breath, sweating, thirst, hypotension, fainting, blurred vision, and vertigo are common. The effects last 30 minutes to several hours.

The effectiveness of disulfiram depends on regular self-administration by the alcoholic and then his reluctance to experience the acetaldehyde reaction. Motivation is obviously important.

Citrated calcium carbimide is a similar compound. Other drugs that can interact with alcohol include the antiprotozoal agent metronidazole and certain hypoglycemic sulfonylureas.

ANTICONVULSANTS

Introduction

The nature of epilepsy is unclear, its clinical expression varied, and the classification of seizures still a matter for debate. Many classes of anticonvulsant drugs have been developed, and it is unlikely that they have a simple common mode of action. There is still considerable ignorance of their biochemical and physiological mechanisms. Attempts to develop experimental models of natural epilepsy have employed convulsant drugs, electroshock, localized irritative lesions, and unusual genetically determined convulsive disorders in animals. None of these models are satisfactory, and the anticonvulsant potential of a new drug can be established only by careful clinical testing.

The earlier anticonvulsants still in use, the barbiturates and the hydantoins, are structurally similar; they are derived by the condensation of urea with malonic acid and glycolic acid respectively. Later introductions, the oxazolidine diones (eg, trimethadione), acetylureas (eg, phenacemide) and succinimides (eg, ethosuximide) were obtained by systematic modification of the original structures. Useful anticonvulsant activity has also been found in some carbonic anhydrase inhibitors (acetazolamide, sulthiame), benzodiazepines (diazepam, clonazepam), carbamazepine, and sodium valproate. Corticosteroids and amphetamines have also been used in the treatment of epilepsy.

Pharmacokinetics
Most anticonvulsants are readily absorbed, peak concentrations being reached in a few hours. An exception is phenytoin, which is poorly water-soluble, and the amount absorbed from various proprietary formulations can vary considerably; variable absorption can result in toxicity on the one hand and lack of convulsion control on the other. Most anticonvulsants are plasma-albumin bound to some extent, the brain concentrations reflecting those in plasma water.

Anticonvulsants are metabolized in the liver, mostly by hydroxylation, and are then excreted in the kidneys in either free or conjugated form. Only 5% of phenytoin but up to 30% of phenobarbitone is excreted unchanged. Primidone is partly metabolized to phenobarbitone, which has a much longer half-life. Diazepam and trimethadione also have active metabolites. Because many anticonvulsants have long plasma half-lives, once-daily administration is feasible.

It is now possible to measure most plasma anticonvulsant concentrations, and more rational use of these drugs is being attained. Optimum ranges have been established for the most widely used anticonvulsants: 10 to 20 ng/ml for phenytoin, 15 to 40 ng/ml for phenobarbitone, 40 to 80 ng/ml for ethosuximide, and 4 to 10 ng/ml for carbamazepine. These ranges allow the most effective control of seizures, although some patients manage quite well at lower levels. However, toxicity may supervene at supraoptimal levels. Moreover, the combination of one or more anticonvulsants does not usually result in better clinical control. A better strategy is to monitor the plasma concentration of the drug of choice so that the optimal range is maintained.

Pharmacology
Anticonvulsants have a variety of effects on different types of convulsions and on neuronal and trans-synaptic function, and their mechanisms are probably varied. In contrast to phenobarbitone and trimethadione, phenytoin does not increase the seizure threshold. Instead, it limits the development and propagation of the seizure discharge without influencing the focus itself. Phenytoin stabilizes many excitable membranes; for example, it slows conduction time along peripheral nerves and reduces post-tetanic potentiation within spinal cord synapses.

Cerebral monoamines, 5-hydroxytryptamine in particular, are operative in some seizure mechanisms. Elevation of 5-hydroxytryptamine concentrations by the administration of an MAOI or a 5-hydroxytryptamine precursor, or the two combined, raises the seizure threshold, as do many anticonvulsants, including phenobarbitone and phenytoin. Similarly, diazepam, clonazepam, and sodium valproate have recently been shown to raise the threshold. Alterations in catecholamine disposition are much less pronounced, but some anticonvulsants raise concentrations of HVA, the dopamine metabolite, in the cerebrospinal fluid. Toxic levels of phenytoin are occasionally associated with dyskinesias similar to those seen with neuroleptics.

Another neurotransmitter under study is GABA (see page 26). Concentrations of this powerful inhibitory transmitter can be elevated in the brain after treatment with anticonvulsants, but not invariably. Similarly, a decrease in the concentration of the excitatory transmitter glutamic acid has been reported to occur after anticonvulsant drug treatment. Finally, phenobarbitone, phenytoin, and primidone occasionally cause folate-deficiency megaloblastic anemia. It is interesting that folate itself has some epileptogenic properties.

Clinical actions
There have been few clinical trials of anticonvulsants except of those introduced recently, and often they are assessed as adjuncts to current therapy. The various types of epilepsy respond differentially to the various drugs: phenobarbitone, phenytoin, and primidone, for example, are used most commonly to manage generalized major and focal epilepsy. The potentialities of one drug should be fully explored before combinations are resorted to. As noted, plasma drug estimations are invaluable in selecting a drug. If the first-choice drugs are ineffective either alone or in combination, others such as sodium valproate or carbamazepine can be tried. Primidone, sulthiame, and carbamazepine may have some advantage in the treatment of psychomotor epilepsy. Petit mal attacks respond best to sodium valproate or ethosuximide. Sodium valproate and clonazepam are most effective in the minor motor epilepsy of childhood ("infantile spasms"), steroids being reserved for severe cases. Intravenously administered diazepam is the standard therapy for status epilepticus, but clonazepam, sodium amylobarbitone, and phenytoin are sometimes used.

The anticonvulsants have effects on behaviour that are not secondary to their control of seizures. They reduce anxiety, irritability, and depression in nonepileptic subjects. Sulthiame reduces disturbed behavior, especially aggressiveness, in intellectually subnormal patients whether or not they have epilepsy. Phenytoin and, particularly, carbamazepine may provide successful pain relief in syndromes such as trigeminal neuralgia and thalamic pain.

Unwanted effects

Anticonvulsant drugs have numerous unwanted effects. Minor side effects include drowsiness, dysarthria, ataxia, and nausea. Phenytoin commonly causes hirsutism and gum hypertrophy. More serious effects include cerebellar degeneration, peripheral neuropathy, Dupuytren's contracture, benign lymphadenopathy, disseminated lupus erythematosus, osteomalacia, and megaloblastic anemia. The latter two may be due to induced metabolism in the liver of vitamin D and folic acid, respectively.

The anticonvulsants interact with many other drugs. Phenytoin is highly bound to plasma albumin and can displace drugs such as tricyclic antidepressants from their receptor sites. Most anticonvulsants are powerful inducers of hepatic microsomal enzymes and accelerate the metabolism of many substances, including steroid hormones, oral anticoagulants, digitoxin, and many psychotropic drugs. Metabolic interactions among the anticonvulsants are complex; usually induction results in low levels of all the agents administered, but occasionally competition can result in slow metabolism, high concentrations, and toxicity.

The infants of epileptic mothers show an increased incidence of malformations, namely harelip and cleft palate, heart lesions, and minor skeletal abnormalities, which are probably related to the mother's use of anticonvulsant medication during pregnancy.

Anticonvulsant medication may also be associated with subtle mental changes and even intellectual deterioration and frank psychiatric illness. Polypharmacy should be avoided and plasma concentrations monitored.

DRUGS AND DEMENTIA

Dementia in later life is associated with progressive neuronal degeneration, the cause of which is usually obscure. For that reason, no rational treatment is possible nor have successful empirical treatments been developed as for the psychoses. The dementias fall into two broad groups, those associated with cerebral arteriosclerosis and those in which primary degeneration of the neurons occurs. In many cases both processes coexist. However, whatever its origin, dementia is associated with a decrease in cerebral blood flow, and oxygen uptake with a shift to anaerobic modes of metabolism. Until recently, drug therapy was aimed at correcting these abnormalities.

Blood flow in the brain is determined by the systemic blood pressure interacting with the cerebrovascular resistance, which is mainly a function of the patency of cerebral arterioles as controlled by smooth-muscle contraction. This is mainly regulated by local metabolic factors, accumulation of carbon dioxide and lactic acid, and an associated fall of intracellular pH, which produces vasodilatation. Rising oxygen tension in the tissues causes vasoconstriction. Much less important is autonomic control of cerebral vessels, though sympathetic stimulation causes vasoconstriction, and parasympathetic stimulation causes vasodilatation.

In the treatment of dementia, drugs have been used to dilate cerebral arterioles or to influence metabolism. The reactivity of arterioles to carbon dioxide accumulation is preserved in dementia. However, cerebral blood flow and oxygen consumption are dependent on the degree of neuronal activity, so that lowered consumption may be a consequence and not a cause of dementia. In that case, improvement of cerebral blood flow and metabolism would be of little avail. Many vasodilator drugs such as the xanthines and nitrites lower systemic blood pressure so precipitously that cerebral blood flow is impaired rather than enhanced. However, several modern vasodilators are claimed to improve cerebral blood flow and have been used extensively in treating dementia, especially the arteriosclerotic multi-infarct type.

Papaverine has a direct effect on cyclic AMP in smooth-muscle cells and increases cerebral blood flow. Cyclandelate and isoxsuprine (both beta-adrenergic agonists) and naftidrofuryl also act directly on vascular smooth muscle and have been shown in placebo-controlled studies to improve intellectual performance and general behaviour.

"Hydergine" is a mixture of three dihydrogenated ergot derivatives that blocks alpha adrenoceptors. It reduces cerebrovascular resistance and increases cerebral blood flow and oxygen consumption, but it also appears to have a separate direct metabolic action. It is effective in improving the mood and behaviour of demented patients but has less effect on memory and other intellectual functions. "Cosaldon" contains nicotinic acid, an essential cofactor in tissue respiration, and a xanthine derivative that increases brain-stem blood flow and has caffeine-like stimulant actions. Its value in treating dementia is unestablished.

Other drugs have a primary metabolic action, increasing brain glucose uptake and, at least in animals, protecting against the effects of hypoxia. Meclofenoxate and pyritinol have shown some limited efficacy in the treatment of senile dementia patients.

Even placebo-treated patients can show considerable improvement both in general behaviour and, perhaps surprisingly, in their intellectual functioning – including memory. This suggests that much of the impairment is "functional" and may account for the efficacy of mild stimulants and antidepressants. Optimizing psychological and social factors may be, therefore, at least as important as the benefits from drug therapy.

Recent biochemical studies have revealed that in both presenile and senile dementias the activity of choline acetyltransferase is reduced in parts of the brain. Hence, acetylcholine synthesis is impaired. Cholinergic receptors are preserved, so the function of the remaining neurons should be enhanced by increasing available acetylcholine or prolonging the effects of that which is produced. Unfortunately, cholinomimetics either do not pass into the brain or they have intolerable side effects. And, as mentioned in the section on tardive dyskinesia (page 61), there are no really effective ways of increasing acetylcholine synthesis by giving precursors such as choline. Whatever improvement occurs is anyway likely to be of brief duration because more neurons degenerate. In Huntington's chorea, both the concentrations of choline acetyltransferase and the numbers of receptors are reduced, so treatments aimed at increasing acetylcholine concentrations are likely to be ineffective. The function of other amine systems in dementia is largely unknown, although reduced turnover of dopamine and serotonin has been found in Alzheimer's disease.

The drug treatment of dementia is at present largely unrewarding, so two cardinal principles of management must always be borne in mind. First, search for a remediable cause such as hypothyroidism; second, mobilize any available psychological and social resources.

HORMONES, PEPTIDES, AND ANTILIBIDO AGENTS

Disturbed functioning of endocrine glands has been demonstrated in some psychiatric conditions, particularly severe depression, and primary endocrine malfunction is commonly associated with affective disturbances. In the past, hormones have been used in the treatment of psychiatric conditions. For example, schizophrenic psychoses have been treated with insulin-induced coma, catatonia with thyroxine, and emotional immaturity with androgens. Current interest in hormones is focused on the management of depression and certain disturbances of sexual function.

Thyroid

Triiodothyronine (T_3) potentiates to a minor extent the antidepressant actions of imipramine and amitriptyline, resulting in more rapid and complete clinical response. This is especially apparent in women and in patients whose thyroid function is in the lowest ranges of normal. There is evidence from animal experiments that T_3 potentiates the actions of imipramine on noradrenergic synapses by sensitizing the adrenoceptors. Thyroid-stimulating hormone (TSH), secreted by the anterior pituitary to release T_3 and thyroxine from the thyroid gland, also potentiates imipramine. Thyroid-releasing factor (TRF), a hypothalamic neuropeptide that releases TSH from the pituitary, has also shown some antidepressant activity. Elevation of mood after intravenous administration is said to begin after about two hours and to last for up to 30 hours. The pituitary response to TRF is less in patients with depression than in normal controls, suggesting some dysfunction in the hypothalamic-pituitary axis. However, pituitary-thyroid function seems normal in depressed patients. Several neuropeptides, including TRF and ACTH, have complex central effects independent of peripheral endocrine actions, but the evidence for therapeutic effects is inconsistent.

Sex hormones

It is a firm clinical impression that sex hormones, at least in women, have an important role in psychiatric conditions. Depressive and neurotic symptoms emerge or increase premenstrually, during the puerperium, after the menopause, and with the use of oral contraceptives. However, confirming these impressions with controlled studies has not been easy. Hormonal changes are not obviously related to symptoms in the puerperium; of the many symptoms attributed to the menopause, only hot flushes and night sweats are clearly hormonally associated. Controlled studies have failed to confirm the clinical impression that oral contraceptives increase the incidence of psychological symptoms. Oestrogens have been used in the treatment of menopausal emotional symptoms, and progestogens have been employed to treat premenstrual tension, but controlled trials have failed to show any advantages of either over placebo. It is probable that the psychological disturbances are associated with several patterns of hormonal abnormality so that one single treatment is likely to be effective in only a few patients.

Much less is known of disturbed hormonal function in males. Sexual deviation is not associated with such changes; in particular, plasma testosterone concentrations in homosexuals are generally within the normal range. Attempts have been made to help sexual offenders and deviants by lowering sexual drive on the assumption that it is maintained by hormonal mechanisms. Oestrogens and some progestogens suppress the release of pituitary gonadotrophins, leading to a decrease in testicular androgen production. They also antagonize the effects of androgens in the tissues. Diethylstilboestrol and oestradiol are particularly effective antiandrogens. Cyproterone acetate is a synthetic antiandrogen that also inhibits gonadotrophin secretion and has progestational effects. All these drugs can be used to reduce sexual interest and activity, with only minimal effects on erectile capacity. Antipsychotic drugs such as chlorpromazine, haloperidol, and benperidol have similar effects, probably by blocking the central dopamine mechanisms of sexual regulation. The value of such treatments has hardly been explored, but they may be best employed to weaken sexual drives while behavioural methods are used to modify the object of the drive. Side effects such as feminization and gynaecomastia may be troublesome, however. The oestrogens can cause nausea, and cyproterone can cause lethargy and impaired liver function. Neither drug should be used in adolescents before growth has ceased. The possibility of neoplastic changes, especially of the breast, should also be borne in mind.

FURTHER READING

Bewley TH: Treatment of opiate addiction in Great Britain, in Fisher S, Freedman AM (eds): *Opiate Addiction: Origins and Treatment.* Washington, Winston, 1973, pp 141-161.

Brawley P, Duffield JC: The pharmacology of hallucinogens. *Pharmacol Rev 24*: 31-66, 1972.

Brimblecombe RW, Pinder RM: *Hallucinogenic Agents.* Briston, Wright, 1975.

Browne TR, Penry JK: Benzodiazepines in the treatment of epilepsy: A review. *Epilepsia 14*:277-310, 1973.

Dole VP: Biochemistry of addiction. *Ann Rev Biochem 39*:821-840, 1970.

Donovan BT: The behavioural actions of the hypothalamic peptides: A review. *Psychol Med 8*:305-316, 1978.

Groves PM, Rebec GV: Biochemistry and behaviour: Some central actions of amphetamine and antipsychotic drugs. *Ann Rev Psychol 27*:91-127, 1976.

Jasper HH, Ward AA, Pope A: *Basic Mechanisms of the Epilepsies.* London, Churchill, 1969.

Kalant OJ: *The Amphetamines: Toxicity and Addiction* (ed 2). Toronto, U of Toronto Press, 1973.

Lundwall L, Baekelund F: Disulfiram treatment of alcoholism: A review. *J Nerv Ment Dis 153*:381-394, 1971.

Mackay AVP: Psychiatric implications of endorphin research. *Br J Psychiatry 135*:470-473, 1979.

Parry BL, Rush AJ: Oral contraceptives and depressive symptomatology: Biologic mechanisms. *Compr Psychiatry 20*:347-358, 1979.

Paton WDM: Pharmacology of marijuana. *Ann Rev Pharmacol 15*:191-220, 1975.

Pinder RM, Brogden RN, Speight TM, Avery GS: Sodium valproate. A review of its pharmacological properties and therapeutic efficacy in epilepsy. *Drugs 13*: 81-123, 1977.

Resnick RB, Schuyten-Resnick E, Washton AM: Narcotic antagonists in the treatment of opioid dependence: Review and commentary. *Compr Psychiatry 20*:116-125, 1979.

Reynolds EH: How do anticonvulsants work? *Br J Hosp Med 19*:505-509, 1978.

Richens A: *Drug Treatment of Epilepsy.* London, Kimpton, 1976.

Thompson J, Oswald I: Effect of oestrogen on the sleep, mood and anxiety of menopausal women. *Br Med J 2*:1317-1319, 1977.

Trimble MR, Reynolds EH: Anticonvulsant drugs and mental symptoms: A review. *Psychol Med 6*:169-178, 1976.

von Rossum JM: Mode of action of psychomotor stimulant drugs. *Int Rev Neurobiol 12*:307-383, 1970.

Weiss B, Laties VG: Enhancement of human performance by caffeine and the amphetamines. *Pharmacol Rev 14*:1-36, 1962.

Wilson IC, Prange AJ, McClane TK, Rabon AM, Lipton MA: Thyroid hormone enhancement of imipramine in non-retarded depressions. *N Engl J Med 282*: 1063-1067, 1970.

116